ENGLISH VOCABULARY ELEMENTS

ENGLISH VOCABULARY ELEMENTS

Keith Denning

Brett Kessler

William R. Leben

Second edition

OXFORD
UNIVERSITY PRESS
2007

OXFORD
UNIVERSITY PRESS

Oxford University Press, Inc., publishes works that further
Oxford University's objective of excellence
in research, scholarship, and education.

Oxford   New York
Auckland   Cape Town   Dar es Salaam   Hong Kong   Karachi
Kuala Lumpur   Madrid   Melbourne   Mexico City   Nairobi
New Delhi   Shanghai   Taipei   Toronto

With offices in
Argentina   Austria   Brazil   Chile   Czech Republic   France   Greece
Guatemala   Hungary   Italy   Japan   Poland   Portugal   Singapore
South Korea   Switzerland   Thailand   Turkey   Ukraine   Vietnam

Published by Oxford University Press, Inc.
198 Madison Avenue, New York, New York 10016

www.oup.com

Oxford is a registered trademark of Oxford University Press

Library of Congress Cataloging-in-Publication Data
Denning, Keith M.
English vocabulary elements / Keith Denning, Brett Kessler, William R. Leben.—2nd ed.
p. cm.
Includes bibliographical references and index.
ISBN-13 978-0-19-516802-0; 978-0-19-516803-7 (pbk.)
1. Vocabulary.   2. English language—Grammar.   I. Kessler, Brett, 1956–   II. Leben,
William Ronald, 1943–   III. Title.
PE1449.D424 2006
428.1—dc22   2006049863

15

Printed in Canada

Preface

Intended Audience for This Book

This book is intended for use in college-level courses dealing with English word structure. It also aims to provide an introduction of how units of a language—sounds, word elements, words—function together and how a language functions in society over time. Part or all of the text may also be used to good effect in English for Foreign Students and English as a Second Language (ESL) courses. It is also recommended for those interested in preparing for educational aptitude tests and other postsecondary admissions tests (including the PSAT, SAT, ACT, GRE, LSAT, MCAT, and MAT) that test vocabulary skills. If this list seems broad, it is because nearly every field of study or work requires a facility for comprehension or expression in the English language. The list is, of course, not meant to exclude those who are merely afflicted with the kind of curiosity about language that has motivated many an amateur and professional linguist in the course of a lifetime of joyful pursuit.

The book's first goal is to expand vocabulary skills by teaching the basic units of learned, specialized, and scientific English vocabulary, but its reach extends far beyond this. To make sense of current English word structure and to build word analysis skills that will continue to prove useful, the book presents basic principles of word formation and word use and shows how these have affected English since its beginnings. This in turn leads to further topics including phonetics and the relationship of English to other Indo-European languages. As a result, the book provides an introduction to some of the most important concepts of modern linguistics by showing their role in the development of English vocabulary.

Using This Book

Key concepts are shown in boldface when introduced (e.g., **gloss** and **doublet**). Learning definitions of these terms is important, but a bigger goal is to gain an idea of the role of these concepts in the overall system of language.

Lists of word elements to be memorized accompany most chapters. Following them are a variety of exercises to choose from. Some help build familiarity with word elements by putting them to use in words. Others apply principles from the chapters to new cases. We hope these will encourage you to master the material as it is encountered instead of saving memorization until the end.

Vocabulary-building Techniques

Students may find flashcards useful for memorizing word elements. Thanks to Suzanne Kemmer, an excellent set is available on the Web at http://dacnet.rice .edu/projects/ling215/FlashCards/.

A more low-tech method is to cover one side of the list of elements and glosses and, going from top to bottom and then from bottom to top, to try to recall the element for each gloss and then the gloss for each element. Other approaches to the task of self-drilling for memorization include repeating word elements and glosses to yourself until you cannot internally hear one without the other, or finding a rhyme or mental picture that helps to associate elements with their glosses (e.g., "*aster* reminds me of the flower having the same name, which looks like a **star**," or "*viv* reminds me of my friend Vivian, who is very **lively**").

Using a Dictionary

As a companion to this text, we strongly recommend a bound dictionary designed for the collegiate level or above (i.e., one containing 150,000 or more entries), such as *The American Heritage Dictionary of the English Language*[1] or *Merriam-Webster's Collegiate Dictionary*.[2] You may also find it useful to consult

1. Fourth ed. (Boston: Houghton Mifflin, 2000). Also accessible through http://bartleby.com/.
2. Eleventh ed. (Springfield, Mass.: Merriam-Webster, 2003). Also accessible at http://www.m-w.com/.

a larger dictionary like the *Oxford English Dictionary* (*OED*)[3] or *Webster's Third New International Dictionary, Unabridged*[4] or such specialized dictionaries as *Dorland's Illustrated Medical Dictionary*[5] or *Stedman's Medical Dictionary*.[6]

Using a dictionary effectively is a skill that must be learned. It is important to become familiar with the basic layout of any dictionary you use. Most good dictionaries make this task easier by presenting explanations of entries, lists of abbreviations, and so forth, in the introductory pages. We recommend that students take the time to read this material before trying to use a new dictionary, thereby avoiding frustration later on.

Most dictionaries are also accessible online or in CD or DVD formats. These are invaluable for many kinds of searches (e.g., finding all words that end in -*archy*, or words whose definition contains the word *government*). We recommend these not as a substitute but as a supplement to a print version, if only because printed pages permit a level of browsing that can't yet be duplicated on computer screens.

One of the best ways to attack the bewildering variety of English vocabulary is to refer to a collegiate-level dictionary when you confront unfamiliar, difficult, or interesting words. When you come across an unfamiliar word or element, it is a good idea either to make a note of it for later reference or to take a moment to look it up. Learning to look for and recognize the elements and words you learn in the course (as well as those you acquire on your own) will eventually minimize the time you will spend with a dictionary—unless, of course, you enjoy reading dictionaries, in which case you may find yourself spending more time on other words than on the one you originally meant to look up!

Moving beyond the Final Chapter

This book doesn't contain one percent of what the authors find interesting about English vocabulary. We will judge the text as successful if the groundwork laid

---

3. Second ed. (20 vols.; Oxford, Eng.: Oxford University Press, 1989; micrographic 1-vol. ed., 1991). Three supplementary volumes have been published as well (1993–1997). All are incorporated in the CD-ROM and in the online version at http://www.oed.com/.
4. Springfield, Mass.: Merriam-Webster, 1961. See also http://www.m-w.com/.
5. Thirtieth ed. (Philadelphia: Saunders, 2003).
6. Twenty-eighth ed. (Philadelphia: Lippincott Williams & Wilkins, 2005). Also accessible at http://www.stedmans.com/.

here motivates readers to explore further and provides enough skills to undertake such explorations.

More comprehensive lists of Latin and Greek word elements than those provided in the glossary can be found in the works listed at the end of this book. These works list elements according to different principles, but the student can, with a little searching, use them to find and identify many less frequently used word elements not found in our glossary.

The World Wide Web is a rich source of lists of words and word elements. One constantly growing resource we recommend is Professor Suzanne Kemmer's Rice University Neologisms Database, which contained some 5,500 entries at the time this book was published: http://esa4.rice.edu/~ling215/.

We owe profound thanks to our students and teaching assistants over the years for many helpful and insightful suggestions. The course that led to this book owes its development to the textbook *Structure of English Words*, by Clarence Sloat and Sharon Taylor,[7] and to course materials prepared by Robert Stockwell, and we are indebted to these sources for first showing the way. We are also grateful to many colleagues for generous and helpful comments and corrections: to John J. Ohala, J. David Placek, Robert Vago, and the late R. M. R. Hall, who offered extensive suggestions for the first edition. Special thanks to Suzanne Kemmer, Joan Maling, Joe Meyers, Nasreen Sarwar, and many students over the past eleven years for corrections to the first edition. Thanks also to Daniel Leben-Wolf for doing the art.

Tragically, Keith Denning, coauthor of the first edition, passed away suddenly in 1998. We dedicate the second edition to his memory.

7. Fourth ed. (Dubuque, Iowa: Kendall/Hunt, 1996).

Contents

Symbols and Abbreviations

International Phonetic Alphabet

The following symbols are used in the text when a pronunciation must be described precisely. The boldface parts of the words beside each symbol illustrate the sound; more precise definitions can be found in chapter 5, Phonetics. Unless otherwise noted, the keywords are to be given current standard American pronunciations. The phonetic symbols used here are those of the International Phonetic Association (IPA).[1] When these symbols are used, they are enclosed in slashes. For example, "the word bathe is pronounced /beð/" or "the sound /ʒ/ occurs at the end of the word *rouge*."

a	*hock;*[2] also in *ride* /raɪd/, *out* /aʊt/
ɒ	*hawk*[2]
æ	*cat*
b	*boy*
d	*dog*
dʒ	*badge*
ð	*they*
e	*made*
ə	*elephant, cut*
ɛ	*pet*

1. Further information about this phonetic alphabet is available in the *Handbook of the International Phonetic Association* (Cambridge University Press, 1999) and at http://www.arts.gla. ac.uk/ipa/.
2. Many North Americans do not distinguish /a/ and /ɒ/ in their speech, so that *hock* and *hawk* sound alike.

f	*fat*
g	*go*
h	*hot*
ɦ	*cohere* for some speakers: a breathy-voiced /h/
i	*machine*
ɪ	*pit*
j	*hallelujah, yell*
ɟ	voiced palatal stop similar to /dʒ/, as in Sanskrit *Jagannātha*
k	*kiss*
l	*left*
m	*mark*
n	*nice*
ŋ	*sing*
o	*rose*
ɔ	*horse*; also in *joy* /dʒɔɪ/
p	*pot*
r	*run, irk*
s	*sit*
ʃ	*ship*
t	*top*
tʃ	*catch*
u	*prune*
ʊ	*put*
v	*vote*
w	*worm*
x	German *Bach*, Scottish *loch*, Hebrew *Hanukkah* (a raspy /k/)
y	French *tu*, German *Übermensch* (/i/ with rounded lips)
z	*zoo*
ʒ	*pleasure*
θ	*thigh*

In addition to these symbols based on letters, we also use the following characters:

ˈ   Precedes a fully stressed syllable: "*record* is pronounced /ˈrɛkɽd/ when a noun and /rɪˈkɔrd/ when a verb."

ˌ   Precedes a syllable that has secondary stress: "*taxicab* /ˈtæksiˌkæb/."

ː   Follows a long sound. For American English the mark is not necessary, but the contrast between short and long sounds is important for many other languages: "Latin /ˈakɛr/ 'maple' vs. /ˈaːkɛr/ 'sharp.'"

r̩   A vertical stroke under a consonant means that it forms the core of a syllable instead of a vowel: "*butter* /ˈbətr̩/, *apple* /ˈæpl̩/."

Modified Orthography

When the precision of the IPA is not required, it is often more convenient to indicate certain aspects of the pronunciation of a word by adding diacritics to the standard spelling, or **orthography**, of the word. For example, if we wish to note which syllable is stressed in the word *orthography*, we can write "*orthógraphy*" rather than "<orthography> /ˌɔrˈθagrəfi/." The diacritics used in orthography are:

´   Placed above a vowel that has primary stress: "*infláte*"

`   Placed above a vowel that has secondary stress: "*táxicàb*"

‾   Placed over a long vowel: "Latin *ācer* 'sharp' "

˘   Placed over a short vowel: "Latin *ăcer* 'maple' "

Abbreviations

A	adjective
adv.	adverb
cf.	compare (Latin *confer*)
G	Greek
L	Latin
lit.	literally
ME	Middle English
ModE	Modern English
N	noun
OE	Old English
PREP	preposition

| SI | International System of Units |
| v | verb |

Typographical Conventions

Typefaces

italics	When words are cited (talked about rather than used functionally), they are set in italics. The same applies to word elements and phrases: "It depends on what the meaning of *is* is"; "The word *prefix* begins with the prefix *pre-*."
bold	Boldface is used to draw the reader's attention to a specific word or element: "*epi-* means 'additional' in words like *epithet* 'nickname'.
CAPS	Small capitals are used for words and abbreviations describing parts of speech: "*récord* N has a different stress from *recórd* v."

Punctuation and Other Symbols

In addition to regular double quotes "…" which have their everyday meaning, the book uses the following types of quote marks for specific linguistic purposes:

<…>	When the discussion deals specifically with spelling, letters are enclosed in angled brackets: "the letter <s>."
/…/	Pronunciation may be indicated by placing phonetic symbols between slash marks: "/tɪr/ and /teɪr/ are both spelled <tear>."
'…'	If meaning (rather than sound or spelling) is the focus, a word or phrase appears within single quotes: "Greek *cosmos* 'universe.'"
×…	The mark × before a word means that it is ungrammatical: "the past tense of *write* is not ×*writed*."
*…	The mark * before a word or element means that it is unattested, but we have reason to believe it existed: "The

word *chief* must come from a popular Latin word **capum*, not the classical Latin *caput*."

Other special symbols include the following:

X < Y   X descended from Y: "*oak* < OE *āc*."

Y > X   Y developed into X: "*āc* > *oak*."

Y → X   X developed from Y by some morphological or analogical
               process: "Irregular English plurals include *ox* → *oxen* and
               goose → *geese*."

X~Y   X and Y are variants: "The past tense of *dive* is *dived~dove*."

Ø   Zero, the absence of a sound or letter: "The plural of *deer* is
               formed by adding Ø."

X-   More material must be added at the end of X to make a
               complete word. Prefixes and stems are cited with a trailing
               hyphen: "*pre-*", "*writt-*."

-X   X is a suffix: "*-ism*."

X-Y   A hyphen inside a word separates morphs: "There are three
               meaningful components in the word *black-bird-s*."

(...)   When part of a word or morph is in parentheses, that part
               is optional: "The morpheme *cur(r)* appears in *recur* and
               recurrent."

/   In a phonological rule, / separates the statement of the
               change from the description of the environment in which it
               takes place.

__   In the environment of a phonological rule, __ stands for
               the sound under discussion: "n → m / __ p" means that /n/
               becomes /m/ before a /p/.

ENGLISH VOCABULARY ELEMENTS

CHAPTER ONE

The Wealth of English

Word Power and a World Power

In the number of speakers who learn it as a first or second language, and in its range of uses and adaptability to general and specific tasks, English is the world's most important language today. It is the mother tongue of several hundred million people. Its rich verbal art, great works in science and scholarship, and major role in international commerce and culture have made English the most frequently taught second language in the world.

English is not the first language of as many individuals as Mandarin Chinese. But it is spoken over a much vaster area. In North America, Europe, Asia, Africa, and elsewhere, it is the official language of many nations, including some where English is not most people's first language.

A history of political importance as well as a certain linguistic suppleness have endowed English with an enormous vocabulary. *Webster's Third New International Dictionary* contains 476,000 words, and these do not include the many technical terms that appear only in specialized dictionaries for particular fields, or recent neologisms, not to mention all the regular plural forms of nouns, the different present and past tense forms of verbs, and other words derived from these words. No other language comes close to English in a count of general vocabulary. German runs a distant second with under 200,000 words. According to Robert Claiborne,[1] the largest dictionary of French has about 150,000 words, and a Russian dictionary maybe 130,000.

---

1. *Our Marvelous Native Tongue: The Life and Times of the English Language* (New York: Three Rivers Press, 1987).

The size of the English vocabulary has some wonderful advantages. Although it may be true that any concept can be expressed in any language, a language can make the process easier or harder by providing or not providing appropriate words. Thanks to the well-developed word stock of English, English speakers have a head start over speakers of other languages in being able to express themselves clearly and concisely.

Whether one uses this head start to advantage or not is, of course, up to the individual, but speakers with a good command of vocabulary can say things in more subtly different (and, hence, often more effective) ways than others can, and this ability is noticed.

- We refer to our friends and acquaintances as good talkers, fast talkers, boring conversationalists, etc.
- College Board and aptitude test scores depend very heavily on vocabulary knowledge.
- A job or school application or interview often turns on how adept at using language the interviewee is.
- We find that we can overcome many sorts of individual and group handicaps to the extent that we become established as a "good communicator."

In cases like these, the difference between success and failure often amounts to how well we have mastered the ability to speak and comprehend speech and to read and write. The expressive power of language is enormous, and every time a word acquires a new shade of meaning—a common development, as we will see—the richness of the language is enhanced. This may make you wonder why people complain so much about novel uses of language. Some seem to react to each new twist that comes into the language as a sign of decline, but a view of language change as growth deserves serious consideration.

The enormous size of the English vocabulary also has its disadvantages, as we are reminded each time we have to use a dictionary to look up a word we don't know, or because we were tricked by the alluring picture on the front cover of a book into thinking that the language inside would be easily within our grasp. A language as rich in its vocabulary as English is full of surprises, and however wonderful it may be that this richness is always increasing, it places a potentially painful burden on us when we first learn words and their meanings.

To sum up, English is extraordinarily well endowed with words. As versatile as the language already is, the supply of words is ever on the rise, with their meanings shifting in time to reflect new uses. These are the facts that we deal with in this book.

On the Attack

In the face of a challenge of such large proportions, a well-organized attack is called for. Although we cannot expect the language to always oblige us in our quest for shortcuts to an enhanced vocabulary, we fortunately will discover that some of the work has already been done for us: most of the complex words in the language have similar structures. If we learn the rules that reveal the structure of a certain kind of word, it will relieve us of some of the burden (and, perhaps, boredom) of learning all the words of this type individually.

We must divide to conquer. We will find that some aspects of the study of word structure (known as **morphology**) are helpful in analyzing words into their parts and in understanding how the parts contribute to the meaning of the whole. It will also come in handy to understand how English came to be the way it is and to learn some of the linguistic characteristics of the principal languages that English has drawn on to reach its present position.

Precision and Adaptability

One significant result of the size of the English vocabulary is the degree of precision and range of choices it allows. We have a wealth of words that are nearly synonymous yet embody subtle differences in meaning. For example, deciding between the words *paternal* and *fatherly* in the following sentences involves sensitivity to a distinction few other languages make.

paternal or fatherly?

a. *The judge's decision restricted Tom's _____ rights.*
b. *George gave Kim a _____ smile and then went back to reading.*

You would probably choose to use *paternal* in the first sentence and *fatherly* in the second. Certainly *fatherly* and *paternal* share the same basic meaning or **denotation**, and we could have used *fatherly* in the first sentence and *paternal* in the second, but the opposite choice is preferred because of **connotation**, the subtler secondary associations of a word. Connotation includes factors such as style, mood, and level of familiarity. *Paternal* is a more stylistically formal choice and therefore appropriate to a legal context like that in the first sentence, while *fatherly* is less formal in style. *Fatherly* connotes idealized qualities of fatherhood, like personal warmth and love, more strongly than *paternal*.

Another feature that increases the expressive power of the language is its adaptability. English provides many means for creating new words. If our dictionary does not list an appropriate word, we often create one. To fill the need for, say, a verb meaning 'correct in advance', we may add the **word element** *pre-*, which means 'before', to the existing verb *edit* and then use it in a sentence: *The author must pre-edit the manuscript.*

Similarly, the element *-like* (as in *childlike* or *treelike*) may be attached to a huge number of nouns to create such new words as *tentacle-like*, *cuplike*, and so on. If we invent a device for examining wings and recognize that in many words *pter* means 'wing' (as in *pterodactyl*) and that *scope* means 'a viewing device' (as in *microscope* 'a device for examining very small things'), we may call the new device a *pteroscope*, a word never before recorded in the dictionary. It is hard to imagine a new idea that couldn't be expressed by combining English words or their parts in new ways.

Such adaptability means that even the largest dictionaries can't capture every possible word in the language. The number of possible combinations of word elements like *pre-*, *pter*, and *scope* and the immeasurable amount of speaking and writing done in English require that dictionary editors restrict themselves to listing only the most frequent words in a language, and even then, only those used over a substantial period of time. Dictionaries are therefore always at least slightly out of date and inaccurate in their descriptions of the language's stock of words. In addition, the use of many words is restricted to specific domains. For example, medical terminology involves a tremendous number of words unfamiliar to those outside the medical community. Many of these terms never enter general dictionaries of the language and can only be found in specialized medical dictionaries.

The Constantly Evolving Nature
of English Vocabulary

Change and innovation are integral to English, as they are to every living language. The productivity of the language has brought in new verbs using the element *-ize*, such as *finalize, standardize*, and *prioritize*. Although some of these words have been singled out as "corruptions" by certain writers and teachers of English, all of them have established firm footholds in the language and are unlikely to be the subject of debate in coming generations.

Taste and style are often matters of personal discretion and are also subject to change. In the course of this book we hope to build a greater sense of security about language use. We all like to think of ourselves as making informed decisions about the acceptability of particular words or usages for particular circumstances. We all would like to move freely between the informal, formal, and technical domains of spoken and written English.

Why English Is So Rich

Modern English is the product of a long and complex process of historical development. Consequently, we can expect to find clues to its character in the past. Indeed, English has a history as rich as its vocabulary. The most important historical factor in the growth of the English vocabulary has been the ease with which it has **borrowed** words from other languages and adapted them to its own uses. The word *clique*, for example, was taken into English from French around the year 1700. Since that time, *clique* has become a familiar English word. It has been incorporated into the language to such an extent that it participates in processes that originally applied only to native vocabulary, resulting in the new words *cliquish, cliquishness, cliquey, cliqueless*, the verb *to clique* and others.[2] In fact, English now has many more words derived from *clique* than French does.

English has been so ready to take words from foreign sources that the greater part of the modern English vocabulary has either been borrowed or formed

---

2. Otto Jespersen, *Growth and Structure of the English Language*, 10th ed. (Chicago: University of Chicago Press, 1982).

from borrowed elements. Understanding why English vocabulary is as rich and diverse as it is gives us an important aid in learning to master it. (Chapter 2 deals in depth with the historical development of English vocabulary.) The reason that English has two words with such similar meanings as *fatherly* and *paternal* is that it retained a native word (*fatherly*) while borrowing from Medieval Latin a near synonym (*paternal*). In a sense, this allowed *fatherly* to "share" its duties with *paternal*. This is the general pattern with native and borrowed synonyms: the native word is more familiar or more basic and usually shorter, while the borrowed word is more formal or more technical and longer. A few additional synonym pairs serve to illustrate this point.

Native	*Borrowed*
tell	*inform*
spin	*rotate*
pretty	*attractive*

In each of these pairs the first member is more appropriate for everyday use, more conversational, and less formal or technical than the second.

But the choice between familiar and formal words is only one small part of the picture. With its wealth of native and foreign resources, English vocabulary has tremendous freedom to expand. Specialized and technical terminology, which generally involve the use of elements borrowed from Latin and Greek, are the most frequent sites of vocabulary innovation.

Pneumonoultramicroscopicsilicovolcanoconiosis

The forty-five-letter word *pneumonoultramicroscopicsilicovolcanoconiosis* has been cited as the longest word in English.[3] It is the name of a lung disease caused by the inhalation of extremely fine particles of volcanic silicon dust. This word seldom sees serious use, but it illustrates the lengths to which innovation using foreign word elements may be taken. Although perhaps bewildering at first, this monstrous word is not as difficult to handle as it might seem. It is made up of

---

3. *The Random House Dictionary of the English Language,* 2nd ed., unabridged (New York: Random House, 1987).

a number of elements, many of which are already familiar to you by themselves or as they appear as parts of other words. These include *pneumon* (which is also part of the name for the **lung** disease *pneumonia*), *ultra* 'extremely' (as in *ultraconservative*), *microscopic*, *silic* (as in the word *silicon*), *volcan*, and *-osis* (as in *tuberculosis* or *neurosis*) 'medical condition' or 'disease'. The most unfamiliar element of the word is *coni*, which means 'dust' in specialized terms such as *conidium*, a type of spore, and *coniology* 'study of the health effects of dust'. It is also related to the element *cin* 'ashes' in *incinerate*. So *pneumon-o-ultra-microscopic-silic-o-volcan-o-coni-osis* literally means 'lung-extremely-microscopic-silicon-volcanic-dust-disease' or, to rearrange things a bit more sensibly, 'lung disease (caused by) microscopic volcanic silicon dust'. (Incidentally, *microscopic* could itself be broken down into three elements: *micr* 'small', *scop* 'view', and *-ic*, which makes the word an adjective.) Notice that the meaning 'caused by' is not carried by any particular elements in the word but must be inferred from the other meanings.

To approach such special words, we need the ability to **parse** (i.e., analyze, break down, or take apart) the word into its proper components, and we need to know the meanings of the components. The same system that we use to parse and interpret words can also be used to coin new words.

The remainder of this book deals with specific methods and rules that will put this ability and knowledge into our hands. Long words need not be intimidating. In fact, the longer a word, the more likely it is that we can take it apart and figure out its meaning from the sum of its parts. You may or may not want to use your newfound skills to impress your family and friends, but you will definitely find that you have some powerful tools that will open up the worlds of technical and specialized vocabulary.

The History Hidden in Words

English words encode interesting and useful historical information. For example, compare the words

> *captain*
> *chief*
> *chef*

All three derive historically from *cap*, a Latin word element meaning 'head', which is also found in the words *capital, decapitate, capitulate*, and others. It is easy to see the connection in meaning between them if you think of them as 'the **head** of a vessel or military unit', 'the leader or **head** of a group', and 'the **head** of a kitchen', respectively. Furthermore, English borrowed all three words from French, which in turned borrowed or inherited them from Latin. Why then is the word element spelled and pronounced differently in the three words?

The first word, *captain*, has a simple story: the word was borrowed from Latin with minimal change. French adapted it from Latin in the thirteenth century, and English borrowed it from French in the fourteenth. The sounds /k/ and /p/ have not changed in English since that time, and so the Latin element *cap-* /kap/ remains substantially intact in that word.

French did not borrow the next two words from Latin. As mentioned earlier, French developed from Latin, with the grammar and vocabulary being passed down from speaker to speaker with small, cumulative changes. Words passed down in this way are said to be **inherited**, not borrowed. English borrowed the word *chief* from French in the thirteenth century, even earlier than it borrowed *captain*. But because *chief* was an inherited word in French, it had undergone many centuries of sound changes by that time. Across the vocabulary, certain /k/ sounds and /p/ sounds became /tʃ/ and /f/ sounds, respectively, so that *cap-* became *chief*. It was this form that English borrowed from French.

After English borrowed the word *chief*, further changes took place in French. Among these changes, /tʃ/ sounds changed to become /ʃ/ sounds, without changing the <ch> spelling, so that *chief* became *chef*. Subsequently English also borrowed the word in this form. Thanks to the linguistic evolution of French and the English propensity to borrow words from that language, a single Latin word element, *cap-*, which was always pronounced /kap/ in Roman times, now appears in English in three very different guises.

Two other word triplets that follow the same /k/ to /tʃ/ to /ʃ/ pattern are *candle, chandler* ('candle maker'), *chandelier* (originally an elaborate candle holder) and *cant* ('singsong intonation', 'jargon'; also visible in *incantation*), *chant, chantey* (as in *sea chantey*).

The history and relationship is diagrammed in table 1.1. Old French refers to that earlier stage of French, up to about 1300, when English borrowed a great many words. Modern French began in 1500. (The intermediate period was known as Middle French.)

Table 1.1 Changes in Sound in Latin and French and Their Results in Borrowings

Source	Sounds	English borrowings with these sounds		
Latin ↓	/k/, /p/ ↓	*captain*	*candle*	*cant*
Old French ↓	/tʃ/, /f/ ↓	*chief*	*chandler*	*chant*
Modern French	/ʃ/, /f/	*chef*	*chandelier*	*chantey*

Another example of a historical correspondence of sounds can be seen by comparing the originally Latin element *semi-* (as in *semicircle*) with the Greek element *hemi-* (as in *hemisphere*). Both *semi-* and *hemi-* mean 'half'. This correspondence of /h/ in one to /s/ in the other results from the fact that Greek and Latin are **related** languages, that is, they share a common ancient vocabulary, including the element *sēm-* 'half'. Over a long period of time, the two languages came to differ in certain respects, including the pronunciation of the first sound of this element. We discuss the nature of language relationships and sound changes in detail in later chapters.

Such correspondences between the sounds of words borrowed from related languages such as French, Latin, and Greek give us a way to organize information about English words. Knowing something about their historical development can provide useful clues to meanings and word relationships. In later chapters we show exactly how to use sound correspondences to learn new word elements.

Additional Goals

While the main goal of the book is to teach new word elements, we should keep in mind an important secondary aim: to develop a set of powerful techniques and concepts that will place the student on a path of vocabulary growth that will continue for a lifetime.

The book should serve other purposes as well. As we come across examples in which English pronunciations and words have changed over time, we also run into reactions that may involve resistance to change and have to consider whether change in general or in specific cases amounts to linguistic enrichment, linguistic corruption, or something between these two poles. We also note that usage varies greatly between one geographical area and another, and even between different speakers in the same area, and we become aware of attitudes and prejudices (others' and our own) based on this variation. We confront the issue of how to use sophisticated vocabulary properly for effective communication and understanding.

In the process of developing techniques for word analysis, we also introduce some of the principal areas of modern linguistics. We treat phonetics and phonology (the study of speech sounds and how they function in language), morphology (the study of word structure), diachronic linguistics (the study of language history and change over time), lexical semantics (the study of word meaning), and sociolinguistics (the study of social factors in language variation and change).

A final goal is spelling improvement. Word structure often correlates with standard spelling. For example, if you realize the words *pyromaniac* and *antipyretic* both contain the word element *pyr* 'fire', you will automatically know that there is a <y> (rather than an <i>) between <p> and <r>. Similarly, if you know that *consensus* contains the element *sens* 'feel', you will remember that it has an <s> where many people mistakenly put a <c>. Even though *accommodate* is one of the most frequently misspelled words in the language, often found misspelled in government documents, magazines, memos from college administrators, and in other professional writing, you will have no problem remembering that this word has two <c>s and two <m>s once you know that it has the structure *ac-com-mod-ate*, with each of its elements contributing to its meaning.

Word Elements

Use the example words to learn the following word elements and their glosses. You need not memorize all the examples. However, learning one of them will typically help you to memorize the element and its gloss. Many students find that the first example in each set is particularly well suited for use as a mnemonic, but you may find that another example works better for you.

Element	Gloss	Examples
anthrop	human	*anthropology, anthropomorphic, philanthropy*
bi	life	*biology, macrobiotic, biography, bioluminescent, microbial*

Element	Gloss	Examples
cac	bad	*cacophony, caconym, cacodemonic*
chrom	color	*monochrome, chromosome, chromatic, chrome*
chron	time	*chronic, diachronic, chronometer, anachronistic*
cosm	universe, adorn, order	*cosmic, cosmopolitan, cosmetic, macrocosm, microcosm, cosmogony, cosmonaut, cosmecology*
gam	marry, unite	*monogamy, gamete, bigamy, epigamic, gamosepalous, exogamous, gamophyllous, gamogenesis*
iatr	heal	*psychiatry, iatrogenic, geriatric, pediatrician*
idi	personal	*idiosyncrasy, idiom, idiopathy, idiomorphic, idiolect, idiochromatic, idiot*
log	speak, study	*logic, eulogy, logorrhea, anthropology, analogy, prologue, logo*
macr	large	*macroeconomics, macrocephalic, macrocyte, macradenous, macro, macron*
micr	small	*microscope, microcosm, microbe, microphotography, micron, micranatomy*
mis	hate	*misanthrope, misogamy, misogyny, misology*
morph	form	*polymorphous, morpheme, ectomorph, endomorph, morphology*
nom	law, system	*astronomy, autonomy, nomothetic, nomogram, metronome*
path	feel, illness	*pathology, sympathy, empathy, pathos, pathetic*
petr	rock	*petrify, petroglyph, petroleum, petrous*
phil	liking	*Anglophile, hemophilia, philosophy, philanthropy, philately*
phon	sound	*telephone, phonetic, euphony, cacophony, phonics, phonology, symphonic, aphonia*
pol	community	*politics, police, political, metropolis, megalopolis*
pseud	false	*pseudonym, pseudopod, pseudoscience, pseudepigrapha*
psych	mind	*psychiatry, psychic, psychotic*
pyr	fire	*pyromaniac, pyrotechnics, pyrometer, pyrite, antipyretic*

Element	Gloss	Examples
the	god	*theology, polytheism, theocracy, theogony, atheist*
top	place	*topography, topical, topology, toponym*
xen	foreign	*xenophobia, xenon, xenogamy, xenoplastic, axenic, pyroxene*

All of the word elements in this list come from Greek. Notice that when Greek elements appear in a word, they are separated by an <o>, especially if the adjacent sound would otherwise be a consonant. Another clue that some of these elements are Greek rather than Latin is the spelling: Latin elements rarely if ever have the digraphs <ch>, <ph>, <th>; silent consonants or <x> at the beginning of a word; or the vowel sequence <eu>. Latin elements rarely have <y> except at the end of the word. The digraphs <ch> and <th> also occur in native English words; but <ch> reveals its Greek origin when it is pronounced /k/.

We should not expect that every word that contains the letters of one of these elements does in fact contain that element. For example, a bicycle is not a **living** wheel; that word begins with another morpheme, the prefix meaning 'two'. On occasion we explicitly point out **homographic** morphemes, but even when we do not, you should always keep your eye open for them.

Element Study

1. *Cosm* generally means 'world' or 'universe'. It means 'adorn' only in the extended form *cosmet* appearing in *cosmetic, cosmetology,* and so on. What is the unifying idea behind the two meanings? Which meaning do you think is more basic, and why?

2. *Idi* is mostly found at the beginning of words and usually names something that does not follow the general system or was not subject to outside influences. Distinguish from *ide*, which means 'idea'. For each of these words, give the trait or feature that is characterized as unusual:

   a. *idiosyncrasy*
   b. *idiolect*
   c. *idiopathy*
   d. *idiom*
   e. *idiot*

3. The element *log* 'speak', 'study' and the wooden *log* are totally unrelated elements. Which of the two is the source of the word *log* referring to a written record, as when we log hours on a job? If you are uncertain, look up your answer.

4. Although *log* is glossed as 'speak' or 'study', it has a wider range of meanings. To get an idea of where these meanings show up in real words, answer these questions:

   a. What general meaning does *log* have at the beginnings of these words: *logic, logistical, logarithm*?
   b. What very general meaning does *log* have in these words: *Decalogue, travelogue, dialogue, catalog, prologue*?
   c. What general meaning does *log* have before the endings *-y* and *-ist* in the words *anthropology, geology, psychologist,* and *biologist*? Does it have the same meaning in *analogy* and *apology*?

5. *Nom* sometimes means 'law' in the sense of rule or control. But very often it refers to scientific law. Which of the two meanings best fits the definition of each word below?

   a. *anomie*
   b. *astronomy*
   c. *autonomy*
   d. *Deuteronomy*
   e. *economics*
   f. *heteronomy*
   g. *taxonomy*
   h. *theonomous*

6. In each word below, replace the noun suffix *-y* with a new ending that makes it into an adjective.

   a. *astronomy*
   b. *autonomy*
   c. *economy*

7. The element *nom* has no relation to *nomad*. Nor is it related to the element *nomen~nomin* 'name' found in *nominal* and *nomenclature*. In which of the following words does *nom* mean 'law'? Verify your answers by looking them up.

   a. *autonomic*   c. *gastronomy*
   b. *binomial*   d. *nominate*

8. The element *path* in this chapter is an element from Greek with no connection to the native word meaning 'way'. Combined with the suffix *-y* at the end of a word, *pathy* sometimes names a type of feeling, sometimes a disease, and sometimes a system for treating disease. For each word below, determine which of these three meanings comes closest to capturing the meaning of *path* in that word.

a. *antipathy*	g. *hydropathy*
b. *apathy*	h. *myopathy*
c. *arthropathy*	i. *naturopathy*
d. *cardiopathy*	j. *neuropathy*
e. *empathy*	k. *sympathy*
f. *homeopathy*	l. *telepathy*

9. List five words beginning with the element *phil* and five words ending in *phile*. Referring to the different meanings of this element in these ten words, describe the range of meanings of *phil* and its variant *phile*.

10. Replace the question marks with the appropriate word elements and glosses you have memorized. For example, in *a* below you'd write "pseud" for "?$_1$" and "shape" for "?$_2$." Then spell out the full word, incorporating any extra letters you are not asked to gloss. For *a*, you would write out "*pseudomorph*."

a. ELEMENTS	?$_1$	*o*	*morph*	*e*	
GLOSSES	false		?$_2$		
b. ELEMENTS	?$_1$	*o*	*phag*	*e*	
GLOSSES	large		eat		
c. ELEMENTS	*the*	*o*	*gam*	*-ous*	
GLOSSES	?$_1$	?$_2$	A		
d. ELEMENTS	?$_1$	*o*	*metr*	*-y*	
GLOSSES	mind		measure N		
e. ELEMENTS	?$_1$	*anthrop*	*e*		
GLOSSES	hate	?$_2$			
f. ELEMENTS	?$_1$	*o*	?$_2$	*-y*	
GLOSSES	bad		sound N		

Exercises

1. For each of the borrowed words below, give a synonym that is a single native word. The native word will generally be less formal. You may be able to guess the answer yourself or find likely candidates in a book of synonyms. In either event, check that your answer really is a native word by looking it up in a good dictionary and ensuring that the etymology does not indicate that the word was borrowed from a foreign language. Be sure that you understand the abbreviations your dictionary uses in etymologies. In particular, do not be misled when dictionaries say a word is **related** to a word in another language—being related is not the same as being borrowed.

   a. *intér*
   b. *depart*
   c. *velocity*
   d. *rapid*
   e. *decay*
   f. *illumination*
   g. *terminate*
   h. *converse* (v)
   i. *canine*
   j. *injure*
   k. *prevaricate*
   l. *perambulate*

2. Indicate which is the native English word and which is the borrowed word in each of the following pairs. Besides the etymological information contained in your dictionary, what kinds of clues to their origins do the form and structure of the words themselves provide?

   a. *wordy — verbose*
   b. *chew — masticate*
   c. *vend — sell*
   d. *malady — sickness*
   e. *answer — respond*
   f. *old — antique*
   g. *tell — inform*
   h. *watch — observe*
   i. *durable — tough*
   j. *eat — consume*
   k. *emancipate — free*
   l. *deadly — mortal*
   m. *sad — dejected*

3. In this chapter *fatherly* and *paternal* were seen to have similar meanings but different connotations. Consider *pyromaniac* and *firebug* in this light. When and why might one choose to use one over the other?

4. What are the characteristics, if any, that differentiate a *chronometer* from a *watch*?

5. Given what you've learned from the word elements for this chapter, what do you think the word *philophony* might mean? (You won't find this word in a dictionary.) Explain your answer.

CHAPTER TWO

The History of English and Sources of English Vocabulary

This chapter looks at the major historical events that have shaped the English language. We pay special attention to the development of our native Germanic vocabulary and to the forces that introduced massive numbers of foreign elements, especially from Latin, Greek, and French. The richness of this combination makes English vocabulary distinctive among the languages that originated in Europe.

The phrase *English language* refers to something that is at the same time the American language, the Australian language, the Canadian language, the language of England, Scotland, and Wales, and so on. English today is the native tongue of more than three hundred fifty million people in many independent nations. It is also a major second language, primary, or alternative official language for an even larger number of people throughout the world. So, what is it that is "English" about this major world language? The answer is its history, because for almost a thousand years it was spoken almost entirely in England.

As we look at historical events, we see that they have had a variety of linguistic repercussions, and we may ask what English would have been like if its history had been even slightly different.

Background to the History of English

Origins of Language

Human language goes back to at least fifty thousand years ago. That is roughly when fully modern humans emerged from Africa and started developing recognizably modern human culture around the globe. The remarkable success of this new type of human—us—is thought to be due in large part to the development of a brand-new type of communication system: language as we know it. That tool proved so powerful that it enabled its inventors to take over the world.

Unfortunately we know no details about the original human language. Language, being very ephemeral, left no traces at all before the invention of writing about five thousand years ago. Furthermore, language constantly changes. If only a few words are lost and replaced with new ones in each human generation, virtually the entire original vocabulary would be lost over the course of fifty thousand years.

Another result of constant language change is that the original language (or languages) has by now diverged into some six thousand distinct languages. As humans spread around the world, they formed independent communities that were no longer in intimate contact with each other. When innovations appeared in the language of one community, another community would not necessarily adopt those innovations. It takes only a few centuries for the speech forms of separated communities to become so different that it becomes compelling to regard them as different languages.

Because of the obscuring effects of time, all theories about remote language origins are highly speculative. However, linguists can make some reasonably solid conclusions about prehistoric languages, provided they don't try to trace things too far back in time—more than, say, ten thousand years. By comparing **attested** languages—those currently spoken or for which there exist historical records—linguists may find common traits that demonstrate that certain languages diverged from a common earlier form. To describe the connections between languages, they make liberal use of biological metaphors. If a language, say, Latin, diverges in time into, say, French and Spanish, linguists say that French and Spanish are **genetically related** (or simply **related**) to each other, that they **descend** from Latin; that Latin is an **ancestor** or **parent** of French and Spanish, and that French and Spanish are **descendants** of Latin. Furthermore, French and Spanish and all the languages that are related to them are said to form a **family**. All this biologically inspired terminology is straightforward enough, provided one does not try to read too much into it. Languages are not formed by the union of a mother and father language. They don't come into being suddenly, like humans do. And the fact that two languages are genetically related does not mean that their speakers are genetically related.

Indo-European

The method of comparing languages to discover their prehistory (called the **comparative method**) has led linguists to discover that English is related to dozens of other languages. That family is called **Indo-European** because even in prehistoric times the family had already spread as far as India in the east and the Atlantic coast of Europe in the west. The ancestor of all the Indo-European languages is called Proto-Indo-European.

Proto-Indo-European was most likely spoken in southeastern Europe about six thousand years ago, although the so-called **homeland** problem is still being debated. Because Proto-Indo-European predated the invention of writing, it is not directly attested, but a great deal of the language can be **reconstructed** by the comparative method. The language was highly inflected, meaning that most words could appear in many different forms depending on how they were used in the sentence. Where English has two forms for nouns—*horse, horses*—Proto-Indo-European had perhaps two dozen forms. Where English has on average four or five different forms for verbs—*love, loves, loving, loved*—Proto-Indo-European verbs could take hundreds of different forms.

Eventually the speakers of that language spread through much of Europe and Western Asia, replacing the languages formerly spoken there. A speaker of an Indo-European language might like to think that Indo-European languages won out because they were superior to the earlier languages, but it is doubtful whether any language is objectively superior to another. Rather, languages gain territory because their speakers have military or socioeconomic superiority. An intriguing possibility is that Proto-Indo-European spread so widely because its speakers were among the first to use horse-drawn war chariots.

Linguists have divided the Indo-European languages into about a dozen groups, or **branches,** of languages, each of which must have shared a common ancestor that descended from Proto-Indo-European. For example, the **Italic** branch includes Latin and its descendants the **Romance** ('originating in Rome') languages (e.g., Italian, French, Spanish, Portuguese, and Romanian), as well as other extinct languages. Other groups important in the history of English include **Celtic** (e.g., Welsh, Irish, and Scots Gaelic) and **Hellenic** (Greek). These branches are very much like families: groups of related languages that have a common ancestor. We even refer to their common ancestor languages by using the *Proto-* prefix: *Proto-Italic, Proto-Celtic, Proto-Hellenic.* The only difference between a branch and a family is that a branch's protolanguage has an identified ancestor: the ancestor of Proto-Italic was Proto-Indo-European, but we don't know what the ancestor of Proto-Indo-European was.

Germanic

The branch of Indo-European that includes English is called the **Germanic** group. Proto-Germanic was probably spoken in northern Germany and southern Scandinavia. It was not as highly inflected as Proto-Indo-European had been. Indeed, simplification of the inflectional system is a constant theme in the history of English.

We also know that a great many of the consonants changed in Proto-Germanic. For example, in Proto-Indo-European, the word for 'foot' began *ped-* or *pod-*, and these are still the forms in Latin and Greek. But English is typical of the Germanic languages in having quite different consonants in the word *foot*. To a casual observer these differences seem great. One of the earliest achievements of modern linguistics was Grimm's law, which showed how the correspondences between Germanic consonants and those of other Indo-European languages were systematic and quite simple to understand. Grimm's law is covered in Chapter 10.

Proto-Germanic developed into not only English, but also several other languages we are familiar with. Some Germanic tribes migrated eastward, into what is now Romania and Ukraine, and developed the language branch known as East Germanic. The most important language in this group was **Gothic**, which was the first Germanic language in which we have a significant amount of written text: a translation of part of the New Testament. All speakers of East Germanic languages eventually abandoned them in favor of other languages, and so we say that that branch is now **extinct**—another biological metaphor.

After the East Germanic branch split off, we begin to find in the core Germanic area a small body of short inscriptions written in **runes**, highly modified variants of the Latin letters. A typical old Germanic inscription is the following, from one of the golden horns of Gallehus: ᛖᚲᚺᛚᛖᚹᚨᚷᚨᛊᛏᛁᛉ᛬ᚺᛟᛚᛏᛁᛃᚨᛉ᛬ᚺᛟᚱᚾᚨ᛬ᛏᚨᚹᛁᛞᛟ: When rendered in ordinary Latin letters, this reads *ek hlewagastiz holtijaz horna tawido* 'I, Hlewagast of Holt, made [the] horn.'

The Germanic area was bordered by the Roman Empire, and the history of the two sociopolitical groups was strongly intertwined. Germanic borrowed

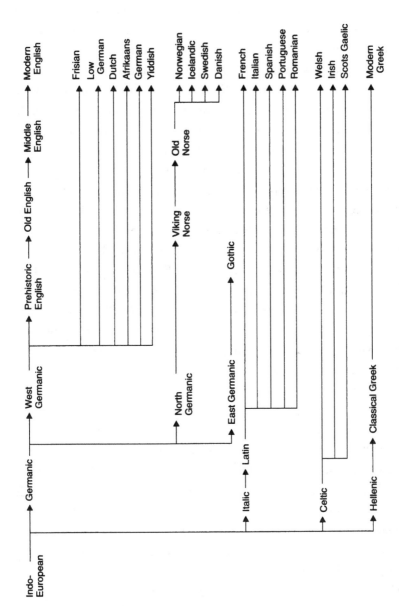

Figure 2.1 Stages in the Development of English and Some of Its Relatives

from Latin several words for cultural items that were new to the Germanic tribes or that were distinctively different in the Roman and Germanic worlds. Among these earliest words borrowed from Latin and still present in English are the practical, familiar terms *wine, street, mile, pit, cheese, chalk, kitchen, dish, pepper, kettle, cheap, pound, tile,* and *mint* (both the plant and the place where money is coined).

The Germanic language that remained after East Germanic branched off diverged into two new groups, **North Germanic** and **West Germanic**. The West Germanic group, which includes English, is discussed in the next section. The North Germanic branch comprises **Viking Norse** dialects, which developed into literary Old Norse and eventually into modern Scandinavian languages, among them Icelandic, Norwegian, Swedish, and Danish.

It should be noted that our history of English still has not taken us to England. Until the fifth century, England was inhabited by Celts, whose language developed into modern **Welsh**. Eventually England was incorporated into the Roman Empire as the province of Britannia. It is easy to mistakenly assume that early Latin influence on English occurred because England was part of the Roman Empire. But the chronology would be wrong; Roman presence in Britain during the Celtic period can only explain Latin influence on Welsh. Latin influence on (the ancestor of) English occurred because of social and economic contact between the Romans and Germanic peoples on the European mainland, peoples who, on the whole, were not part of the Roman Empire.

West Germanic

In the fifth century, Germanic expansion brought about the fall of the Roman Empire. Subsequently, without the Roman army to defend them, many lands passed under the control of Germanic tribes. The movements of the West Germanic tribes are particularly important to the story of English. By the end of the fifth century, West Germanic speakers had taken control of much of France and England. In France, many words of the conquering Frankish Germans were incorporated into the vocabulary. These words included the name of the land itself: called *Gallia* (*Gaul*) under the Romans, it now came to be called *Francia* (*France*) 'land of the Franks'. Still, Latin (or an increasingly modified descendant of Latin) remained the language of France. It is perhaps surprising that the conquerors adopted the language of the conquered people, but the high prestige of

Latin as the language of a great empire and civilization may have contributed to its survival.

As for England, most of its invaders came in the fifth century from what is now northwestern Germany—including Lower Saxony, the region whose name reappears in *Anglo-Saxon*—although some invaders must have set out from other nearby areas around the North Sea as well. The languages spoken in this area are very closely related to English, especially Frisian, which is spoken along the North Sea coasts of the Netherlands and Germany. Other West Germanic languages include Dutch and its South African variety Afrikaans. Yiddish and standard German, which developed in southern Germany, are somewhat more distantly related to English, although the Low German dialects of northwestern Germany are still more similar to English than to standard German in several respects.

Major Stages in the History of English

Prehistoric English

In the fifth century, Germanic invaders from the east conquered and occupied the eastern part of the British island. The Celtic language originally spoken in that area was replaced by the West Germanic dialects spoken by the invaders, as the original inhabitants were killed, were relocated, or adopted the language of the now dominant society. The western part of the island, as well as much of the far north, was not subjugated at this time. This is why the island to this day contains not only England but also the separate countries Wales and Scotland, which still use native Celtic languages alongside English. The Celtic language of Scotland, Scots Gaelic, was introduced from Ireland, but that of Wales, called Welsh or Cymric, is the descendant of the language spoken throughout southern Britain at the time of the Germanic invasions.

Although, as we have seen, the Germanic tribes occupying France adopted Latin, those occupying Britain retained their own language. Why the difference? After all, both regions had an ostensibly similar sociopolitical background—Celtic populations who had been incorporated into the Latin-speaking Roman Empire. Apparently the difference is that Latin never really took hold among the native population in Britain, which lay on the periphery of the empire and was conquered by Rome quite a bit later than Gaul was. Furthermore, the Latin-speaking soldiers, administrators, and governors all retreated from Britain early in the fifth century. Consequently, the people conquered by the Germanic tribes were speakers of a Celtic language that was not associated with a wealthy and prestigious empire. The invaders did not adopt the native language or even borrow very many words from it.

Roughly speaking, the tribes that settled in Britain formed three groups: the Angles north of the Thames, the Saxons south of the Thames, and the Kents in the southeast. The Angles and the Saxons occupied by far the greatest part of the country, so that the Germanic civilization that emerged in Britain is often called Anglo-Saxon. The Angles lent their name to the language—English—and to the whole of the territory held by the invaders—England.

Because we have very few written records of this stage of English, it is called **Prehistoric English.** The Germanic speakers did bring with them their runic script. But we have only about a dozen legible inscriptions from this period (400–700), and they are all very short. Presumably, relatively few inscriptions were produced, and most of those were on materials like wood that have rotted away. By contrast, runic inscriptions on durable stone were produced prolifically by the North Germanic speakers who spread through Scandinavia.

It was during the Prehistoric English period that England was converted to Christianity. Latin, the official language of the church, provided not only ecclesiastical vocabulary (e.g., *abbot, mass, pope,* and *priest*) but also a surprising number of what are now everyday words (e.g., *candle, cap, fennel, school,* and *spend*). These were added to the stock of Latin words that earlier had passed into Germanic during the period of the Roman Empire.

Old English

Around the year 700 there begin to appear substantial English texts, which were written in a version of the Latin alphabet that was introduced from Ireland. This is therefore the approximate date of the beginning of historical English—that is, English for which we have reasonably detailed historical records. It is conventional to divide the history of a language into three equal parts, referred to as Old, Middle, and Modern. When this system was adopted around 1900, there were twelve centuries of history to work with. So the first four hundred years or so of historical English (700–1100) is referred to as **Old English.**

Old English is the direct ancestor of the English spoken today and serves as the source of some of the most basic elements of English vocabulary. While it may at first appear quite alien to the modern reader, closer examination shows its deep resemblance to modern English.

In Old English the sentence *He has a white tongue* would have been written he haꝼaþ hꝑite tunᵹan (in a modern font, *He hafaþ hƿite tungan*) and pronounced /he: ˈhavaθ ˈhwiːtɛ ˈtuŋgan/ (refer to Symbols and Abbreviations for the sound values of these symbols). We see that some things haven't changed much since Old English, while others are rather different. Alongside the obvious differences in pronunciation are differences in spelling—for example, Old English <f> for the /v/ sound, and two survivals from the runic script: <þ> for the /θ/ sound and <ƿ> for the /w/ sound. Note also the Old English **inflectional endings** -*aþ*, -*e*, and -*an* on these words. All of these disappeared on the way to twentieth-century English. These endings marked such things as the **grammatical function** of nouns, so that, for example, the ending -*an* on the word *tungan* 'tongue' indicated that it was the direct object of the verb *hafaþ* 'has'. Only one of these endings is likely to seem familiar to a speaker of modern English: -*aþ*, which is an earlier form of the ending -*eth* in words like Shakespearean *holdeth* 'holds'. The -*aþ* verb ending marked the **person** and **number** of the subject of the verb, which in our sentence is the third person singular pronoun *he* 'he'. In current English the ending -*s* has replaced -*eth* in this function.

One of the most important periods in the development of Old English was the reign of Alfred the Great in the ninth century. Alfred was concerned about the poor state of Latin learning in his day. He undertook a massive campaign to revive learning by making English translations of Latin books. One result of this campaign was the flourishing of English-language literature, with the eventual emergence of a literary standard based on the West Saxon dialect of King Alfred and his successors, whose court was in Winchester. From the ninth to the eleventh centuries, English language and culture were among the most vibrant and active of the Western world. With every new cultural, material, technological, religious, scholarly, or artistic development, the language grew and changed, especially in vocabulary. The more sweeping the change, the more dramatic the influence on the language.

Throughout the ninth and tenth centuries and into the eleventh, Vikings invaded and settled large parts of England. English again responded by borrowing words, this time from the North Germanic tongue of the invaders, Viking Norse.

This created an interesting mixture, because Old English was still very similar to this close Germanic relative. Like languages themselves, words can be related to each other, or **cognate** (literally, 'together born'), meaning that their origin traces back to the same word in an ancestor language. A fair number of words borrowed from Viking Norse closely resembled cognates that already existed in Old English, but they often had somewhat different pronunciations and meanings. These pairs of native and borrowed cognates are called **doublets**. A few English–Norse doublets are illustrated in the following word pairs:

Native	*Norse loan*
shirt	*skirt* (both name a garment open at the bottom)
no	*nay* (as in *naysayer*)
shrub	*scrub*
lend	*loan*
rear	*raise*

In addition, several hundred Norse words for which no native English cognates survive were also incorporated into Old English, among them *ill, till, flat, they, skin*, and *egg*.

Middle English

The Middle English period is defined as lasting the four centuries from 1100 to 1500. Arguably the most important single event to affect historical English, the **Norman Conquest**, took place at the end of the Old English period. The monumental changes that this invasion produced in the shape of English society were accompanied by tantamount effects in the vocabulary of Middle English.

The Normans were originally Vikings—their name comes from *North man* (i.e., 'Norse'). In a sense, then, the Norman conquest can be seen as yet another Germanic invasion. But there was a difference this time. The Normans had earlier been ceded control of a large duchy along the northern coast of France—Normandy. As French subjects, they had adopted French culture. So the language they brought with them was not a Germanic language, but French. As we have seen, French is an Indo-European language, being a descendant of Latin. But that degree of relationship to English is not nearly as close as that of Viking Norse.

After their victory in 1066 at the Battle of Hastings under William the Conqueror, the Normans quickly assumed leadership and privilege in England. The Norman dialect of French thenceforth was the language of the upper class, while English was relegated to use by the peasants. As a result, the English language lost most of its literary and scholarly vocabulary. When English again came to be used widely for literary purposes a few centuries later, writers naturally turned to their knowledge of French to supplement the vocabulary. Especially during the 1200s, English assimilated a multitude of Old French words, especially those dealing with areas of life in which French language and culture were dominant. These included government (where we find French borrowings such as *court, duke, baron, county, crown, trial,* and *village*), war (*peace, enemy, arms, battle, moat*), and the finer things (*gown, robe, emerald, diamond, feast, savory, cream, sugar*).

The story of borrowings from French is complicated by the fact that some French words are themselves borrowed from Latin. The French word *animal* would not have preserved the shape of the Latin word *animal* so perfectly if it had been passed down in the normal lines of transmission from ancestor language to descendant language, subject to almost a thousand years of change. Instead, the French borrowed it from Latin, which language was still used for many secular and religious purposes during the European Middle Ages. Medieval speakers of Latin tried, with varying degrees of success, to keep words the way they were during the Roman Empire. For a historian it may well matter whether English speakers borrowed the word from French or directly from Latin, but for our purposes, the most important thing is that the English word *animal* looks and behaves like a Latin borrowing, so we call it Latin. In cases where we are not sure, or do not care, whether a word is really Latin or was modified by its descent through French or other Romance languages, we can always hedge and call it **Latinate** (i.e., borrowed from Latin, whether directly or indirectly).

Middle English differed from Old English not only in vocabulary but also in its grammatical structure. Most of the vowels in inflectional endings became /ə/ (spelled <e>), which change obliterated the distinction between many of the endings. The following lines from Geoffrey Chaucer, the greatest and most renowned of Middle English writers, illustrate how the language looked after these changes.

> And Frenssh she spak ful faire and fetisly,
> After the scole of Stratford atte Bowe,
> For Frenssh of Parys was to hire unknowe.[1]

We can make this passage more understandable by substituting the modern forms of the Middle English words while keeping the Middle English word order:

> And French she spoke full fair and featously,
> After the school of Stratford-at-Bow,
> For French of Paris was to her unknown.

(The word *featous* 'elegant' was borrowed from French and is now obsolete.) Only a few changes in word choice and order are required to translate this into Modern English prose:

> And she spoke French very pleasantly and elegantly—according to the Stratford Bow school, for Parisian French was unknown to her.

Chaucer is poking fun at a prioress who strives to be a sophisticate but whose French was obviously learned in an English convent. While this passage is relatively easy to follow, even in its original written form, hearing it spoken would be quite another matter, for it was pronounced approximately like this:

> /and frenʃ ʃe: spaːk fʊl faɪr and ˈfeːtɪsli
> aftər θə skoːl ɔf ˈstratford ˈatːə bɔʊ
> fɔr frenʃ ɔf ˈparɪs was toː hɪr ʊnˈknɔʊ/

During virtually the entire Middle English period, England and France were closely connected. But gradually the ruling classes of England began to think of themselves as English, especially after losing Normandy for the first time in 1204. They began to look more favorably on English and began to use that language more widely, even for literary purposes. But the connection with Old English traditions had been severed, and the members of the new literate class didn't even speak the

---

1. *Canterbury Tales* (London: Dent, 1958), p. 4.

dialect that the old literature had been written in—the language of King Alfred in Winchester had been a southern, Saxon-based dialect, whereas the new language of the London court was based mostly on Anglian dialects of the English Midlands. Native verse forms were abandoned, and even the script and spelling system took on a radically different shape. Much had been lost, but Middle English writers had at their disposal the tradition of spoken and literary French to help them create a vigorous and rich national language. With the Hundred Years' War, enthusiasm for things French waned considerably, but English retains many hundreds of French words, not to mention thousands of Latin and Greek words that entered the language indirectly through French.

Modern English

The current stage of the language, **Modern English**, is conventionally said to have begun in 1500. Thanks to the advent of movable type, books began to be produced in English on a massive scale, leading to greater standardization of the language and to its acceptance as a major language. Thanks to the Renaissance, great numbers of Latin and Greek words were added to English, along with continued borrowings from French.

One of the most extensive linguistic changes in the history of English is known as the **Great Vowel Shift**, which marks the transition from Middle English (ME) to Modern English (ModE). These major sound changes affected the pronunciation of **long vowels**. These changes are shown in table 2.1. This table tells us, for example, that the older sound /iː/ became /aɪ/. One example is that the word *fine*, formerly pronounced /fiːnə/, is now pronounced /faɪn/. (The sound /ə/

Table 2.1 The Great Vowel Shift

ME sound	ModE sound	ME example word	Same word in ModE
/iː/	/aɪ/	*fine* /fiːnə/	*fine* /faɪn/
/eː/	/i/	*me* /meː/	*me* /mi/
/ɛː/	/i/	*cleene* /klɛːnə/	*clean* /klin/
/aː/	/e/	*name* /naːmə/	*name* /nem/
/uː/	/aʊ/	*hous* /huːs/	*house* /haʊs/
/oː/	/u/	*moone* /moːnə/	*moon* /mun/
/ɔː/	/o/	*goote* /gɔːtə/	*goat* /got/

was lost from the ends of words at roughly the same time, but that deletion is not considered apart of the Great Vowel Shift.)

By Shakespeare's time (around 1600), the Great Vowel Shift was complete. Here is an example of the written language of that period:

> The king hath on him such a countenance,
> As he had lost some Prouince, and a Region
> Lou'd, as he loues himselfe.[2]

Few if any of these words are hard to recognize, especially if we take into account that the letters <u> and <v> were often interchanged in this period. The words were pronounced then very much as they would be today in American English, and even words like *hath* that have dropped out of general use may still be familiar from poetry or the King James Version of the Bible. The presence of such Latinate loanwords as *countenance, province*, and *region* is testimony to the continued importance of the French and Latin loanwords that were borrowed throughout the Middle English period.

External influences continued to enrich English vocabulary. The Renaissance opened a new age for art and science in England and the rest of Europe. Along with many new words from French and Latin, Greek words now began to make their greatest impact. The scholarly disciplines owe much of their vocabulary to **classical** Latin and Greek. Among the first contributions to Modern English from Latin were *exterior, appendix, delirium, contradict, exterminate,* and *temperature.* At about the same time, Greek provided *tonic, catastrophe, anonymous, lexicon,* and *skeleton.*

As the European colonial empires expanded throughout the world, English borrowed words from many other languages. Among these words are names for animals and places (*moose, skunk, woodchuck, Michigan, Chicago, Manhattan*) from American Indian languages encountered by English settlers; food terms (*yam, gumbo, banana*) from African languages spoken where the foods originate; new species and technologies (*kangaroo, koala, boomerang*) from Australian languages; unusual weather phenomena and customs (*typhoon, kowtow*) from Chinese; and many others.

---

2. William Shakespeare, *The Winter's Tale*, Act 1, scene 2, lines 474–476. Electronic Text Center, University of Virginia Library, http://etext.virginia.edu/frames/shakeframe.html. Spelling is that of the first folio, 1623.

Still, English continues the tradition of the Renaissance in its heavy reliance on Latin and Greek. This is fortunate, because it means that the systematic study of scientific and other special vocabulary can concentrate on these two languages out of the many that English has drawn from in its history. Because the Latin of ancient Rome itself borrowed words from Greek, many Greek words entered English indirectly through Latin. As a result, the three most important sources of borrowed vocabulary—French, Latin, and Greek—have contributed to English along the paths illustrated in figure 2.2.

The period during and after the Renaissance saw not only heavy borrowing of actual words from Latin and Greek but also the use of parts of older borrowings, resulting in the **innovation** of words that never existed in Latin and Greek when they were living languages. This process of innovation remains alive in English today and is one way that the classical word stock can be so valuable. Anyone can cannibalize the elements of borrowed words to invent words such as *phrenolatry* 'the act of worshipping the mind' or *somnivorous* 'sleep devouring' or *steatocephalic* 'having a fatty head'. This is because English not only borrowed huge numbers of words but, in effect, also borrowed the rules by which those forms were related to each other. For example, Greek usually put an *o* between word elements when it formed compound words like *philosophia*, from *phil* 'liking' and *sophia* 'wisdom' (borrowed by English as *philosophy*). Consequently, when we make up new compounds from Greek elements, we usually apply the same rule, as when we made up the word *phrenolatry* from *phren* 'mind' and *latri* or *latry* 'worship'.

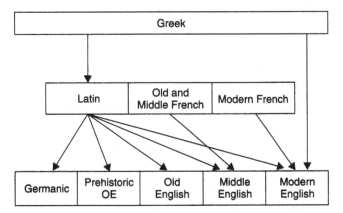

Figure 2.2 Major Paths of Borrowing from Greek and Latinate Sources into English

The complexity of developments in borrowing and neologism can be seen (figure 2.3) in the path taken by an ancient word (and, later, word element) meaning 'wine', which was borrowed from an unknown source by both Ancient Greek and Latin during the first millennium BC, from which it was in turn borrowed by Germanic and English at several points in its history. Light lines indicate descent within a language over time; darker lines indicate borrowing between languages; and the arrowhead pointer indicates derivation from the word above it, within the same language.

After reading about so many layers of borrowing into English, it is easy to get the impression that English has turned into a foreign language. Admittedly, English does rank high in its hospitality to loanwords. But it remains at its core a typical Germanic language. In general, the most basic, most frequently used, and simplest words of Modern English are inherited from its Germanic ancestor languages. Words such as *sun, moon, lamb, life, death, mother, health,* and *god*; prefixes such as *un-* and *be-*; suffixes such as *-ness, -ly, -some, -ship,* and *-hood*; and thousands more words and elements are all native to English.

We have largely focused our attention here on the sources of vocabulary, but there are other mechanisms of linguistic change as well. For example, words can acquire new meanings. The word *bead* used to mean 'prayer' and the word *edify* used to mean 'construct a building'. We examine many similar developments in the chapter on semantic change. Borrowing can also bring into the language new sounds and new relationships between sounds. The /t/ at the end of words like *democrat* and *pirate* becomes an /s/ in *democracy* and *piracy* because of a change that took place in postclassical Latin. Changes in meaning and sound are discussed more fully in chapters 6 and 9 through 11.

Summary

Historical events and political and cultural factors have left their linguistic traces on the development of English. The original Indo-European and Germanic vocabulary is still found in abundance, but the language has also undergone a series of changes in grammatical structure and pronunciation. Its original Germanic word stock has been enhanced by copious borrowings from many languages, most notably Latin, Greek, French, and Norse. The major stages of word borrowing into English are listed below.

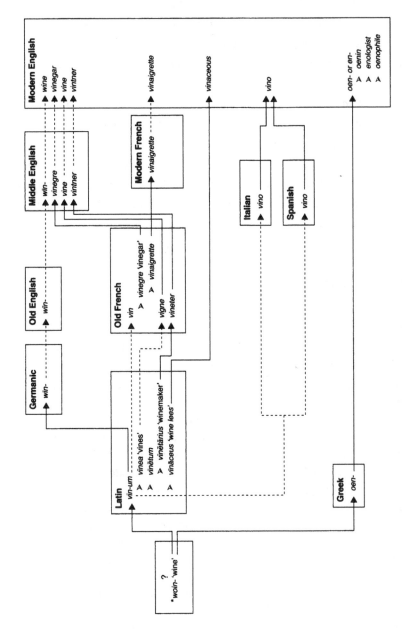

Figure 2.3   Developments Involving Word Elements Meaning 'Wine' Up to Modern English

- **Germanic** (before ca. 450): Borrowings from Latin, mostly words for types of everyday objects new to the Germanic peoples.
- **Prehistoric English** (ca. 450–700): More borrowings of names of everyday objects from Latin. Beginning of an influx of ecclesiastical terms accompanying Christianization.
- **Old English** (700–1100): More literary borrowings from Latin. Large influx of everyday words from Viking Norse.
- **Middle English** (1100–1500): Steady flow of borrowings from literary Latin are joined by heavy borrowing from French, especially terms from law, government, the military, and higher culture.
- **Modern English** (1500–present): Heavy influx of scientific vocabulary, including many neologisms based on elements from Latin and Greek. Borrowings from many other languages with which English has had contact in Europe, Asia, Australia, Africa, and the Americas.

Word Elements

Learn the following elements and their meanings.

Element	Gloss	Examples
anim	soul	animate, animadversion, animosity, unanimous
corp	body	corpuscle, corpse, corpulent, corpus, corps
culp	fault	culpable, mea culpa, exculpate
duc	to lead	duct, conduct, induce, produce, educate, deduct
fug	flee	fugitive, fugacious, centrifuge, fugue
grat	goodwill	grateful, gratuity, ingratiate, ingrate, gratis
greg	social group	congregation, egregious, gregarious, segregate
hom	human	hominid, Homo erectus, homicide
leg	law, deputize	legal, allege, legislature, relegate, legacy, privilege
libr	balance, weigh	Libra, equilibrium, libration
liter	letter	literal, literary, literati, alliteration, obliterate, transliterate
nov	new	novelty, innovate, novitiate, novice, nova, renovate
omn	all	omniscient, omnipotent, omnivorous
par	give birth to	parent, post partum, parturition, oviparous
pet	seek, go to	centripetal, petition, impetus, appetite, perpetual

Element	Gloss	Examples
pot	able, powerful	*potential, potent, omnipotent, impotent*
prob	good, test	*probe, approbation, probity, reprobate*
sci	know	*omniscient, conscious, prescient, scilicet, plebiscite, adscititious, sciolism*
sec	cut	*bisect, section, sector, transect, secateurs, secant, insect*
somn	sleep	*insomniac, somnolent, somnambulism*
ven	come	*intervene, contravene, prevent, eventual, ventive*
ver	true	*verify, veritable, veracity, verisimilitude*

All of these elements are taken from Latin. For a few of them this is obvious, because Greek elements never contain the letters <f> or <v>.

Element Study

1. The element *anim* has developed the following four meanings: (1) 'life'; (2) 'soul', 'mind'; (3) 'hostility'; (4) 'courage'. Which words below exemplify which of these meanings?

   a. *animalcule*   d. *animism*   g. *animosity*
   b. *animate*   e. *animus*   h. *magnanimous*
   c. *animation*   f. *animadversion* i. *pusillanimous*

2. *Leg* meaning 'law', 'deputize' is easily confused with other elements of the same spelling, meaning 'read' or 'gather'. In which of the words below does *leg* (or an altered form of it) mean 'law' or 'deputize'?

   a. *legislate*   d. *delegate*   g. *league*
   b. *college*   e. *legacy*   h. *colleague*
   c. *legate*   f. *legend*

3. *Libr* 'weigh', 'balance' is the source of the abbreviation *lb.* for 'pound'. This element is not to be confused with two others, *libr* 'book' and *liber* 'free'. For each of the following words, decide which of these three elements appears:

   a. *library*   c. *equilibrate*   e. *deliberate*
   b. *liberty*   d. *Librium*   f. *liberal*

4. a. *Par* often occurs in *parous* at the ends of words describing reproduction. Find three such words.

   b. There is a closely related element *par* meaning 'prepare' in *apparatus, disparate, pare, prepare,* and *separate.* What do the two meanings 'reproduce' and 'prepare' have in common?

5. The element *sci* 'know' is historically related to *sec* 'cut'. Elements containing *sci* that still mean 'cut' are *scind* and *sciss* 'split'. Can you think of a way that the basic meaning 'cut' can be extended to mean 'know'?

6. After studying this chapter's word elements, test your knowledge by replacing the question marks with the appropriate word elements or glosses you have memorized. Then spell out the full word. With the aid of a dictionary, give a brief definition that partly or fully reflects the meaning of the individual elements. If you cannot find the word in your dictionary, you may find portions of it that allow you to guess what the full word might mean.

a. ELEMENTS	*extra-*	*corp*	*ore*	*-al*
GLOSSES	'outside'	?		A
b. ELEMENTS	?	*-ent*	*-ate*	
GLOSSES	'powerful'	A	N	
c. ELEMENTS	*contra-*	?		*-tion*
GLOSSES	'against'	'come'		N

Exercises

1. Which part or parts of the verb in the sentence *She perspires in the heat* marks the person and number of the subject?

2. Look up the following words in your dictionary. On the basis of the etymologies given there, state for each one

   a. whether it is a native Germanic word (i.e., one present in Old English with no evidence of borrowing from any other language) and
   b. if it is not native, indicate: (1) what language the word originally came from and (2) when it was borrowed: Old English or earlier, Middle English, or Modern English.

To answer these questions, you may have to read the introductory material in the dictionary to learn how to interpret the **etymologies** in individual word entries.

Be sure you understand how the dictionary distinguishes between when a word is borrowed from another language and when a word is related to or akin to a word in another language.

a. *time*	g. *chant*	m. *barn*	s. *sweet*
b. *face*	h. *critic*	n. *great*	t. *grain*
c. *want*	i. *wise*	o. *joke*	u. *crown*
d. *canoe*	j. *stigma*	p. *taste*	v. *tomato*
e. *finger*	k. *vest*	q. *bazaar*	w. *poem*
f. *theology*	l. *corn*	r. *please*	x. *canine*

3. These are Modern English words and the Middle English words they descend from. Using phonetic symbols, give the pronunciation of each word. You may assume that any sound not discussed in this chapter was pronounced roughly the same in Middle English as in Modern English. Be sure to consult Symbols and Abbreviations for the correct IPA symbols. As an example, for the first pair below you would transcribe ModE /tek/, ME /taːkə/.

a. ModE *take*, ME *take*
b. ModE *reed*, ME *reed*
c. ModE *shoe*, ME *shoo*
d. ModE *hone*, ME *hoone*
e. ModE *shine*, ME *shine*
f. ModE *town*, ME *toun*
g. ModE *cake*, ME *cake*

CHAPTER THREE

Morphology: Analyzing Complex Words

The Basics of Morphology

By and large, the words we deal with in this course are **complex**. Unlike such **simplex** words as *eat, pray, cone,* and *people,* complex words are built from two or more **morphological components** (also called *constituents* or simply *parts*), as the following list illustrates:

Word	Components
blackbird	*black, bird*
refresh	*re-, fresh*
bookish	*book, -ish*
warmth	*warm, -th*

From such examples we can see that there is no simple relation between sounds and morphological components. A component is often a syllable, but even a one-syllable word may have more than one component (*warmth*), and sometimes a component has more than one syllable (*elephant*). Something is clearly going on here beyond merely counting syllables or sounds.

What morphological analysis attempts to do that goes beyond phonological (sound-based) analysis is provide an explanation for why a word has the meaning it does. A **blackbird** is a **bird** species typified by **black** coloration. *Warmth* is the state of being **warm**. A morphological component actually tells us something about a word's meaning or role in a sentence. When a word we haven't seen yet contains morphological components found in other words, we can make a reasonable prediction of what the new word means. This information is rarely perfect: not all black birds are blackbirds, and not all blackbirds are black. But the morphological components of a complex word tell us much more about the meaning of a word than we could hope to conclude from studying parts of a simplex word such as *eat* or *elephant.*

There are several useful ways of classifying components. One way is to ask whether the component itself is composed of other components. If a component is simplex, composed of no smaller components, it is called a **morph.** Thus we say that *bookishness* is a complex word, whose immediate components are *bookish* and *-ness;* where *bookish* itself is a complex component, composed of the simplex components, or morphs, *book* and *-ish.* And *-ness* itself is also a morph. So the full list of the morphs is *book, -ish,* and *-ness,* which we can express in shorthand by spelling the word with dashes between each morph: *book-ish-ness.* The process of dividing a word into morphs is called **parsing.**

Word	*Morphs*
unreadable	*un-read-a-ble*
appendectomy	*ap-pend-ec-tom-y*
coefficient	*co-ef-fic-i-ent*

There are many technical issues involved in deciding exactly what a morph is. How do we decide when we can stop dividing words up into smaller components? To many **morphologists,** the key issue is whether native speakers of English intuitively recognize subcomponents, or whether they can use subcomponents to create new words that other native speakers can understand. If that is the criterion, it is clear that we have gone way too far with the examples above. A typical speaker would be able to break apart *unreadable* into *un-read-able* and make new words with each of those three parts, but breaking *-able* into *-a-ble* might not occur to him or her. The situation is even more striking with the more learned words *ap-pend-ec-tom-y* and *co-ef-fic-i-ent.* Would you have broken these words into as many parts as we have? Which of the morphs that we've identified can you recognize from other words?

Etymologists and those interested in the history of the language may go in the opposite direction and isolate as a morph every sound that ever had a distinct function, even if they have to go as far back as Proto-Indo-European to find it. Both viewpoints are valid, as long as the criteria are clearly stated. In the context of this book, which deals primarily with learned and scientific vocabulary, it makes sense to think of a morph as the smallest unit that has an identifiable function when viewed in the context of the entire English vocabulary—whether or not the average speaker of English is aware of those patterns. One of our goals in writing this book is to put you in the camp of those who find five morphs in *ap-pend-ec-tom-y*. What we call **elements** throughout this book are pretty close conceptually to morphs in this sense of the word. But we often use the informal term *element* so that we can reserve the right to present the morphological components that are the most practical to learn, whether or not they technically qualify as morphs.

Often a knowledge of Latin and Greek can be a big help in identifying morphs, because the people who have created much of our learned vocabulary were consciously working with Latin and Greek vocabulary components. Being highly familiar with English, we think it's obvious how to break *bookishness* into morphs. The composition of a word like *concurrent* may be equally obvious only to a Latin scholar. But English has borrowed so many Latin words that the structure of words like *concurrent* is actually inferable from English vocabulary, if we know how to look for it. Morphs occur in a variety of words in which they carry the same approximate meaning, which is what makes a course in the structure of English words both possible and potentially useful. The morph *con-* occurs at the beginning of a variety of words, including the verbs *contract* and *confuse*. The basic meaning of the morph *con-* is 'with' or 'together'. For example, the meaning of the verb *contract* comes from its two main parts, *con-* 'together' and *trac* 'pull' (as in *tractor*), giving *contract* the literal meaning 'pull together'. Similar is *confuse* (literally 'melt together'). *Curr* or its variant *curs* means 'run' in words like *cursive* (as in running, or flowing, handwriting) and *recurring* ('running again'). And *-ent* makes adjectives in many words such as *resplendent* and *salient*. If we consider all these words, it becomes clear enough that *concurrent* is to be analyzed as *con-curr-ent*, an adjective, and has a meaning approximately like 'running together with'.

Function of Morphological Components

Lexical Components

In addition to their complexity, another way of categorizing components is by their function. A **lexical** component is one whose function is primarily to provide meaning. In *bookish*, the nonlexical morph *-ish* vaguely tells us that the word describes a tendency, but it is the lexical morph *book* that conveys the overwhelming bulk of information about the meaning of the word *bookish*. A lexical morph—the smallest, indivisible, simplex lexical component in a word—is called a **root**. Because a root tells us more about the meaning of a word than anything else, the first thing we ask about a complex word is often: What is its root? Often a complex word has more than one root, as in *blackbird*.

Word	*Root*
bookish	*book*
bookishness	*book*
blackbird	*black, bird*
refresh	*fresh*
warmth	*warm*
eat	*eat*
elephant	*elephant*
unreadable	*read*
appendectomy	*pend* 'hang', *tom* 'cut'
coefficient	*fic* 'do'

In our native and nativized vocabulary, roots can usually appear as independent words, for which reason they are called **free** morphs. This makes it particularly easy to find the roots of words like **black-bird**, **re-fresh**, and **book-ish-ness**. In Latin and Greek, roots most often do not occur as separate words: they are **bound** morphs, meaning they can only appear when tied to other components. For example, the root of *concurrent* is *curr* 'run', which is not an independent word in English or even in Latin. So finding the root of a Latin- or Greek-derived word isn't as simple as looking for the free word inside the word. Instead, you need to make a special effort to memorize frequently occurring roots borrowed from those languages. This is the primary purpose of the word element lists presented at the end of most chapters in this book.

Inflectional Affixes

Morphological components that are not lexical are called **affixes**. The term *affix* 'something attached' comes from the point of view that the most important part of the word is the root; affixes are auxiliary components. From a more physical point of view, affixes clearly seem to attach to other components because each affix has a constant preference as to which end it wants to be attached to. Affixes that attach before their **base** are called **prefixes**, and those that attach after their base are called **suffixes**. (A base is simply any component that an affix attaches to. As we shall see shortly, the base may be a root, or it may be a complex component that already has an affix.)

Affixes have several types of functions. **Inflectional** affixes tell such things as the **number** of nouns, the **degree** of comparison of adjectives, and the **tense** and **person** of verbs. In English, and in Latin and Greek as well, virtually all inflectional affixes are suffixes.

Word	Inflectional morph
books	*-s* (plural)
oxen	*-en* (plural)
alumni	*-i* (plural)
finest	*-est* (superlative degree)
admires	*-s* (third person singular indicative mood)
admired	*-ed* (past)
admiring	*-ing* (active participle)

There is rarely anything mysterious about the meaning of inflectional affixes: we all know what a plural is, and the concept of plurality doesn't differ between words. For this reason, dictionaries rarely give separate entries to words with inflectional affixes unless there is some irregularity. Your dictionary may not mention *books* at all, and it may quickly dismiss *alumni* by saying it is the plural of *alumnus*. The set of words that vary from each other only by inflectional forms is called a **lexeme**, and the individual words are **word forms** of that lexeme. Very often when we speak of words we are really talking about lexemes. When the dictionary defines *book*, the definition holds equally for *book* and for *books*; the definition of *admire* applies to all its word forms: *admire, admires, admired,* and *admiring*. Dictionaries define lexemes, not word forms, because the meaning of a word form can trivially be deduced from the meaning of the lexeme. By convention, noun lexemes are cited by the singular word form and verb lexemes by the infinitive, at least in English. So if you read a statement about *admire*, it is potentially ambiguous, and it pays to stop and ask yourself whether the text is talking about the word form *admire* or the lexeme *admire*.

Inflection is so important that there is a term for the base to which an inflectional affix is attached: it is called the **stem**. As we shall see, a stem sometimes consists only of a root, but it may also be a more complex lexical component. Inflectional affixes at the end of the word are called **endings**. We follow usual linguistic convention here by writing individual stems with a hyphen after them and endings with a hyphen before them, to indicate where material needs to be added to fill out the word. For most English words, the process of inflecting a word by adding an inflectional morph to a stem is so straightforward that it scarcely merits talking about. But there are interesting wrinkles, such as when an inflectional category uses an irregular stem or ending or both: *written*, not *˟writed* (the ˟ means the form is ungrammatical). Sometimes inflection is indicated by changing the stem alone, as in the past tense of the lexeme *be*.

Inflected word	*Stem*	*Ending*	*Function*
admires	*admire-*	*-s*	third person singular indicative mood
written	*writt-*	*-en*	passive participle
was	*was-*	-	past

Later we will see that Latin and Greek inflections can be somewhat more challenging, not only because we are less intimately familiar with them but also because they evince a bit more variety and unpredictability.

Derivational Affixes

Derivational components are the other major type of affix. A derivational affix can be defined as any nonlexical component that is used for turning one lexeme into another. Or, equivalently, it is any affix other than an inflectional affix. Here are some examples. We use a hyphen to show the direction in which derivational affixes are attached: -X is a suffix, X- is a prefix.

bookish	*book*	*-ish*
	ROOT	DERIV

forgetfulness	*for-*	*get*	*-ful*	*-ness*	
	DERIV	ROOT	DERIV	DERIV	
admires	*ad-*	*mire*	*-s*		
	DERIV	ROOT	INFL		
appendectomy	*ap-*	*pend*	*ec-*	*tom*	*-y*
	DERIV	ROOT	DERIV	ROOT	DERIV
philosophy	*phil*	*-o-*	*soph*	*-y*	
	ROOT	DERIV	ROOT	DERIV	

Some derivational affixes have meanings, others have none. The affix *-ish* indicates a tendency or inclination in many words; *-ful* often indicates that something is found to a large degree. The contributions of **privative** (negating) affixes, such as *-less*, *un-*, or *non-*, are always very important. However, the contribution of the root to the meaning of the word is more important still: even a privative affix doesn't convey much information until you know what is being negated.

Quite often, the meaning of a derivational affix is rather fuzzy and varies from word to word. Consider the affix *-ous*. In *tetrapterous* 'having four wings' (like insects), the roots are *tetra* 'four' (compare *tetralogy* 'a literary work in four parts') and *pter* 'wing' (as in *helicopter*, literally 'helix-wing'). If we conclude from this example that *-ous* means 'having', a look at other *-ous* words shows that this isn't true. The word *disastrous* does not mean 'having disaster' and *miraculous* does not mean 'having a miracle'. These examples push us back to a vaguer meaning such as 'characterized by'. But such a notion, common in dictionary definitions, is merely a kind of least common denominator, an attempt to capture what all of the different meanings of *-ous* share. It doesn't capture the different meanings themselves. What actually unites the different occurrences of *-ous* is the fact that they all form adjectives. Quite a few derivational affixes, especially those that occur at the end of a word, are best characterized by their function, which is to mark the word's part of speech.

Finally, there are some derivational affixes that appear to have no meaning or function at all. For example, in the word *floatation*, the derivational suffix *-tion* turns the root *float* into a noun, but the intervening *a* has no obvious function. Such morphs are called **empty** morphs, because they seem to be most easily defined by what they lack: they have neither meaning nor function. But they do have roles in word derivation, often with very specific rules. One must not assume that because a morph is empty it can be added anywhere in a word for mere decoration.

More about Morphs and Meaning

It is not only derivational elements that may have a fuzzy meaning. Even lexical morphs are seldom as well behaved as the simple glosses in the word element lists might lead one to expect. We have to adjust our definition of morphs to reflect their potentially complicated behavior. An example is the morph *curr*, glossed above as 'run'. The fact that this morph doesn't literally mean 'run' in the word *concurrent* may not be too troublesome, because it is easy enough to see the connection between the actual meaning of *concurrent* and the image 'running together'. But this example shows that recognizing literal meanings is only a first step in understanding morphs. Instances of the morph *curr* in words other than *concurrent* may present new images, related in other ways to the literal meaning 'run'. In *recurrent*, whose prefix means 'again', there is normally no running in the literal sense. But the running action denoted by the basic meaning of the morph *curr* makes for a more picturesque image of the bland event 'happen'.

Very often the use of morphological elements relies on our ability to see ways in which one thing stands for another. In *astronomy*, the morph *astr* means 'star'. This strikes us as entirely appropriate, even though astronomy is the study of all heavenly bodies, not just stars. The 'point' designated by the lexical component *punct* in *punctuation* refers not just to a period but to a variety of marks, even blank spaces. In *punctual* the connection with a literal point is different. And in both cases the semantic connection becomes even more tenuous when one realizes that the ultimate root of the component *punct* means 'poke'. In the remainder of this chapter and in chapter 7 we explore the ways in which morphs depart from their literal meanings.

Affixes often present special meaning problems. When they come at the end of a word, they generally have a grammatical function, determining what part of speech a word belongs to, and in all positions they often add to meaning as well. For example, *-ity* creates nouns and often adds the meaning 'quality or state of being' to the base it is attached to. Thus, *sincerity* means 'the quality of being sincere', and *ability* means 'being able'. Some *-ity* nouns designate objects characterized by a certain quality: examples are *monstrosity* 'something monstrous' and *oddity* 'something odd'.

The suffixes *-like, -ish, -esque,* and *-y* all form adjectives, such as *childlike, yellowish, picturesque,* and *risky*. These four suffixes are in fact all somewhat similar semantically; they help to describe a property in terms of its resemblance to some object. But there are also differences between them. *Childlike* can be used in flattering ways (as in *We found his childlike manner disarming*), but *childish* tends to have negative connotations (*Your childish behavior has to stop*). *Spongelike* and *spongy* refer to the same noun to get their meaning, but the meaning is somewhat different. Something *spongelike* is going to be similar to a sponge but something *spongy* may simply be springy but not really like a sponge. Thus, it is probably good for a cake to be spongy but bad for it to be spongelike. (Different individuals may have slightly different senses of the subtler aspects of such distinctions of meaning.)

Suffixes like these show that different elements exhibit different degrees of variation in meaning. The meaning of *-like* is quite uniform from example to example, while *-y* varies in meaning from 'like' (as in *yellowy*) to 'containing an appreciable amount of' (as in *meaty*). Several suffixes, in fact, have a number of distinct meanings or functions. Such cases are best regarded as accidental resemblances in form between different suffixes. For example, besides the adjective-forming suffix *-y*, there is a noun-forming suffix *-y*, which appears in *monogamy, democracy,* and *comedy,* and also a suffix *-y* that forms diminutives, as in *kitty, Billy,* and so on. These three separate occurrences of *-y* obviously have very different meanings.

Other Variations in the Meanings of Morphs

One reason for so much variation in meaning is that language must constantly stretch to accommodate new situations in a changing world. A morph may start out with a particular meaning. Once it is used in different words, however, and those words themselves come to be used in different situations from the ones for which they were initially coined, the meaning of the morph may lose its original simplicity. The morph *ship* once meant specifically 'oceangoing vessel', but in *spaceship* it loses that 'oceangoing' qualification and simply means 'vessel'. Thus, although morphs remain meaningful elements from word to word, we cannot expect their meaning to stay constant from word to word.

Differences in the meaning of the same morph in different words become a little easier to deal with when we realize that there are often patterns to these variations in meaning. Two uses of a morph may not have exactly the same meaning, but the meanings may be related. For example, *pyr* sometimes means 'fire' (as in *pyrotechnics* 'fireworks') and sometimes 'fever' (as in *antipyretic* 'a medication that reduces fever'). The meanings are not the same, but they are related; in this case, the relationship has come about from the use of *pyr* 'fire' as a metaphor for the "burning" of a fever's heat. We deal more with variation in meanings in chapter 7, where we discuss semantics.

Words as Symbols

The word *apteryx* denotes the kiwi, a flightless bird of New Zealand with only rudimentary wings. We can parse this word into its components: the privative prefix *a-*, which means 'without' or 'not', as in *atheist* 'without (belief in) God'; the root *pter* 'wing'; and the suffix *-yx* (a rather rare noun-forming suffix, as in *calyx*). If we assumed that the meaning of a word is completely determined by the meanings of its parts, *apteryx* would mean something like 'wingless thing'. But kiwis aren't literally wingless, and even if they were, there is much more to a kiwi than the state of its wings. Such incompleteness in representation of meaning is the rule rather than the exception. The reason is that words are only symbols, not complete linguistic representations of the physical or conceptual world.

Another example is *bibliophile* (from *bibli* 'book' and *phil* 'liking'), which is a very general term for someone who likes books. Would it, by the same token, be reasonable to infer that a *pedophile* (*ped* 'child') is anyone who likes children? Not really. In *pedophile*, the liking is of a very specific kind, one involving sexual attraction, a sense hardly appropriate to *bibliophile*. Therefore, when we analyze the structure of an English word, even if we succeed in breaking it down into its individual morphs, the task of figuring out the meaning of the word may not be over. We may get significant clues to the complete meaning, but the rest is left up to general knowledge, or common sense, or the idiosyncrasies of the word as a whole. The context in which a word appears can also provide important clues.

The Utility of Morphological Analysis

The analysis of words into morphs not only provides clues to the meaning and function of words we have never seen before but also deepens our knowledge of words we already know. For example, it can provide reliable spelling clues for less familiar words. If we realize that /ˈrɛnəˌvet/ *renovate* contains the component *nov* 'new', we know that the vowel /ə/ in that word is spelled with an <o> rather than an <a> or some other letter. Word analysis also provides constant reminders of the multitude of images on which our language is built. If we already know that *salient* means 'conspicuous', we may not need to know that it is built on the root *sal*, which means 'jump'. But knowing that this word (and others containing the morph *sal*, such as *sally* and *salacious*) is built on an image of jumping may enhance its expressive power for us. Skill in word analysis also helps in recalling words that are not yet thoroughly familiar. Even though many characteristics of the kiwi are not expressed by any particular part of the word *apteryx*, it is easier to recall its relationship to the notable "wingless thing" because of its very common key elements: *pter*, which appears in many words having to do with wings or flying, and *a-* 'not', 'without'.

How We Make Words

New Components from Old

People coin words in many ways, often idiosyncratically. But it is useful to think of words as being built up in the following, ideal, way.

Word formation begins with a lexical morph, a root. If we wish, for example, to coin a word to describe a place with a lot of wind, we might start with the root *wind* then attach to it the adjective-forming affix *-y*, forming *windy* (which we might here write as *wind-y*, to mark clear dividing lines between the morphs). We can call this process **affixation**, or **suffixation**, if we want to be a bit more specific. The component that an affix is added to is called a base. Affixation can be used both to form new lexemes, as here, in which case the process is called **derivation**, or it can be used to create new word forms (e.g., *winds*), in which case it is called **inflection**.

A property of language that makes derivation very flexible is that it permits a certain amount of **recursion**. This means that derivation can create an output (a complex morphological component) that it can then turn around and use as an input to another round of derivation. Derivation doesn't have to apply only to morphs. For example, *wind-y* was created by affixation, and we can apply affixation to *wind-y* to create yet another word, such as *wind-i-ness*. (The alternation of *i* and *y* is just a spelling rule of English, which avoids *i* at the end of words.) If we wish to make this recursion explicit, we can choose to enclose every component within square brackets. This [wind] plus [y] makes [[wind][y]], and [[wind][y]] plus [ness] makes [[[wind][i]][ness]]. This gets cumbersome fast, and we rarely make use of this notation in this book, but you can see how it does have the advantage of making explicit the fact that *-ness* was added to the complex component *wind-y* and not to the morph *y* itself.

We can do the same thing with Latin or Greek morphs. The word *admirable*, for example, starts with the Latin root [mir] 'amazing' and adds the suffix [a] to make it verbal, giving the component [[mir][a]] 'be amazed'. The complex component *mira* is used as the base of **prefixation**: it adds the prefix [ad] (roughly 'to') to give [[ad][[mir][a]]] 'admire'. Finally, that is used as the base for another suffixation, adding [ble] 'capable of', 'worthy of' to give [[[ad][[mir][a]]][ble]]. Again, we should emphasize that you won't normally be asked to figure out the exact steps involved—it's accomplishment enough to work out that *admirable* contains the morphs *ad-mir-a-ble*. But it is good to understand in principle how complicated words can be constructed by the repeated application of simple processes like prefixation and suffixation.

In almost all cases, the last morph of a word is its **grammatical head**. The head of a word is important for a couple of reasons. First, it tells how the word is used in the sentence. Because the last morph of *wind* is a singular noun, it can be used as the subject of verbs like *is*: *Wind is good for dandelions*. The same is true of *wind-i-ness*, because the morph *-ness* marks singular nouns as well: *Windiness is good for dandelions*. But because the last morph of *-y* is adjectival, *windy* can only be used as an adjective: *Windy weather is good for dandelions*, not ×*Windy is good for dandelions*.

For our purposes as students of English word formation, the more important consequence of headedness is that the last morph of a word, its head, determines what further morphological elements can be added to a word. To take an inflectional example: to make the plural of *child*, one must add the suffix *-ren*.

But once one has affixed the suffix *-hood*, that becomes the head of the word, and so determines how the plural of *childhood* is formed, which turns out to be the normal suffix *-s*: *childhoods*. Because *child* is not the head of the word *childhood*, it would be a serious mistake to decide that the plural of *childhood* should be ×*childhoodren* on the grounds that *child* forms its plural by adding *-ren*. A more general example of how heads control affixation is that when the head of a word is an inflectional morph, it does not tolerate any further affixation at all. That is why we create words like *childhood* and *bookish*, not ×*childrenhood* and ×*booksish*, even if we are talking about the early life of several people, or people who are fond of reading more than one book.

Compounding

Combining two or more roots in the same word is called **compounding**. Sometimes the resulting new word is written as one word:

workbook
blackboard
mailman

But many expressions similar to these are ordinarily written as two words:

exercise book
bulletin board
mail carrier

There are two rules (if we dare to call them that) that we are aware of for spacing in compounds. First, if at least one element is more than one syllable long, the words of the compound tend to be written separately. That is the case with the last three examples.

Second, many compounds are written as a single word if they have been in the language for a while or are used very commonly. So even though the first element of *checkerboard* is two syllables long, there is no space in the compound.

The rules for punctuating compounds are arbitrary enough to warrant lots of variation in practice. The most important thing to understand is that *exercise book*, like the other examples listed here, is actually a compound word and not a phrase. Many people mistakenly take *exercise* to be an adjective because it looks like a separate word and it modifies the meaning of the word *book*. This is cogent reasoning, but the space is not very good evidence; it is just a writing convention of English (many other languages, including Latin and Greek, do not use spaces in such cases) and is inconsistently applied at that. In contrast to a true adjective–noun phrase like *small book*, *exercise book* behaves more like *workbook* in such matters as stress (*éxercise bòok, wórkbòok*, vs. *smàll bóok*), inflection (*smaller book* but not ×*exerciser book*, ×*workerbook*), and ability to change word order (*This book is small* means the same as *This is a small book*, but *This book is exercise* doesn't mean the same thing as *This is an exercise book*).

The most common way to form compounds in English is to combine a noun with a noun to form another noun, as in most of the examples above. But compounds can be of any part of speech and be built up of different types of elements.

Star Trek N	*star* N + ***trek*** N
White House N	*white* A + ***house*** N
window-shop V	*window* N + ***shop*** V
stir-fry V	*stir* V + ***fry*** V
jet-black A	*jet* N + ***black*** A
update V	*up* ADV + *date* N
easygoing A	*easy* ADV + *go* V + ***ing*** A
able-bodied A	*able* A + *body* N + ***ed*** A
in between PREP	*in* ADV + ***between*** PREP
killjoy N	*kill* V + *joy* N

Usually the last element in the compound is the head (marked in boldface above), just as in affixation, so that element determines the part of speech of the whole compound. But there are several counterexamples to this rule, and words for which it is not even clear which element, if any, is the head (as in *update* and *killjoy*).

From the examples one might conclude that compounding combines words, but that is not strictly true. Consider the ungrammaticality of words such as ×*windows-shopping* and ×*killedjoy*. From a logical point of view these make perfectly good sense—why shouldn't someone who used to ruin parties in the past, but has reformed, be a ×*killedjoy*? Compounding doesn't actually operate on words; it operates on stems. The stem, we recall, is the form of the word before inflectional endings are added. The elements in *killjoy* are actually the uninflected stems *kill-* and *joy-*. Inflections can only be affixed to the finished compound, which is why they are found only at the end of compounds, not in the middle of them. There are, admittedly, a few glaring exceptions like *humanities professor*. Most of these involve plurals that have specialized meanings—the humanities are a scholarly discipline, whereas *humanity* is the state of being human or humane. Apparently this difference in meaning makes the plural enough like a distinct lexeme to be an acceptable component of a compound.

The existence of rules like headedness and exclusion of inflectional affixes shows that compounding, which may seem at first glance so simple and natural, is rule governed, like every other aspect of language. Another piece of evidence that it is rule governed comes from the fact that compounding works differently in different languages. In French, noun–noun compounds are quite rare; most compounds are verb–noun, like *amuse-bouche*. The corresponding pattern is pretty rare in English, though examples like *killjoy* and *pickpocket* do exist. Latin formed compounds somewhat more freely than French but had a special rule whereby it normally inserted an *i* between the two components of the compound. Greek formed compounds very freely, normally inserting an *o* between elements. These patterns are usually followed in English when we build new compounds out of Latin or Greek elements: *ped-i-cure, micr-o-scope*. The connective element, a type of empty morph, is called an **interfix** because, unlike prefixes and suffixes, which are attached to the beginning or end of elements, an interfix only comes between components.

A feature of compounds that makes them especially versatile is the kinds of relation understood to exist between the elements that make up the compound. For example, in *footstep*, the noun *foot* specifies the subject of the action noun *step*. By contrast, *doorstep* uses *door* to specify the location of the noun *step*. If you look through a list of compounds, you will find many different types of relationship expressed between the two elements.

But there is also a sense in which *footstep* and *doorstep* have similar internal relations. The *foot* of *footstep* narrows down the type of step being expressed to the step made by a foot. A footstep is a kind of step; or, in more technical terms, *footstep* is a **hyponym**, or subtype, of *step* and *step* is a **hypernym**, or supertype, of *footstep*. Similarly, the *door* of *doorstep* narrows down the type of step to one directly outside a door: *doorstep* is also a hyponym of *step*, and *step* is a hypernym of *doorstep*. Compounds that are hyponyms of one of their components are called **endocentric**: their hypernym is found inside the compound.

Now consider the compounds *pickpocket* and *redhead*. A pickpocket is not a type of pocket or a type of picking; a redhead is not a type of head or a type of red. Rather, they describe a **person** who picks pockets and a **person** with red hair. Neither of the components of these compounds is a hypernym of the compound, and so they are called **exocentric**.

Conversion

English is well known for the facility with which it permits words to be converted from one part of speech to another, without making any visible or audible change in the word. This is called **conversion**.

table N	*The committee laid the bill on the table.* →
table V	*The committee tabled the bill.*
Xerox N	*I copied this with a Xerox brand photocopier.* →
xerox V	*I xeroxed this.*
control V	*The new treatment controls things excellently.* →
control N	*The new treatment provides excellent control.*
overnight A	*Better request overnight delivery on this package.* →
overnight V	*Better overnight this package.*
retrospective A	*MOMA has a retrospective exhibition of her work.* →
retrospective N	*MOMA has a retrospective of her work.*
out ADV	*The president was forced out of the closet.* →
out V	*The president was outed.*

This process usually creates a noun or a verb out of some other part of speech. Conversion is also called **zero derivation** by the following reasoning: if the verb *magnetize* is derived from the noun *magnet* by adding *-ize*, then arguably the verb *xerox* is derived from the noun *Xerox* by adding nothing at all—zero.

Often, however, something is added in pronunciation even if not in spelling: the derivation of one form from another is marked by a stress difference. Compare the pronunciation of the verb and noun forms of the following words:

addíct v   *Clarence is addicted to reality TV.*

áddict N   *Clarence is a reality addict.*

prógress N   *Aviation made rapid progress in the 1910s.*

progréss v   *Aviation progressed rapidly in the 1910s.*

séparàte v   *I wish the store would separate the ensemble and sell the blouse
                       and skirt as individual pieces.*

séparate N   *I wish the store would sell the blouse and skirt as separates.*

When there is a stress difference, nouns are stressed on the first syllable, while verbs are characterized by stress (primary or secondary) on a subsequent syllable. Because stress causes conversion in the same way as suffixes and prefixes can, it can be thought of as an affix. Specifically, it is called a **superfix**, because it neither precedes nor follows the word but floats above it in some metaphorical sense (like the accent marks we have supplied in the examples).

Clipping

So far we have been discussing classical patterns of word formation. Affixation, compounding, and conversion account for virtually all word formation in Latin and Greek, and the great bulk of the English vocabulary as well. But present-day English vocabulary is also characterized by several other notable patterns.

An example is **clipping**, the process of extracting chunks of words to stand for the whole. Recent informal clippings like

key	*kilogram*
dis	*disrespect*
hyper	*hyperactive*
info	*information*
hood	*neighborhood*
leet (or *1337*)	*elite*
net	*Internet*
morph	*metamorphose*
neocon	*neoconservative*

join a host of earlier clippings that now seem very ordinary:

ad lib	*ad libitum*
auto	*automobile*
blitz	*blitzkrieg*
bus	*omnibus*
flu	*influenza*
graph	*graphic formula*
intercom	*intercommunication system*
lab	*laboratory*
phone	*telephone*
radio	*radiotelegraphy*
tux	*tuxedo*
van	*caravan*

The major criterion in clipping is phonological, not morphological. Usually one or two syllables are extracted to make a pithy English-sounding word, without regard for morph boundaries in the original word. *Van* was originally just a meaningless syllable in *caravan*, which is a one-morph word. Of course, now that *van* has become a well-accepted word in its own right, it can act as a morph in new words such as *vanpool*. Unfortunately, this makes it easy to mistakenly want to analyze *caravan* as if it were ˣ*cara-van*.

Blends

Our vocabulary is enhanced as well by **blends** formed from parts of two or more words. The standard example is *smog*, a blend of *smoke* and *fog*.

But English has many others, including the following entries from the *American Heritage Dictionary*:

sexploitation	*sex, exploitation*
billion	*bi, million*
motel	*motor, hotel*
squiggle	*squirm, wiggle*
emoticon	*emotion, icon*
netiquette	*Internet, etiquette*
homophobia	*homosexual, phobia*

pixel	*pictures, element*
lit crit	*literary, criticism*

The difference between a blend and a compound is that in a blend, one or both of the components are clipped. Blends in which the components overlap in pronunciation or spelling are especially popular. For example, in *sexploitation*, one cannot say where *sex* leaves off and *exploitation* begins: the *-ex-* could belong to either.

Blends are often created with an aura of frivolity, but they serve the vital purpose of allowing us to succinctly refer to concepts that would otherwise be a mouthful, and they are used in many serious contexts. The members of the International Criminal Police Organization are not joking around when they refer to themselves as *Interpol*. And blends are crucial in such fields as chemistry and molecular biology, where words like *aldehyde* and *aflatoxin* are much more convenient than the alternatives (*alcohol dehydrogenatum* and *Aspergillus flavus toxin*).

Initialisms and Acronyms

Another way of reducing potentially long names to something manageable is to represent a phrase by its initial letters. Words so formed are called **initialisms**.

USA	*United States of America*
GAO	*Government Accounting Office*
IBM	*International Business Machines*
WWW	*World Wide Web*
OK	*Oll Korrect*

Often people do not think of initialisms as being words, because they seem so much like abbreviations. The difference is that abbreviations, like *Dr.* and *ME*, are intended to be pronounced in full when read out loud (*doctor, Middle English*), whereas an initialism has a pronunciation of its own, the concatenation of the names of its component letters. Indeed, in speech the initialism often becomes more frequent than the full phrase or replaces it entirely.

Some initialisms are read off by the sounds of their letters rather than by the names of their letters. This type of initialism is called an **acronym**. A frequently cited example is *radar*, which stands for *radio detecting and ranging*. Others, from *Dickson's Word Treasury*,[1] are:

scuba	*self-contained underwater breathing apparatus*
Qantas	*Queensland and Northern Territory Aerial Services*

As these examples suggest, acronyms are even more likely than initialisms to completely supplant the original phrase they were derived from.

Perhaps the ultimate development in acronymy is when the acronym makes sense as a word that describes some aspect of its meaning.

zip (code)	*Zone Improvement Program*
NOW	*National Organization for Women*
ACT	*American Conservatory Theater*
MADD	*Mothers Against Drunk Driving*

Often the full phrases are invented only as a justification for the acronym. Such acronyms are often called **reverse acronyms**, because the normal order of development is reversed.

The only drawback to acronyms is that that word-formation pattern makes it far too easy to make up a perfectly credible etymology for a word out of thin air. Consequently, questionable etymologies abound that explain words as being acronyms. One often hears that *phat* comes from *pretty, hot, and tempting,* or that *posh* comes from *port out, starboard home,* purportedly an observation about how posh people book sea voyages between England and India. People often claim that the word *news* is an acronym formed from the points of the compass, which misses the much more obvious explanation that **news** is information about **new**ly occurring events. Many of these explanations began as wordplay that mistakenly came to be taken as literal word histories. Acronyms can be fun, but the student of English vocabulary elements should be cautious to verify the accuracy of acronymic etymologies picked up on the street.

---

1. Paul Dickson, *Dickson's Word Treasury: A Connoisseur's Collection of Old and New, Weird and Wonderful, Useful and Outlandish Words*, rev. ed. (New York: Wiley & Sons, 1992).

Onomatopoeia and Sound Symbolism

The normal situation with morphs is for sound and meaning to be totally divorced from one another. In *cat*, there is nothing inherent in the individual sounds or sound combinations that suggests the meaning 'cat'. But occasionally the sounds do suggest meanings.

In **onomatopoeia**, a word attempts to mimic the sound it describes, or occasionally the object that makes that sound.

> *pow*
> *creak*
> *blip*
> *flap*
> *bleat*
> *cuckoo*
> *bobwhite*
> *cough*
> *babble*

Slightly different from onomatopoeia is **sound symbolism**. Here, the connection between the sound of the word and its meaning is less direct. Some probable examples are:

> *putrid*
> *foul*
> *mother*
> *teeny*
> *humongous*

The root of *putrid* is *pu* and dates back to a Proto-Indo-European exclamation of disgust. This root is sound symbolic because it mimics the natural (nonlinguistic) sound humans might make on smelling rotten food; if it were onomatopoetic it would name the sound itself, or the person making the sound. *Foul* has the same origin but has been significantly altered by Grimm's law and the Great Vowel Shift. The element *cac* from chapter 1 may also be a symbolic cry of disgust; compare *caca* 'excrement' in baby talk. A huge number of the word's languages have an /m/ in their word for *mother*, because this is the sound a baby most easily makes when making sucking movements.[2]

Some sound-symbolic words don't mimic sounds at all. In *teeny*, the consonants and especially the /i/ vowels suggest smallness synesthetically; that is, the thin, sharp sound of the /i/ indicates smallness in other, nonacoustic domains. In *humongous*, the opposite is true.

The existence of sound symbolism is beguiling, because when one knows English so well that it becomes second nature, one starts to feel that most words sound like what they mean—even if in fact their sounds are completely arbitrary, as in *cat*. Often some crosslinguistic investigation will tell us whether a sound–meaning correspondence is really sound symbolism. For example, experiments have shown that children presented with the two totally made-up words *takete* and *uloomu* overwhelmingly choose the first as the name of an angular object and the second as the name of a curvy one—whether the children are English speakers from England or Swahili speakers from Tanzania.[3] Thus, awareness of the possible effects of sound symbolism, if approached cautiously, may provide clues to the meanings of some words.

Analogy

In applying these techniques for building words—affixation, compounding, clipping, and so forth—people normally add a dose of analogy. For example, when a word was needed to express an abnormal dread of spiders, one could have proceeded in many ways, selecting from several different English, Latin, or Greek roots and combining them in different ways. Why not form the compound *spider dread* or (from Latin roots) *araneihorror*, or the blend *spidread*? All of those, and more, make perfect sense. But because the psychoanalytical literature already contained several words like *agoraphobia*, *acrophobia*, and *xenophobia*, analogy suggested *arachnophobia*—a compound using Greek roots, the second of which is *phob*, with the suffix *-ia*. To take another example, we have occasionally noticed people saying that their dogs

2. Roman Jakobson, "Why 'mama' and 'papa'?" In his *Selected Writings* (2nd ed.) (The Hague: Mouton, 1971), 538–545.
3. R. Davis, "The Fitness of Names to Drawings: A Cross-Cultural Study in Tanganyika," *British Journal of Psychology, 52*, 3 (1961): 259–268.

caninify certain qualities. If a person can personify bravery then a dog, apparently, should be able to caninify it. The word *caninify* obviously owes its existence to analogy, but at the same time it can be described as a normal outcome of the process of affixation.

Analogical reasoning may result in **back-formation**, where a simple word is derived from a more complex word. The words *edition* and *editor* existed in English long before the simple word *edit*. Clearly somebody noted that -*tor* and -*tion* often are used to derive nouns from Latinate verbs ending in -*t*, and so decided that an **edit**or is one who **edits editions**. That is completely logical, but historically speaking what has happened was not affixation: it was the undoing of a supposed affixation. Similarly, *peddle* is formed from *peddler* and *televise* from *television*. The availability of a potential back-formation by no means guarantees its acceptance, however. Hans Marchand[4] lists a number of attempts that never caught on. Examples of missed opportunities include:

> *to auth*
> *to ush*
> *to buttle*

The examples of analogy we have given so far would be hard to identify without special historical information. Just looking at the word *arachnophobia* will not tell you that it was coined, in part, by analogy with *agoraphobia* and not the other way around. However, some back-formed words leave us clues:

> *This tape will **self-destruct** in five seconds.*
> *Nobody would **carjack** my beat-up Hyundai.*

At first glance, *self-destruct* and *carjack* seem like ordinary compounds, with a little blending added in the latter case (*car, hijack*). But there's something a little strange with these words. Since when have English verbs expressed their objects by compounding? We don't ˣdinner-eat after we ˣself-wash-up. We would expect that Mr. Phelps's tape should **destroy itself**, and that people should not **hijack**

---

4. *The Categories and Types of Present-Day English Word-Formation*, 2nd ed. (Munich: Beck, 1969).

my old car. But we do have lots of English nouns that compound with objects, in particular, *self-destruction* and *carjacking*. People have back-formed verbs from the nouns by simple analogy:

> *reaction* N is from *react* V + *-ion* N
>
> ::
>
> *self-destruction* N is from *self-destruct* V + *-ion* N

—without noticing that the compound verb would not normally have existed in the first place.

Reverse acronyms are back-formations, and in fact some people whimsically call them *backronyms*. Sometimes one needs historical information to reliably discern whether the phrase or the acronym came first. Often, however, one can spot a backronym from the fact that it just sounds much better than the full phrase. Also, acronyms more than a few letters long rarely arise by sheer coincidence. One strongly doubts, for example, that the authors of the USA PATRIOT Act were surprised to discover that that acronym just happened to emerge from the official title *Uniting and Strengthening America by Providing Appropriate Tools Required to Intercept and Obstruct Terrorism*.[5]

Analogy can lead to **reanalysis**, where people misperceive the morphological composition of a word. Often reanalysis is harmless and undetectable: if somebody thinks that antennas are so named because ants have them, or that an uproar is so called because people roar in the streets during an uproar, we would never even know it, unless of course that person expresses such opinions on a morphology quiz (*roar* means 'move' in *uproar*, being a loan from Dutch or Low German; *antenna* is the Latin word for *sailyard*). But it is also easy to imagine how reanalysis could lead one astray.

Many reanalyses have become established as part of everyday speech. The word *sovereign* picked up its <g> because someone imagined that the final syllable of that word was from *reign* (the suffix is actually *-an* as in *Mississippian*). Similarly, *marijuana* picked up the <j> in English because it was interpreted as coming from the names *María* and *Juana*; the original Spanish word was *marihuana* or *mariguana*. So many people have taken *covert* as containing *overt* that

5. U.S. Congress, H.R. 3162 (October 24, 2001).

its pronunciation has been affected: traditionally /ˈkəvr̩t/, being a derivative of *cover*, but now mostly /ˈkovr̩t/ or /koˈvr̩t/, to rime with *overt*. Enough people have somehow found the word *bosom* in *buxom* that one would now be foolish to use it in its original sense of 'obedient'.

Widely accepted restructurings of established words due to reanalysis are called **folk etymologies**. The word *pea* was *pese* in Middle English, where it was originally a singular noun. But the final /z/ sound came to be taken as a plural ending, and so the ending was eventually subtracted to give a new singular form, *pea*. For the term *chaise lounge*, English speakers modified the French expression *chaise longue* by substituting the English word *lounge* for the French adjective *longue*. Because the French adjective means 'long' and has no connection with lounging, this is quite a switch. Why English speakers didn't also change the first word, *chaise*, is anyone's guess. Finally, the only connection between Jerusalem artichokes and the city of Jerusalem is the similarity in sound of the name of this city with the Italian term *girasole*, which means 'sunflower'; the Jerusalem artichoke is in fact a kind of North American sunflower.

The amazing thing about many folk etymologies is that often they make very little sense. What could a sockeye possibly be? How could anyone think a cockroach (from *cucaracha*) has anything to do with cocks (male chickens) or roaches (a type of fish)? Apparently the main motivation in many cases is simply to transform long strings of unfamiliar syllables into familiar English morphs that sound vaguely similar; the fact that the parts have little or nothing to do with the meaning of the whole is often neglected. Nevertheless, folk etymologies should not leave us shamefaced, for even the term *shamefaced* is a folk etymology, coming from Middle English *shamefast*, 'bound by shame'.

Morphology or Etymology?

Morphology studies the components of words; etymology studies the history of words. When the definitions are stated so starkly, the distinction between morphology and etymology seems very clear. But in practice, a morphological analysis of a word is often very hard to tell apart from a etymological analysis. Consider the following pairs of statements:

MORPHOLOGY: *Blackbird* is a compound of *black* and *bird*.
ETYMOLOGY: *Blackbird* was formed by compounding *black* with *bird*.

MORPHOLOGY: *USA* is an initialism of *United States of America.*
ETYMOLOGY: *USA* was formed from the initials of the main words in
United States of America.

In these sentences, the difference between morphology and etymology is trivial, and it disappears entirely when the statements are brief enough. More often than not, you'll find that the sort of concise etymologies found in most dictionaries serves very well as a morphological analysis. The confluence of etymology and morphology is particularly strong in a book like this one, where the history of a word is taken as an important piece of evidence for its morphology.

But often there is a sharp distinction between morphology and etymology. Here are some examples of etymological statements that would be out of place in a morphological analysis:

The word *deficit* first appeared in print in English in 1782, and was borrowed from French.
Oak comes from the Old English word *āc.* It is related to the German
word *Eich.*

This kind of information is also included in many dictionaries, and students need to be careful not to automatically copy out such information when asked to do purely morphological research. These facts say nothing about what the functional elements of the words might be. By the same token, morphological statements such as the following would be considered laughably inadequate by etymologists:

Deficit has the structure *de-fic-i-t,* where the root is *fic* 'do'.
Oak is a morpheme.

There are even situations when the morphology conflicts with the etymol-
ogy. While *cockroach* certainly derives from *cucaracha* historically, today it is a compound of *cock* and *roach. Scissors* can be traced etymologically to the Latin root *cid* 'cut', which puts it in the same group of words as *decide* and *incisor,* but in its modern spelling it groups more naturally with words such as *scissile* and *scission,* so arguably it now shares with those words the morph *sciss,* which means 'split' or 'cut'.

This book deals with both morphology and etymology, so the reader should always be attentive to the distinction. Perhaps the biggest source of confusion comes from the fact that in discussing a word's morphology, we often talk about whether elements are native, Latin, or Greek. Because the classical Latin and Greek languages were spoken a few thousand years ago, this certainly sounds like a historical, therefore etymological, approach. However, the source language is mentioned primarily because word elements from different languages often have different morphological properties in English, as we shall see shortly. Besides, most of the words that contain Latin and Greek elements weren't borrowed thousands of years ago. Most, in fact, are modern creations. The word *anemometer*, for example, was coined in the eighteenth century. Knowing that *anem* 'wind' and *met* 'measure' are Greek roots helps us understand why the interfix -*o*- is used in this compound.

Summary

Unlike etymology, which studies the history of words, morphology is the study of the functional composition of words. Components may be complex, consisting of other components, or simplex, in which case they are called morphs. Lexical components, including every content word, contain at least one root, which provides the core meaning. Affixes may accompany the root. They add to the meaning or provide grammatical information such as the part of speech; empty affixes do neither. Affixes are either inflectional, making different word forms for a lexeme, or derivational, forming different lexemes. Affixes can also be classified by where they attach to their bases: prefixes attach before, suffixes after, interfixes between, and superfixes cause change of stress in English.

The meanings of a morph may vary from word to word. The meaning of a morph in a specific word can often be derived from general knowledge, context, or an understanding of the systematic ways in which meanings vary.

The most important types of word-formation processes are affixation and compounding, both of which are potentially recursive. Compounds combine two lexical stems, sometimes with an empty interfix between them. They may be endocentric, containing their own hypernym as one of their components, or exocentric. Conversion changes a stem from one part of speech to another with no change other than an occasional change of stress. Less traditional processes include clipping, which is often accompanied by blending; initialisms and acronyms; and onamatopoeia and sound symbolism. In practice, word formation often considers the analogy of existing words as well. Analogy can also lead to back-formation of simpler words from more complex ones and can be easily detected only if the product is irregular. Finally, analogy can cause people to assign false structures to words, sometimes bringing about folk etymology, where a word changes its spelling or pronunciation to agree better with the reanalyzed structure.

Word Elements

Learn the following derivational affixes and their glosses. The glosses A, N, and V indicate that the element makes words having a specific part of speech: adjective, noun, and verb, respectively.

Suffix	Gloss	Source	Examples
-ance	N	L	penance, exuberance
-ant	A, N	L	Protestant, defiant, tenant
-ary	A, N	L	temporary, tertiary, mortuary, granary
-ate	N, A, V	L	delegate, irate, navigate, novitiate, precipitate, prelate, roseate
-ence	N	L	science, intransigence
-ent	A, N	L	parent, proponent, incumbent
-ic	A, N	L, G	chronic, topic, photographic, neurotic, psychic, historic
-ity	N	L	stupidity, alacrity, monstrosity, femininity, paucity
-ize	V	G	vocalize, Americanize, extemporize, psychologize
-oid	resembling (A, N)	G	android, spheroid, pterygoid, adenoids
-ory	A, N	L	sensory, auditory, oratory
-ous	A	L	porous, poisonous, ridiculous, pompous
-sis	N	G	analysis, tmesis, symphysis, thesis, phthisis, praxis
-tion	N	L	nation, action
-tive	A, N	L	native, laxative
-y	N	L, G	astronomy, sympathy, privacy

Prefix	Gloss	Source	Examples
ab-	from, away	L	*abreact, abolish, abdicate, ablative, absolute*
ad-	to, toward	L	*adapt, adit, abbreviate, adduce, affect, annul, arrive, attract*
an-	not, without	G	*anarchy, anhydrous, anaerobic*
ana-	up, again, back	G	*anachronism, anaclastic, analeptic, anacardium, anabolic, analog*
ante-	before	L	*anterior, antebellum, antedate, antecedent*
apo-	away from, off	G	*apology, apocrypha, apostasy, apoplectic, apotheosis, apogee*
cata-	down, backwards	G	*cataclysm, catapult, catalyst, catalepsy, catalog, catacomb*
con-	with	L	*convene, concomitant, concord*
contra-	against, facing	L	*contraceptive, contradict, contrapositive*
de-	reverse, from	L	*detract, descend, decode, denote, demand, deoxygenate, deport, destruction*
dia-	through	G	*diameter, dialysis, diathesis, dialogue, diopter, diaphoresis, diapositive*
ec-	out	G	*ecstatic, tonsillectomy, appendectomy*
ecto-	outside	G	*ectoderm, ectoplasm, ectoparasite, ectomorph*
en-	in	G	*encephalitis, energy, encyst*
endo-	inside	G	*endogamy, endoscopy, endopsychic, endomorph*
epi-	on, over	G	*epitome, epitaph, epigram, epibiotic, epicene*
eu-	good	G	*euphoria, eulogy, euthanasia, eugenic, euphony, euphemism, euphuism*
ex-	out	L	*excavate, except, exfoliate, extend, educe, exact, egregious*
extra-	outside	L	*extraordinary, extraterrestrial, extramarital, extraneous*
hetero-	other	G	*heterosexual, heterodox, heterogeneous, heterodont, heterodyne, heteronomy*
homo-	same	G	*homosexual, homologous, homogeneous*
hypo-	under, below	G	*hypodermic, hypalgia, hypothermia, hypothesis, hypogeal, hypophysis*
in-	in, into	L	*invade, inception, incinerate, incite*

Prefix	Gloss	Source	Examples
in-	not	L	*incompatible, ignorant, inequity, illegal, impossible, irreverent*
infra-	below	L	*infrared, infrastructure, infralapsarian*
inter-	between	L	*internal, interior, international, interfere, interject, intercalate*
intra-	within	L	*intramural, intravenous, intrauterine*
iso-	equal	G	*isometrics, isosceles, isopathy, isobar*
meso-	middle	G	*mesosphere, mesomorph, mesobiotic, Mesopotamian, Mesolithic*
meta-	beyond	G	*metaphysics, metamorphosis, metaphor, metalanguage, method*
ob-	toward, against	L	*object, obstacle, obdurate, obit, obreption, obloquy, obstruct*
para-	beside, nearly	G	*parallel, paramedic, paranormal, paragraph, parody*
per-	through, thorough	L	*pervade, pernicious, perspicacity, perturb*
peri-	around, near	G	*perimeter, periscope, perihelion*
post-	after, behind	L	*postwar, posterior, posterity, postpartum, postpose, postprandial*
pre-	before	L	*prehistoric, preadolescent, prewashed*
pro-	forward, for	L, G	*proceed, prowar, provide, procure, produce*
re-	again, back	L	*review, reappoint*
se-	apart	L	*separate, select, seduce, segregate*
sub-	under	L	*subhuman, subclass, subreption, success, suffuse, suborn*
super-	above	L	*superficial, superpower, supercilious, supersede*
syn-	with	G	*synchronize, sympathy, syllogism, symphony, synergy, systolic*
trans-	across, through	L	*trans-Atlantic, transparent, transaction, transfigure, translucent*

Element Study

1. Look up the words below to see which parts of speech they can represent. For words that can function as two or more different parts of speech, does the pronunciation of *-ate* differ depending on part of speech?

a. *saturate*
b. *primate*
c. *prevaricate*
d. *delicate*
e. *irate*
f. *prelate*
g. *relate*

2. Many adjectives in *-ic* have a noun counterpart. Which of the words below function both as adjectives and nouns? Where does stress normally go on words ending in this suffix? Is the rule for stress more regular for adjectives or for nouns?

a. *comic*
b. *historic*
c. *eccentric*
d. *concentric*
e. *arithmetic*
f. *basic*
g. *sardonic*
h. *automatic*

3. The suffix *-ize* is one of our most common and most productive endings. To get a feel for its productivity, list ten adjectives or nouns that this suffix can be attached to and list another ten that it cannot be attached to.

4. Replace the prefixes in the words below with a different prefix from the element set from this chapter. In each case, show how prefixes affect meaning by contrasting the meaning of the original word with the meaning of the word you turned it into.

a. *catabolic*
b. *contravene*
c. *diagnostic*
d. *ectoderm*
e. *hypomanic*
f. *infrasonic*
g. *metapsychology*
h. *periscope*
i. *persist*
j. *secede*

Exercises

1. Starting with the word *arm* 'weapon', list a dozen other English words related to it by regular word-formation processes, for example, *arms* and *disarm* but not *harm*. Be aware that *arm* 'upper limb' is an unrelated word and so you should not include words related to it, such as *armpit*. It is all right to include words like *armament*, in which the word formation actually took place in another language (Latin).

2. Using each of the following suffixes, give four examples of words to illustrate what part of speech they form. In general, what is the part of speech of the stem that each suffix is added to? Is there a general pattern to the meaning of the suffix besides the part of speech which it forms? (E.g., *-like* in *childlike, lifelike, dreamlike,* and *doglike* forms adjectives from nouns. These adjectives all mean 'similar to or resembling [the noun] in some respect'.)

    a. *-ish*   b. *-ity*   c. *-ize*

3. Each entry in the following list actually represents two or more distinct suffixes that happen to have the same spelling and, in some cases, the same pronunciation. For each one, determine the different suffixes it represents by naming the different type of word (e.g., noun, verb, adjective) that each is used to form. Give examples and explain the differences in meaning the suffixes give a word. For example, for *-y* we would say that there is one suffix *-y* that attaches to a noun and forms an adjective meaning 'having or associated with [the meaning of the noun]', as in the word *dirt-y*; and that there is another suffix *-y* that attaches to a proper noun to make another proper noun with a diminutive or affectionate sense in the names, as in *Bill-y* and *Joe-y*.

    a. *-er*   b. *-ly*   c. *-ate*   d. *-al*

4. Using a dictionary or the glossary in appendix 1, parse and gloss the word *antidisestablishmentarianism*: divide the word into morphs and write the meaning or other function of each morph underneath it. You can treat *establish* as a single element. How many prefixes does the word have? How many suffixes? Using the discussion of the word *apteryx* in this chapter as a model, indicate what portion of the meaning of the word given by the dictionary definition comes directly from the glosses of the individual morphs. What portion of the word's definition is not contained in the morphs themselves but inferred from general knowledge or the actual

use of the word? (Note that *disestablishment* is the withdrawal of especial state patronage and control from a church.)

5. Characterize the relationship between the two elements in the compounds given below and say whether they are exocentric or endocentric. Often it is easiest to do this if you break the word into two elements X and Y, then ask if the word names a type of Y. If possible, try to find a few other examples of compounds that have the same relationship. Do you think the type of compound is productive—could people freely invent new compounds of that type which would be readily understood? As an example, for the compound *sidestep*, one might answer that to sidestep is to step to the side; *side* is a noun naming the place to which one steps. Other examples of such a pattern are *backslide* and *top-dress*. It appears moderately awkward to compose new examples like *×couchsit* or *×away-run*.

   a. *earthworm*
   b. *garage sale*
   c. *endgame*
   d. *french fry*
   e. *bluebird*
   f. *redneck*

6. Identify prefixes, roots, and suffixes in the following words. Looking them up is not cheating.

   a. *anaerobic*
   b. *catastrophe*
   c. *equilibrate*
   d. *contrapositive*
   e. *helicopter*

7. Identify whether blending, clipping, or a combination of the two processes is involved in the formation of the following recent words. What do you think the words mean?

   a. *digerati*
   b. *Jamerican*
   c. *prequel*
   d. *prebuttal*
   e. *Heartzels*
   f. *cyborg*
   g. *Frankenfood*
   h. *infomercial*

8. Create a new word by blending parts of two existing words (in bold below) together. As in the exercise above, the result often sounds more natural if blending includes clipping both words. But in some cases only one of the words needs to be clipped. You might want to check the World Wide Web to see if your answer is attested. If it is, please provide the URL.

   a. a type of cuisine combining **Mexican** and **Mediterranean** elements
   b. a newspaper item that is an **advertisement** but that looks like **editorial** content
   c. products that are sold as **cosmetics** but that have **pharmaceutical** uses
   d. a show that is both a **drama** and a **comedy**
   e. a **movie** that is made into a Broadway **musical**
   f. research relating to the researcher's own identity, in effect making **me** the focus of the **research**

9. The adjectives in -*y* below show how highly productive this suffix is in English. They also illustrate that productiveness is no guarantee of uniformity. Examine this list for patterns of any kind. Some properties worth considering include predominant parts of speech the suffix is attached to, segments of the vocabulary that the suffix draws from (e.g., formal, informal and technical, nontechnical), variations in meaning in the suffix itself or in the stems it attaches to, predominance of metaphorical or nonmetaphorical uses, and any restrictions on the kinds of words that can be formed by adding -*y*. If a pattern admits a few exceptions, give the exceptions along with the pattern.

   These examples all begin with <a>, <b>, or <c>. Feel free to add any words that help you make a point, regardless of what letter they start with.

achy	*bossy*	*catty*
airy	*bouncy*	*chesty*
angry	*brainy*	*chocolaty*
balmy	*brawny*	*choky*
batty	*breathy*	*choosy*
beefy	*brushy*	*crabby*
billowy	*bumpy*	*creaky*
bloody	*busty*	*creamy*
boozy	*buttery*	*creepy*
bosomy	*carroty*	

CHAPTER FOUR

Allomorphy

In the last chapter, we learned that morphs do not necessarily hold their meaning constant from word to word. Now we learn to deal with another characteristic that also serves to make morphs more elusive than we might like: they may change their form from word to word.

Consider plural endings. There are several similar morphs that can make a noun plural:

peach-es	/ˈpitʃ-əz/
plum-s	/pləm-z/
grape-s	/grep-s/

Because these morphs all have the same function and similar pronunciation, they can be thought of as variant forms of the same thing. This "same thing" is called a **morpheme**. The suffix *-eme* indicates that the word *morpheme* names a linguistic unit that cannot be subdivided any further—in this respect a morpheme is like a morph. In addition, *-eme* means that the item is somewhat abstract, in that we don't specify an exact pronunciation.

The morpheme is such a useful concept that most discussions of morphology talk about morphemes much more than they talk about morphs. Even when a morph has no alternate forms—*walk* /wɒk/, for example, stays the same no matter what word it is part of—we still usually refer to the *walk* morpheme rather than the *walk* morph. This is because meaning and functionality tend to interest linguists more than the exact sounds, at least most of the time.

Nevertheless, morphs are important. A learner of English who only learned one pronunciation for each morpheme and consequently spoke earnestly of

/'pləməz/ and /'grepəz/ would attract a certain amount of attention. Language learners must learn allomorphy—how a morpheme varies depending on which other morphemes accompany it in a word. The need to study allomorphy applies just as strongly when it comes to learning the Latin and Greek elements presented in this book. When Latin and Greek morphemes are borrowed into English, their allomorphy usually comes along with them. These rules are rarely intuitively obvious to vocabulary learners, but learning them can pay dividends. Knowing allomorphy rules can

- vastly reduce memory load,
- prevent incorrect analyses of unfamiliar words, and
- help one create more acceptable coinages.

Consider what would happen if learners of English didn't know the rules of English plural allomorphy. They would have to make a special effort to learn the plural of each noun. When hearing a word like *dunce* /dəns/, they might think it is a plural of *dun* /dən/, while we who know the rules realize the plural of *dun* must be *duns*, ending in a /z/ sound. When creating new words, learners unfamiliar with the rules could attract stares of incomprehension if they gave the wrong plural. A portion of our task is to help you avoid such problems with Latin and Greek elements, even though there are no Latin and Ancient Greek speakers left to stare you down.

Allomorphs

Morphs that are forms of the same morpheme are called **allomorphs.** The morphs /əz/ and /z/ are both allomorphs of the plural morpheme.

Recall from the previous chapter that there is no universal agreement as to how finely a word can be chopped up into morphs. The same flexibility applies to deciding whether two morphs should be considered allomorphs of the same morpheme. To a historically inclined linguist, it would be obvious that *internecine, pernicious, innocent,* and *noxious* all share the same Latin root; that is, their root morphs are all allomorphs of the same morpheme, which we may represent as *nec* 'harm'. To a psychologically inclined linguist, it would be equally obvious that the vast majority of English speakers don't understand the connections between these morphs, and so they wouldn't be considered as belonging to the same morpheme. As you may have surmised, for the duration of this book, at least, the authors adopt the former point of view.

Morphs must have the following properties before they can be considered allomorphs of the same morpheme:

- Allomorphs of the same morpheme all have the same function.
- The choice of allomorph depends on other morph(s) in the word.
- Allomorphs share a common history and similar pronunciation.

The first principle may come as a surprise, because earlier we learned that morphs can have rather different meanings in different words; *cosm* is an example. But there is always a thread connecting the meanings of morphs in different words, and when there is no thread, they are different morphemes, no matter how close the morphs are in spelling or sound. Thus the *path* of *pathology* has nothing to do with the *path* of *footpath*; they are different morphemes. This principle applies a fortiori when there are differences between the forms. Even though, as we shall see, some allomorphs differ by changing *e* to *o*, no one would dream of considering *pet* 'seek' and *pot* 'able' as being allomorphs of the same morpheme, because they have completely different meanings.

The second principle, that choice of allomorphs depends on other morphs in the word, plays an equally important role in constraining what can be considered allomorphs. To take the simplest possible case, whole lexemes, such as *vend* and *sell*, are never considered allomorphs of each other, even if they seem to mean the same thing. The second principle tells us this is necessarily so, because there is nothing else in the word to cause us to choose one form over the other. On the other hand, *in-* and *im-* are allomorphs of the same morpheme, because the choice of which to use is determined by the first sound in the next word (e.g., *inviolable* before /v/ but *impossible* before /p/). We see how this works in more detail in chapter 6.

The third principle warns us that allomorphs should have a shared history, which tends to result in some phonological similarity. For example, we have learned that *chron* is a morph meaning 'time', and so is *tempor*. That similarity in function is not enough to make them allomorphs of the same morpheme, however. *Chron* was borrowed from Greek and *tempor* was borrowed from Latin, and they have no deeper common history, as their completely different pronunciation suggests.

It helps to be as systematic and exhaustive as possible in our attempts to recognize allomorphy. For example, if we didn't know that the prefix *re-* had the allomorph *red-* before some roots beginning with a vowel, we would likely strike out in attempts to parse words like *redolent*. We might be tempted to analyze it as *re-dol-ent*, but this turns out to be wrong; there is no root *dol* in this word. The correct parse is *red-ol-ent*, where the root *ol* means 'smell', as it does in *olfactory*. The word *redolent* means 'fragrant'; by metaphorical extension, it means 'reminiscent'.

Knowing about allomorphy also helps us to recognize morphemes when meaning doesn't give a sufficient clue to their identity. Take the list of words *transmit, emit, permit, admit, commit, remit, omit*, and assume for the moment that we knew nothing about Latin. We may get the vague feeling that these words have in common the idea of causing something to move, and therefore we might want to conclude that the morph *mit* is a form of a morpheme that means 'cause to move' or 'send'. For some of the words we may have to recall specialized meanings to make this work (e.g., *The courtier was admitted into the king's presence* or *The judge committed the CEO to prison*), and for some of the words, such as *omit*, the idea of sending seems very tenuous at best. Are we just imagining a connection between these words?

Fortunately, **shared allomorphy** provides the clue we need in cases like these. Notice what happens when we try adding the suffixes *-tion* and *-tive* to these words:

transmit	*transmission*	*transmissive*
emit	*emission*	*emissive*
permit	*permission*	*permissive*
admit	*admission*	*admissive*
commit	*commission*	*commissive*
remit	*remission*	*remissive*
omit	*omission*	*omissive*

This change of final \<t> to \<ss> before these suffixes is not common to all words ending in \<t>; from *abort* and *combat*, for example, we get *abortion* and *combative.* Therefore, we can count this change as another piece of evidence that *mit* has something in common in all these words and can therefore be considered one morpheme. For the cases like *omit*, where shared meaning didn't suffice to establish the identity of the morpheme, shared allomorphy strengthens the case considerably. The fact that we get *omission* and *omissive* is evidence that we are dealing with a single morpheme *mit~miss* in all these cases.

To pursue this question one step further, let's consider another verb ending in the sequence of letters <mit>, namely, *vomit*. Is this an instance of the morpheme *mit~miss*? Recall that shared meaning may not always be a decisive criterion. Actually, meaning can even be misleading in this case, inasmuch as the meaning of the word *vomit* could be construed as involving a 'sending' of sorts. But if we search for shared allomorphy, we find no words such as ˣ*vomission* or ˣ*vomissive*. (Instead, we find *vomition* and *vomitive*.) This provides strong evidence that the last three letters in *vomit* do not constitute the same 'send' morpheme as in the other words we have been considering. Indeed, further investigation would reveal that *mit* is not a morphological component at all in *vomit*; rather, the root is *vom*.

Precisely because morphemes are so abstract and take several different forms, it can be hard to refer to them individually. Some techniques used in this book include citing the morpheme

- by listing some or all of its allomorphs, separated by the symbol ~ (e.g., "the morpheme *mit~miss*"),
- by using parentheses to mark letters or sounds that are found in some allomorphs but not others (e.g., "the morpheme *re(d)-*"), and
- by choosing one allomorph to stand for all (e.g., "the morpheme *nec*").

Phonology-based Allomorphy

Allomorphy has two main sources. First, a morpheme with only one form may come to have two or more different forms as the language changes. This may be thought of as a **morph split**. In the second, what was originally a sequence of morphs comes to be reinterpreted as a single morph. This can be thought of as **morphemic merger**.

Morph splits are almost always due to phonological factors. In many cases, a huge list of allomorphic variations in many different morphemes can be explained by a single phonological principle, which can seriously simplify the task of learning allomorphs. But a systematic study of these phonological influences requires a knowledge of phonology, which we won't pursue until the next chapter. So here we have to be content with a general overview of the types of allomorphy that arise from phonological causes.

Phonological Repairs

The easiest type of allomorphy to understand is when certain combinations of morphs would create **illegal** pronunciations. *Illegal* is a technical term in linguistics for a form that violates the general rules and constraints of the language. To take up again the example of plural endings, if we tried to apply the most common allomorph, /z/, to words it doesn't belong on, we would end up with forms like ˣ/pitʃz/ and ˣ/grepz/. Like many other languages, English does not have words that end in such sequences of sounds; they are so odd that a native speaker trying to pronounce them usually ends up **repairing** them by turning them into some legal sequence: for example, ˣ/grepz/ might get turned into ˣ/grebz/, which is still not right but at least is pronounceable. The allomorphy that the plural morpheme actually undergoes in English—at least for the three main allomorphs, /əz/, /z/, and /s/—can be understood as a set of rules for repairing illegal pronunciations. Another example of an allomorphy that makes phonological repairs is the third person singular present of verbs, which behaves like the plurals of nouns (*snatch-es, grab-s, take-s*). A similar situation occurs in the regular past tense of verbs (*prodd-ed, shove-d, push-ed*).

Yesterday's Phonology as Today's Allomorphy

Here are some words that show phonological alternations whose motivation may not be obvious:

deep /dip/	*depth* /dɛpθ/
deal /dil/	*dealt* /dɛlt/
Christ /kraɪst/	*Christmas* /ˈkrɪsməs/
sane /sen/	*sanity* /ˈsænəti/

It is true that in these cases, a lack of allomorphy would result in pronunciations in the second column that are rather unusual in English. No word ends in /ilt/, so from that standpoint it makes sense that *deal* changes the pronunciation of its vowel when /t/ is added. But why to /ɛ/ exactly? And would /dilt/ really sound all that bad?

Recall that before the Great Vowel Shift, the vowels on the left differed from the ones on the right primarily in being longer. When morphological processes could result in a long vowel appearing in a longer word or syllable, often the vowel was shortened. For example, in Middle English, *deal* was /dɛːl/ but *dealt* was /dɛlt/. This shortening of the vowel kept the word or syllable from becoming excessively long. But in Modern English, the alternation makes much less sense. The vowels in the left column aren't necessarily longer than those in the right column, and because of the Great Vowel Shift they are certainly not just longer versions of the same vowel.

That sort of situation is very common in morphology: typically, an allomorphic alternation makes the most sense phonologically if one looks at an earlier stage of the language. Here are even more striking examples:

foot	*feet*
goose	*geese*
tooth	*teeth*
man	*men*
mouse	*mice*

In this list of words, the different vowels in the plural arose in Prehistoric English. At that time, the plurals had an /i/ ending. English also had a phonological rule (known by the German word **umlaut**) whereby vowels preceding an /i/ became closer to the /i/ in pronunciation. At a later date, the ending was lost. In terms of the phonology of Modern English, the current allomorphy is doubly senseless. First, there is no overt ending to explain the alternation in the stem. Second, even if there were, English has lost the umlaut rule. For example, we feel no pressure at all to turn *Ann* into ×*Enny* when we add the suffix *-y* /i/.

Thus one big source of English allomorphy is the phonology of English. When English loses the phonological rule, or when conditions in the word change so that the rule no longer applies, the alternation often remains in place, and from then on it is a rule of the morphology.

Borrowed Phonology

The phonological origins of allophony may seem even more obscure to us when the phonology is that of a foreign language. English has borrowed so many words from Greek and, especially, Latin that English has incorporated many of the phonological rules of those languages. But because English does not apply those rules to native words, the rules are not general phonological rules in English but, rather, are allomorphic rules that apply only to certain classes of borrowed morphemes.

An example is the changes in the Latin prefix *in-* meaning 'not'. This prefix has the allomorphs *in-* /ɪn/ as in *ineligible, im-* /ɪm/ as in *imprecise, il-* /ɪl/ as in *illegal,* and *ir-* /ɪɾ/ as in *irregular.* This allomorphy applies to hundreds of words and yet is not a fully general phonological rule. Consider, for example, how the native prefix *un-* behaves. It has the same meaning and almost the same form as *in-* and yet does not undergo the same changes: compare *uneventful, unprovable, unloved,* and *unreal.* Because this pattern of changing the final *n* in the prefix only applies to Latin prefixes, speakers of English tend not to perceive it as a phonological pattern but as just another allophonic rule to memorize.

In the same way that English has allophonic patterns that made sense as phonological patterns many centuries ago, some of the allophonic patterns we borrowed from Latin and Greek had long ceased to have a clear phonological motivation in the classical periods of those languages. An example is the Greek privative prefix *an-* 'not', which is *an-* before vowels and /h/, and *a-* before other consonants. Thus we get *a-* in *apnea, atheist,* and *asymmetry* but *an-* in *anesthetic* and *anhydrous.* No other Greek prefix behaves quite like *an-*, which owes its behavior to phonological changes that took place in Prehistoric Greek. An example of a pattern that is very widespread in Latin even though it had lost any phonological explanation in Classical Latin is **Latin Vowel Weakening:**

factor	*defect, infect*	*deficient*
capture	*receptive*	*recipient*
apt	*inept, adept*	
spectator	*respect*	*conspicuous, despicable*
sacrifice	*desecrate*	
status	*obstetric*	*constitute*
tenuous	*content*	*continent*

Basically, any vowel is allowed in the root when it is the first syllable of a word, but the vowel may be weakened to an *e* (before two consonants) or *i* (before one consonant) when prefixation makes the root move to a later syllable. In many languages vowel weakening is caused by a shift in stress: compare the first vowels in the English pronunciations of *spécies* and *specífic*. But in Latin Vowel Weakening, the stress patterns of Classical Latin don't support such an interpretation: consider Latin *conspícuus*, where the vowel is weakened even though it is stressed. Latin Vowel Weakening is a holdover from an earlier stage of Latin, when the stress was always on the first syllable: * *cónspicuus* (the asterisk means that form is unattested: we have no direct proof that the stress was on the first syllable in Old Latin). That would account neatly for the weakening rule: vowels were weakened in noninitial syllables because they weren't stressed. But from the standpoint of Classical Latin, the stage of the language from which English has taken most of its Latin loans, the weakening no longer makes phonological sense.

Many forms of allomorphy have their origin in phonology, whether within English itself (often in an earlier stage of it) or in Latin or Greek. Depending on what other morphs a morph is combined with, the sounds in the other part of the word may change its pronunciation. As a result, a single morph splits into several allomorphs.

Suppletion

Normally the various word forms of a lexeme are based on the same root. However, occasionally this rule is violated:

> *go, went*
> *be, is, was*
> *good, better*

Any child could tell you that the past tense of *go* "should" be ˣ*goed*, but in fact it is formed by adding *t* to *wen*, which means we have an odd-looking allomorphy *go~wen*. The appreciable difference in sound and spelling in this lexeme is due to the fact that *went* was historically a totally different word. Originally, *went* was the past tense of *wend* (compare *spend* and *spent*), a word that the poets among us still occasionally use to mean 'proceed' or 'go' even in the present tense (*Leopold Bloom wends his way through the urban landscape*). The process of incorporating a totally different word in part of another word's inflectional system is called **suppletion.**

Greek verbs had quite a bit of suppletion, but fortunately, Greek verb inflection is outside the scope of this book. Latin was more comparable to English in having a lesser degree of suppletion, but a few English allomorphies can be traced to it. The words *essence* and *future* come from different (suppletive) forms of the verb 'be'. The curious fact that the adjective *Jovian* is so different from *Jupiter* is also due to a suppletion in Latin.

Morpheme Merger

Extended Allomorphs

A common cause of allomorphy is when two adjacent morphemes occurring in the same morphological component come to be perceived as a single morpheme. For example, the second *or* of *corporate* was at one time a separate morpheme, but nowadays *corpor* is generally thought of as an allomorph of *corp*. Erstwhile morphemes such as *or* are relics of older patterns in the parent languages. A number of them used to be meaningful, signaling changes in tense, part of speech, and other things. Today, they have lost their last traces of meaning. Nor do they, in general, play any phonological role such as repairing illegal sequences of sounds. Because they seem to do little more than make the morpheme they attach to longer, they are called **extensions.** Admittedly, allomorphs that have incorporated extensions sometimes sound better. For example, *bathyscope* arguably is more mellifluous than *×bathscope*. But our language has dozens of words that are at least as awkward sounding as *×bathscope*—an example is *landscape*. The use of the allomorph *bathy* instead of *bath* in *bathyscope* is simply a relic from earlier times.

Allomorphs formed by adding extensions may be called **extended allomorphs.** In the word element lists, we encounter numerous examples of extended allomorphs. Here are a few examples. The Greek root *nec* 'die' has the allomorphs *nec* and *necr*. In the latter, *r* was originally a suffix, and this *r* appears in most of the English words whose origin goes back to the Greek morpheme, as in *necrology* 'a list of people who have died' and *necrophilia* 'attraction to corpses'. One example of nec without the *r* is *nectar*, the drink of the gods, which was viewed as overcoming death (*tar* means 'overcome'). English has also borrowed a cognate root from Latin, where it means 'harm'. One allomorph of that Latin root is *noc*, which appears in *innocent* (which literally means 'not causing harm'). When extended by /s/, which was originally a suffix, we get *nox*, as in *noxious*.

The root *ten* 'stretch', 'thin', which appears in words like *tenuous* and *extenuating*, is extended by *d* in *extend*. The allomorph *tend* in turn is the source of yet another allomorph, *tens*, which appears in the words *tensile* and *intense*. The change of \<d\> to \<s\> comes about as a result of another rule of allomorphy that is introduced in a later chapter.

As we have just seen, extensions include vowels like the final vowel sound of the morph *bathy* and consonants like the final *r* of *necr* or the final *d* of *tend*. They also include vowel–consonant sequences, as in the already mentioned *or* of *corporal*. Because extensions are, by definition, so difficult to pin down, we will not explicitly be memorizing lists of extensions or rules for applying them. When you parse a word, there will consequently be a temptation to claim that any difficult letter or two is an extension. Occasionally that will be true, but you should first make a good effort to rule out the alternatives. The most important extended allomorphs are listed in the word element lists.

Nasal Infixation

In nasal infixation, an \<n\> or \<m\> is placed immediately after the vowel in the root:

in-cub-ate	*in-cumb-ent*	'lie'
con-tag-ion	*tang-ent*	'touch'
frag-ile	*frang-ible*	'break'
vic-tor	*con-vince*	'conquer'

In Proto-Indo-European, this consonant was a derivational affix, much like prefixes or suffixes. Because of its placement inside the root, it is called an **infix**. One theory holds that it served to turn intransitive verbs transitive, but only a trace of this function remained in Latin, and none at all is discernible in English.

Ablaut

In Proto-Indo-European, most roots contained the vowel *e* in their basic form. Some of the morphological processes of that language involved changing the vowel to *o*. Other changes consisted of deleting the vowel or making it longer. These changes are all known as **ablaut** (not to be confused with *umlaut*).

In native English words this alternation between *e, o*, and nothing (usually called **zero**) is a bit disguised through millennia of sound changes. But the principle can still be seen in the strong verbs, where the changing of vowels to make the past tense and past participle of verbs (*sing, sang, sung*) is a direct descendant of Proto-Indo-European ablaut. The clearest examples of ablaut can be found in elements borrowed from Greek, which hasn't changed its vowels as much as Latin and the Germanic languages have. Some examples of the different ablaut forms (or **grades**) in Greek elements:

Root meaning	e-Grade	o-Grade	Zero Grade
'birth'	*genetic*	*cosmogony*	
'cut'		*atom*	*tmesis*
'throw'	*belemnite*	*symbol*	*problem*
'work'	*energy*	*organ*	

From Latin:

'hang', 'weigh'	*dependent*	*ponderous*	
'birth'	*indigenous*		*pregnant*
'think'	*memento*	*admonish*	
'accept'	*decent*	*docent*	

Empty cells in these tables simply mean that there are no clear examples that were borrowed into English. Several examples of ablaut have been left out because sound change has made them difficult to recognize.

Linguists aren't completely sure what the function of ablaut was in Proto-Indo-European, and as far as Greek and Latin word elements in English are concerned, we can consider ablaut to be another source of allomorphy with no inherent meaning of its own.

Doublets or Allomorphs?

A number of instances of allomorphy can be traced to the fact that English borrowed a lot of its Latin vocabulary through Old French. As we saw earlier in the case of *captain* and *chef*, very often the same morpheme was borrowed into English from both languages. Latinate English words commonly use Latin morphs throughout the entire word except for the very end, which takes an Old French form. For example, the word *faculty* comes from the Latin base *fac-ul-* 'easily done', plus a respelled form of the Old French suffix *-té*, which forms nouns. This suffix is the French descendant of Latin *-tate*. Now observe what happens when we add another Latinate morpheme, say, *-(t)ive*, to *fac-ul-ty*. The suffix *-ty* is no longer the last morpheme of the word, so it appears in its Latin form instead of its Old French form: *fac-ul-tat-ive*. This use of French allomorphs at the end of words is the source of many alternations in English.

French	Latin	Examples
-le	*-ul-*	*angle, angular; circle, circular*
-le	*-il-*	*able, ability*
-ous	*-os-*	*generous, generosity*
-ence	*-ent-i-*	*preference, preferential*
-ance	*-ant-i-*	*substance, substantial*
-fy	*-fic-*	*glorify, glorification*

This pattern of French/Latin allomorphy is most noticeable in suffixes, because they occur in hundreds of words, but minor patterns are also discernible in some roots. For example, the Latin root *ten* 'hold', as in *abstention, content, detention, pertinent* (by Latin Vowel Weakening), and *retentive*, takes on the Old French allomorph *tain* when it is the last Latinate morpheme in the word: *abstain, contain, detain, pertain,* and *retain*.

The morph pairs discussed so far are clearly allomorphs by any definition of the term. But should we say that any French morph should be considered an allomorph of the Latin morph it descends from? As we will see in chapter 11, many French morphs have changed considerably from the Latin form. For instance, the Latin morph *fid* 'trust', as in *confident* and *fidelity*, is the ultimate source of the French loanword *faith*, and it appears also as *fi* in *defiant* and as *fe* in *fealty*.

Are they all the same morpheme? At least the common *f* unites all these morphs, but consider now the Latin morph *cav* 'hollow', found in *cave* and *cavity*, which is also the root, via French, of the word *jail*. Is this allomorphy?

There is no hard and fast rule for answering this question, and we shouldn't expect there to be one. As with many other issues in linguistics, much depends on what we are trying to accomplish. At some point we need to stop describing these alternations as allomorphy and instead describe them as doublets. Recall from chapter 2 that words such as *shirt* and *skirt*, which entered the language through different routes, are referred to as doublets. Despite their similarity in form and meaning, they don't participate in any systematic alternations. In an analogous way, morphs that come from the same parent morpheme, but which because of different routes of borrowing come to have different forms and usages, are considered to be doublets if they don't alternate with each other systematically.

The word element lists in this book don't contain many French forms, so difficult cases like *cave* versus *jail* don't often arise. However, a similar situation arises between Latin and Greek. These two languages often have closely related morphemes that they both inherited from Proto-Indo-European, with the morpheme undergoing different changes in each language. By adopting both morphemes, English acquired new doublets.

Three of the number terms in chapter 6 have variants that differ mainly in that the first letter of one is an <h> while the first letter of the other is <s> These are *hemi-~semi-* 'half', *hexa~sex* 'six', and *hepta~septem* 'seven'. The morphs in <h> are from Greek, and those in <s> are from Latin. An example of the same pattern in a nonnumeral is the root for 'to creep', which is *herp* in Greek and *serp* in Latin.

A different set of variants distinguishes Latin *nomen* from Greek *onom*, two morphemes meaning 'name'. The Latin root *nomen* has the allomorph *nomin* (as in *nominal, nominate*). This is an example of Latin Vowel Weakening, which was discussed previously in this chapter. The Greek root *onom* has the allomorphs *onomat* (as in *onomatology* 'the study of the origins of names') and *onym* (as in *synonym* and *antonym*).

Another doublet pair is *dent* and *odont* 'tooth'. We use Latinate *dent* for the more familiar *dentist*, and we use Greek *odont* for the more scholarly *odontologist* 'one who studies teeth'. The pattern of using Latin roots for more common things and Greek roots for more specialized purposes is quite strong in English. Latin *fa* 'speak' appears in *fable* and *famous*; the Greek doublet *pha* appears in the medical conditions *aphasia* and *dysphasia*.

Due to the complex history of English and of the languages it has drawn its vocabulary from, it is often difficult to decide whether variation should be considered to be allomorphy or a matter of doublets, and it is often convenient to fall back on the more neutral term *variant*. There are also cases of allomorphy and doublets too idiosyncratic to pigeonhole. Examples from the word element lists are *de~div* 'god', *aut~taut* 'same', and *lith~lit* 'stone'. These simply have to be learned individually. But the bright side of the picture is that most alternations in the form of English morphemes are quite regular. Their regularity is largely a result of the fact that they are, or used to be, governed by phonetic principles. We will study them in more detail after learning some terminology and concepts of phonetics in the next chapter.

Summary

Allomorphs are morphs that fulfill the same function in building words but alternate systematically with each other based on the other morph or morphs in the same word. The abstract functional entity that comprises the set of allomorphs is called the morpheme. Some patterns of allomorphy apply regularly to a wide range of morphemes. Others may apply idiosyncratically to only a few or even just one morpheme, in which case shared allomorphy can help identify morphemes. Allomorphs may be caused by phonological changes that split one morph into many; such patterns include but are by no means limited to English umlaut, Latin and Greek prefix alternations, and Latin Vowel Weakening. At other times allomorphs come about through suppletion, incorporating parts of one word into another word's inflectional patterns. Finally, an allomorph can result from a morph's being extended by what used to be an empty morpheme, such as old Proto-Indo-European suffixes, ablaut vowels, and nasal infixes. Morphemes borrowed from related languages can function as allomorphs, as when French allomorphs at the end of a lexeme vary with Latin allomorphs nonfinally, but more often they act as different morphemes and may be considered doublets.

Word Elements

Learn the following elements, their meanings, and variant forms.

Element	Gloss	Source	Examples
al~ol	nurture, grow	L	*alma mater, abolish, alimentary, adolescent*
am~im	love	L	*amorous, amative, amicable, inimical*
ann~enn	year	L	*per annum, perennial, annals, millennium*
apt~ept	fit	L	*aptitude, inept, adapt, adept, coapt*
bol~bl	throw	G	*parabola, emblem, hyberbole, metabolism, problem*
cap~cep~cip~cup	take	L	*captive, except, incipient, recuperate, principle, precept, percipient, occupy, capacious*
cid~cis	cut, kill	L	*homicide, incision, excise, circumcise, concise*
cri	judge, separate	G	*critic, criterion, crisis, endocrine, hypocrisy*
cri~cre~cer	separate	L	*discern, secern, secret, secrete, certain, criminal*
cub~cumb	lie down	L	*incubate, incumbent, concubine, recumbent, cubicle*
de~div	god	L	*deity, divinity, deification, divine, deism, diva*
equ~iqu	even	L	*equity, iniquity, equanimity, equidistant, equal, equator, equation, adequate*
erg~org~urg	work	G	*energy, metallurgy, organ, orgy, demiurge, ergative, georgic, liturgy*
fac~fec~fic	do, make	L	*factory, defect, artificial, perfect, prefect, fact, factotum, factor, facsimile, deficit, suffice, artifice*

Element	Gloss	Source	Examples
frag~frang~fring	break	L	*fragile, frangible, infringe, fragment, refrangent*
fund~fus	pour, melt	L	*refund, effusive, fuse, fusion, infuse, infusion, refuse, affusion, fusile, diffuse*
gen~gn~na	birth	L	*general, genus, genius, genial, genital, progeny, ingenious, indigenous, genuine, gentile, benign, pregnant, innate, native, nation, natal, agnate*
gen~gon	birth	G	*gene, genocide, genesis, heterogeneous, epigene, gonad*
men~mon	think	L	*mental, memento, dementia, mention, admonish*
mne	remember	G	*amnesia, mnemonic*
mov~mo	move	L	*move, motion, motility, motive, emotion, motor, promote, mobile*
nec~necr	die	G	*nectar, nectarine, necrosis*
nec~noc~nic~nox	harm	L	*innocuous, internecine, pernicious, innocent, noxious*
pend~pond	hang, weigh	L	*depend, appendix, expend, ponder, pendulum, preponderate, vilipend*
sacr~sanc~secr	holy	L	*sacred, sanctify, consecrate, desecrate*
semen~semin	seed	L	*semen, inseminate, seminal, disseminate, seminary*
spec~spic	look	L	*inspect, despicable, spectacle, spectrum, retrospect*
sta~ste	stand	G	*static, ecstasy, thermostat, stasis, system*
sta~ste~sti~st	stand	L	*status, stamen, obstetrician, institute, stationary, stable, prostitute, constitution, statute, insist*

Element	Gloss	Source	Examples
tag~teg~tig~tang~ting	touch	L	contagion, integer, tangent, contingent, tangible
tempor	time	L	temporary, temporize, contemporary, extemporaneous
ten~tin	hold	L	tenable, continuous, tenure, tenacious, retention
tom~tm	cut	G	anatomy, tmesis, atom, microtome, entomology, epitome, tmema
vic~vinc	conquer	L	victor, invincible, evict, evince, convince, conviction
vor	eat	L	voracious, omnivore, carnivore
zo	animal	G	zoology, protozoon, azote, zoomorphic, azoic

Element Study

1. What variations, if any, do you detect in the meaning of the root *al* in *alumnus, alimony, coalesce,* and *altricial*? In *proletariat* and *prolific* the vowel of *al* runs together with the prefix *pro-*, making the root very hard to detect. How would you relate the meaning of the root in these last two words to the basic meaning of *al*?

2. The root *am* 'love' is easily confused with other sequences *am*. Which of the following words contain the root *am* 'love' or one of its allomorphs?

   a. *amaze*
   b. *ameliorate*
   c. *amend*
   d. *amenity*
   e. *amiable*
   f. *amity*
   g. *amoral*
   h. *amour*
   i. *amphitheater*
   j. *amulet*

k. *amuse*
l. *enamor*
m. *enemy*
n. *imitate*
o. *paramour*

3. Which one of these words does not contain a form of the root *ann*?

   a. *annual*
   b. *annul*
   c. *biennial*
   d. *perennial*
   e. *superannuate*

4. Two very common roots are easily confused because both have the allomorphs *cap* and *cep*: one meaning 'take' and the other meaning 'head'. Practice distinguishing the two by giving the meaning of the root in each of these examples:

   a. *capital*
   b. *reception*
   c. *deceptive*
   d. *decapitate*
   e. *capture*
   f. *captain*
   g. *capacity*
   h. *capitulate*
   i. *incipient*
   j. *precipitate*

5. After studying the word element list for this chapter, test your knowledge of the elements presented so far by parsing the following words. Gloss the elements and give variants for the roots. You may assume that any components that are not in the glossary are empty morphemes and should gloss them as such. With the aid of a dictionary, give a brief definition for the whole word which partly or fully reflects the meaning of the individual elements.

   a. *conspicuous*
   b. *deification*
   c. *equanimous*
   d. *energy*
   e. *incipient*
   f. *seminal*

Exercises

1. Define allomorphy. Illustrate your answer with three examples. What is the relevance of allomorphy to the goals of this course?

2. Write and give the gloss of the root in each of the following words. Give the variant forms of the root that are listed in the glossary of this book. Make note of the dictionary's definitions of each full word as well.

   a. *contiguous*
   b. *pertinacious*
   c. *cognate*

3. Match each word in column A with one in column B that has the same root and identify the process or processes relating the roots: vowel weakening, nasal insertion, or ablaut.

A	B
a. *genome*	g. *sacrilege*
b. *tangential*	h. *tenant*
c. *abstinence*	i. *theogony*
d. *edifice*	j. *contagious*
e. *nocuous*	k. *facile*
f. *desecrate*	l. *internecine*

CHAPTER FIVE

Phonetics

Introduction

Phonetics describes the sounds of language. Learning how the sounds of English are pronounced puts us in a better position to understand some of the allomorphy we encounter in English words. The same principles also bring out striking similarities between Latin, French, and English words despite several hundreds of years of sound changes. An example is Latin *capum*, the source of the French word *chef* and, through French, the source of the English words *chief* and *chef*. Basic phonetics also helps us to appreciate the similarities among the Germanic languages and Latin and Greek, despite several millennia of sound changes. For example, in chapter 10 we trace the English word *fire* back to the same source as the Greek root *pyr*, showing along the way that the difference in pronunciation between /f/ and /p/ is a highly regular one.

Many changes in the pronunciation of morphemes are due to **assimilation**, a process whereby one sound becomes more **similar** to another sound, usually the immediately following one. The Latin negative prefix *in-* /ɪn/ becomes *im-* /ɪm/ before /p/ (*impossible*) and /b/ (*imbalance*). We will learn that /p/ and /b/ share a certain phonetic property that has something to do with why /n/ changes to /m/ when it immediately precedes them. Before sounds like /t/ and /d/, the /n/ of prefix *in-* does not change, and so we get the forms *intolerant* and *indecisive*, not ×*imtolerant* or ×*imdecisive*. In some cases assimilation is total, making the two sounds identical, as in *immodest* /ɪmˈmadəst/, although we normally further reduce a sequence of identical sounds to a single sound in English: /ɪˈmadəst/. Understanding the principles of assimilation is particularly helpful because they often apply to several different morphemes. Compare what happens to the Greek prefix *syn-* 'with' in the words *sympathy, symbol, symmetric, syntax*, and *syndrome*.

Phonetic principles also help to make sense of certain changes that don't involve assimilation. For example, *presume* and *redeem* acquire a <p> when <t> is added, as in *presumptive* and *redemptive*. The *p* is inserted because people sometimes insert a /p/ sound when moving from an /m/ to a /t/. As we will see, /p/ has some of the phonetic properties of /m/ and some of the properties of /t/, and so can easily appear as an intermediate sound. The process of inserting a sound is called **epenthesis**.

Phonetics also helps sort out the differences between pronunciation and spelling. English spelling can become ingrained in our consciousness, shaping and even distorting our perceptions of the sounds that letters represent. It may come as a surprise to many readers that the words *cats* and *dogs* generally do not end in exactly the same sound: the sound at the end of *cats* is essentially the one we hear at the end of *hiss*, while the sound at the end of *dogs* is what we hear at the end of *buzz*. One reason that we miss the difference between the two sounds /s/ and /z/ is that both are spelled the same way, <s>, in the plural morpheme. Just to clarify the point here, we do not mean to be attacking the spelling system of English for being phonetically inaccurate. There is so much variation in how different people speak that our much maligned spelling system would be even harder to deal with if it faithfully recorded all such distinctions. But when we focus on phonetics, we must be careful not to be misled by spelling, which is often a poor indicator of how a word is actually pronounced.

Each sound in language can be broken down into a set of properties. We can understand the relation between one sound and another by comparing their characteristic properties. For example, even though we noted above that /s/ and /z/ are not identical, they are indeed very similar, differing only in whether the vocal cords are vibrating or not.

Many assimilatory changes become understandable when we compare properties of the sounds involved. As noted earlier, the /n/ of *in-* becomes /m/ before the initial /p/ of words like *possible*, the initial /b/ of *balance*, and the initial /m/ of *modest*, but not before other sounds. This makes some sense, because /p/, /b/, and /m/ have in common the degree of openness of the vocal tract and the place in the mouth where they are made (**place of articulation**). This pair of characteristic properties occurs together only in these three sounds.

The assimilatory change involves the loss of the distinctive property of /n/ that differentiates it from /p/, /b/, and /m/, namely, the fact that it is made at a different place of articulation.

The fact that each sound is broken down into a set of characteristic properties makes learning new sounds an easier and less intimidating chore. If we understand the basic mechanism for producing a fricative sound, and if we understand how we produce a velar sound like English /k/ or /g/, this puts us in a fair position to produce a velar fricative like /x/ (as in Scottish *loch*, Hebrew *Ḥanukkah*, or German *Bach*), even though this consonant sound may seem unfamiliar to many English speakers.

Basics of Sound Production

Figure 5.1 shows the parts of the vocal tract that play a role in the description of consonants below.

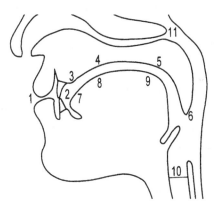

Figure 5.1 The Articulatory Apparatus: Consonants. An idealized cross-section of the vocal tract (adjectival forms in parentheses): 1, lips (labial); 2, teeth (dental); 3, alveolar ridge (alveolar); 4, hard palate (palatal); 5, soft palate (velar); 6, uvula (uvular); 7, tip of tongue (apical); 8, blade of tongue (laminal); 9, back of tongue (dorsal); 10, vocal cords, in the larynx (glottal); 11, nasal passages (nasal)

The Airstream

Any speech sound involves an **airstream** whose flow is modified in some way by the speech organs. All English sounds move air from the lungs through the larynx and **vocal tract** and out the mouth or nose. As the air passes along, its flow can be arrested, slowed down, or diverted by the movement of various speech organs or **articulators**. The nature of these effects and the location of the articulators that produce them are what differentiates speech sounds.

Manner of Articulation

Let us first consider **oral** sounds, that is, sounds whose articulation involves the flow of air through the mouth.

One way to produce sounds is to temporarily stop the airflow through the mouth by bringing two articulators together. These articulators may be the two lips, as in the case of /p/ and /b/. More often, part of the tongue presses against the teeth or top of the mouth. Sounds that are produced by stopping the airflow are called oral **stops**. The oral stops used in Standard English are /p/, /b/, /t/, /d/, /k/, and /g/.

Slowly read the first sentence of the preceding paragraph aloud, and see if you can determine which sounds involve temporary but total blockage of airflow.[1]

Most of the sounds of English do not involve complete stoppage of air. Some consonants are produced by bringing the articulators close together but leaving enough of an opening so that air can pass through continuously. The narrowness of the opening causes the air to be emitted under some pressure, which results in a rushing or rasping effect that gives **fricatives** (with the root *fric* 'rub', as in *friction*) their name. The *fricatives* of English are /f/, /v/, /θ/, /ð/, /s/, /z/, /ʃ/, /ʒ/, and /h/. The word *fricatives* itself has three different fricative sounds in it.

The sounds known as **affricates** involve a transition from a stop closure to a more open fricative sound without otherwise changing the location of the articulators. The fricative sound at the beginning of the word *shore* contrasts with the corresponding affricate at the beginning of *chore*. The affricate is represented as /tʃ/, showing that it consists of a stop plus a fricative. The only other affricate

---

1. In the first sentence they include (in order): /t/, /p/, /d/, /d/, /t/, /t/, /p/, etc.

of English is /dʒ/, which occurs as both the initial and the final consonant of *judge*. Many English speakers produce the same sound at the end of *garage*, while others follow the original French more closely, by producing a fricative, /ʒ/. Which sounds more natural to you?

Because the types of consonants we have discussed so far—stops, fricatives, and affricates—involve substantial **obstruction** of the airflow, they are called **obstruents**. For other consonants, the degree of oral constriction is not so great as for obstruents. Consonants produced with a relatively wide opening between the oral articulators are called approximants. The **approximants** in English are /l/, /r/, /w/, and /j/.

If you pronounce /l/ as in *love* attentively, you will notice that you pronounce the sound with the tongue pressed against your teeth or alveolar ridge. This raises an interesting question: If there is firm contact between the articulators, how can /l/ be an approximant rather than a stop? That is to say, how can the air flow past this area? To answer this question, pronounce an /l/. The answer will be more apparent if you inhale while pronouncing it. You should feel cool air where it is going past the sides of your tongue, for which reason /l/ is termed a **lateral** sound. In English, /l/ is the only sound that has a lateral articulation.

Sounds like /m/ also permit relatively unrestricted flow of air. Is /m/, then, an approximant? No. In fact, when you pronounce the sound /m/, you can feel a complete closure in the mouth. The lips are completely closed, as they are for the oral stops /p/ and /b/. The air that is totally blocked from exiting the mouth, however, is permitted to pass freely through the nose through a passage opened by lowering the velum. Because of this characteristic airflow through the nose, /m/ is called a **nasal** stop. The other nasal stops in English are /n/ and /ŋ/.

Even though nasal consonants aren't approximants, it is true that those two classes of consonants have much in common. For instance, nasals and approximants can form the core of unstressed syllables in English, without the need for a vowel, as indicated by the little stroke in these transcriptions of the words *kitten* /ˈkɪtn̩/ and *little* /ˈlɪtl̩/. The general term for sounds that permit the relatively unrestricted flow of air is **sonorant**. That is, sonorants are the opposite of obstruents. Approximants are sonorants because air travels through the mouth unimpeded enough that frication is not produced. Nasal consonants are sonorants because even though air is blocked in the mouth, it passes unimpeded through the nasal cavity.

Place of Articulation

We have already mentioned several places of articulation in passing when we discussed manner of articulation. In this section we consider in a little more detail the places of articulation used in English.

The oral airflow is manipulated by varying the distance or type of contact between **upper** and **lower** articulators. These are easiest to explore when we consider stops, because the articulators come into firm contact with each other, making them easy to feel or see in a mirror. For the stops /p/, /b/, and /m/, the upper and lower articulators are the upper and lower lips, and so they are called **labial** consonants. For the other stops, the lower articulator is the tongue, and the upper articulator is the top part of the mouth (regions 2 through 5 in figure 5.1). For /t/, /d/, and /n/, the tip or blade of the tongue presses against the **alveolar** ridge (the raised area just behind the upper teeth), and so these are called alveolar consonants. For /k/, /g/, and /ŋ/, the back of the tongue presses against the soft palate, or velum, and so these are called **velar** consonants.

Because affricates begin with a stop, it is also easy to feel where they are articulated. Even though the affricates /tʃ/ and /dʒ/ are represented phonetically with the symbols /t/ and /d/, which are typically alveolar (cf. also the spellings in *etch* and *edge*), the position of the stop component is adjusted to match up with the fricative part of the affricate. You may be able to feel the difference by comparing the initial sounds of *tore* and *chore*. If you pronounce these two words as we do, you should feel that in *tore* it is the tip of your tongue that makes contact with the upper articulator, and it is pointed more upward than in *chore*. For *chore* a greater portion of the tongue makes contact, and contact extends to what is known as the **postalveolar** region—somewhat behind the alveolar ridge. Some speakers do this differently. Pronounce *tore* and *chore*, and see if you make the initial consonant closure in the same position for both.

Fricatives are almost as easy to explore, because even if the articulators do not press firmly against each other, you can usually feel the air rushing past the point of articulation. The fricatives /ʃ/ and /ʒ/ are postalveolar, just like the corresponding affricates /tʃ/ and /dʒ/. If you move the tongue slightly forward, to the alveolar region, you will produce the alveolar fricatives /s/ and /z/, corresponding in place to the stops /t/ and /d/.

Imagine what it would take to make a labial sound that qualifies as a fricative. Try bringing your lips close enough together to produce noise when air passes through, without blocking the air entirely. You have produced a bilabial fricative, which English lacks but which many languages have. The closest that English comes to having a bilabial fricative is the **labiodental** fricatives /f/ and /v/, which are made by bringing the lower lip into partial contact with the upper teeth. Try this and see if it produces something that sounds like a respectable English /f/ or /v/. If not, try it again in front of a mirror.

Another place of articulation for fricatives involves touching the tip of the tongue to the edges of the front upper and lower teeth. This produces what are called **dental** fricatives, written /θ/ and /ð/. These occur in *thin* and *then*, respectively. A bit more subtle is the **glottal** place of articulation, where the friction is made by air rushing through the glottis; this is used for /h/.

The place of articulation for approximants can be a little bit harder to pin down, because the upper articulator is approached only very approximately. The approximants /r/ and /l/ are usually considered as being articulated in the alveolar region. /r/ is the most variable sound in English, and so describing its position involves describing a number of the most common variants found in English dialects. For most American speakers, the tip and blade of the tongue are raised in the direction of the top and back of the upper teeth. The center line of the tongue from back to front is depressed, creating a round, tubular channel for air to pass through. For other speakers, the tip of the tongue is not only raised but also curled backward. Try this and see if the sound that comes out resembles your normal /r/ or some other /r/ that you have heard from speakers of American English.

For /j/, the front and back regions of the mouth are relatively open, and a narrowing takes place in the middle of the mouth. This is done by raising the body of the tongue toward the hard palate. If you pronounce a sequence like *a yacht* /ə ˈjat/ you will feel your tongue and your jaw moving upward after the first vowel and then downward on its way to the second. Sounds made in this part of the mouth are called **palatal**. In English, /j/ is the only palatal consonant.

If you pronounce the /w/ of *wet*, you will first notice that the lips are rounded. But there is more to its articulation than this labial gesture. Notice where the back of your tongue is for /w/. Say the word *wet* very slowly—try to draw the /w/ out very long—and feel what is happening. The lips are moving from a relatively rounded posture to a relatively spread one. But note also the movement of your tongue. At the beginning of the word, for the consonant /w/, you should feel that the back of the tongue is raised toward the soft palate; as you move to the vowel /ɛ/, this changes so that the back of the tongue is no longer raised at all. This shows that /w/ is not only a labial sound but also a velar sound. Because of its twofold articulation, this sound is known as a **labiovelar**.

Phonation

There is one key property of consonants left to be described: their **phonation**. The airstream must pass through the **larynx** (Adam's apple) on its way from the lungs to the oral articulators. The opening in the larynx through which the air passes is known as the **glottis** and is surrounded by flexible tissue known as the **vocal cords**. If the vocal cords are open, the air passes freely through the glottis, as it does when you are breathing and not talking. But it is also possible to position the vocal cords so that an airstream passing through them causes the vocal cords to vibrate. This is done by bringing the vocal cords together yet leaving them slack enough that the pressure of air below them briefly forces them apart. They then close and, again, are forced open by the airstream, a hundred or even several hundred times per second. It is this vibration that is known as voice or **voicing**. When you make a voiced sound, such as /v/, it is possible to feel the vibration with your fingers. Place your fingers on your throat, at the sides of the bulge formed by the larynx, and pronounce a long and drawn out /v/; now compare the voiceless sound /f/. Or if you use your index fingers to cover the openings of your ears as you produce a good /v/, you will feel your whole head vibrate; again compare /f/. Using these cues, decide which of the consonants in this sentence are voiced and which are voiceless.[2]

You might notice that in normal speech, voiced sounds like /v/ and /z/ are not always voiced from beginning to end; voicing may start or stop part of the way into the sound. Languages vary quite a bit in how thoroughly they voice consonants; speakers of Romance languages like French and Spanish tend to voice consonants like /v/ and /z/ from beginning to end. In English, we need to be more attentive: we consider a consonant to be voiced if voicing is found anywhere within the sound, so voiced consonants may actually contain a bit of voicelessness.

---

2. Here is a phonetic transcription of the sentence (pronounced in a very careful style): /ˈjuzɪŋ ðiz kjuz dɪˈsaɪd wɪtʃ əv ðə ˈkansənənts ɪn ðɪs ˈsentəns ar vɔɪst ænd wɪtʃ ar ˈvɔɪsləs/. (Note: Many people pronounce *which* as /hwɪtʃ/.)

Closely associated with phonation is **aspiration**. Oral stops such as /p/, /t/, and /k/ may be so vigorously voiceless—that is, the glottis can be open so wide—that the voicelessness continues well into the next sound. This happens, for example, when those sounds occur at the beginning of a word in English. In words like *pie*, *toe*, and *key*, you may even be able to feel a puff of air if you hold your finger up to your mouth, or see it if you hold a candle flame up to your lips. We say that the consonants are aspirated. We could indicate this in International Phonetic Alphabet by adding a small /ʰ/ after the consonant, because that aspiration is a puff of air much like an /h/: /pʰ/, and so on. One usually does not bother to do this for English, because no two words are ever distinguished in English solely by differences in aspiration. Some other languages, though, such as classical Greek, do use aspiration to distinguish words.

If you push the air out of your lungs fast enough, you may get your vocal cords to vibrate even if they are not very tense. The effect is **breathy** voice. You may get this naturally in English if you talk while exercising or are trying to sound sexy, but of course no two words are distinguished by whether your voicing is breathy. In some languages such as Hindi and Urdu, however, breathy voice is produced by aspirating voiced stops. A symbol like /bʰ/ signifies a /b/ whose phonation is breathy and for which some period of breathiness follows the consonant. An example is /bʰərət/, the Hindi name for India. We will see later that these sounds were very important in the history of English.

In English, the presence or absence of voicing may be the only property that distinguishes one obstruent from another, even leading to the only distinction between words: thus *knife* and *knive* are distinguished only by the phonation of the last sound. The voiced obstruents of English are /b/, /d/, /g/, /v/, /ð/, /z/, /ʒ/, and /dʒ/; the corresponding voiceless obstruents are /p/, /t/, /k/, /f/, /θ/, /s/, /ʃ/, and /tʃ/. The obstruent /h/ is normally voiceless, but people sometimes pronounce it with a bit of breathy voice. With sonorants, the situation is different. Sonorants are normally voiced, although they can lose some of their voice when they appear after aspirated obstruents.

By citing phonation, place, and manner of articulation, one can uniquely identify just about all the consonants of English. One exception is the pair /r/ and /l/. Both are voiced alveolar approximants, and one must specify whether the consonant is lateral if one wishes to fully tell them apart.

Table 5.1 summarizes these observations about consonant properties.

Table 5.1 Places and Manners of Articulation of English Consonants

	Labial	Labio-dental	Dental	Alveolar	Post-alveolar	Palatal	Velar	Glottal
Oral stop	p, b			t, d			k, g	
Fricative		f, v	θ, ð	s, z	ʃ, ʒ			h
Affricate					tʃ, dʒ			
Nasal	m			n			ŋ	
Approximant				r		j	w	
(lateral)				l				

Note: Obstruents are cited in pairs, except for voiceless /h/; the sound before the comma is voiceless, and the following one is voiced. The remaining sounds (sonorants) are all voiced.

Vowels

The understanding of the vocal apparatus used for consonants helps to describe the production of vowels as well. Unlike consonants, vowels are made with a relatively open vocal tract. The vowels of English are ordinarily voiced, as you can see by applying the voicing tests you learned for consonants to the vowels in words such as *I* and *we*. In some circumstances, however, particularly when an unstressed vowel is surrounded by voiceless obstruents, the vowel becomes voiceless. Pay attention to the first vowel of *potato* and see whether you pronounce it as a voiced or voiceless sound. Does the speed with which you say it have any effect?

Vowel sounds vary much more from dialect to dialect than consonant sounds do. Consider regional American dialects or the Englishes of the United Kingdom or Australia: chances are good that it will be the vowel differences rather than consonant differences that stand out. It is difficult to characterize English vowels in a way that does justice to their diversity. Our descriptions are to be taken as a starting point. Our basic goal is to introduce the parameters that distinguish the vowel sounds and to illustrate them with real English examples. These descriptions are not intended to prescribe how the different vowels *ought* to be pronounced—no one is in a position to do this. If your pronunciations differ significantly from the ones presented here, we hope to provide you with vocabulary and concepts to help you describe your versions.

The most important property in the production of vowels is the differing location of the body of the tongue. For the sound /i/ of *heat*, the body of the tongue is raised toward the palate; for the sound /æ/ of *hat*, the body of the tongue is lowered. The jaw is normally raised or lowered with the tongue. Starting with your tongue in the high position for /i/, gradually lower it until you reach the position for the sound /æ/. The result may sound strange, but if you listen carefully you may encounter some other English vowels in the course of going from the highest tongue position to the lowest.

The vowels /i/ and /æ/ are characterized as **front** vowels, because they are made with the body of the tongue in a relatively forward part of the mouth. They are produced in approximately the same region of the mouth as palatal consonants, and in fact /i/ is virtually the same sound as the palatal approximant /j/: notice how the tongue moves little if at all when moving from the consonant to the vowel in the word *ye* /ji/. In table 5.2, the column labeled "Front" lists the front vowels in order from highest to lowest.

Other vowels are articulated with the back of the tongue; this is the case for the vowels /u/ of *who* and /o/ of *coat*. **Back** vowels tend to be pronounced with lip **rounding**. For most people nowadays, this rounding of the lips is rather slight and might only be noticed if you pronounce /i/ and /u/ in succession: your lips will probably be more pursed for the latter sound.

Students may find the low vowels confusing because the descriptions they read in books often don't correspond to their own pronunciation. Different dialects of English have different numbers of distinctive low vowels. Most speakers in England, for example, have three different vowels in the words *spa*, *spot*, and *caught*. Nowadays almost all Americans have the same vowel in *spa* and *spot*, which is most typically a front vowel /a/, although many people pronounce it as a back vowel. Consequently, most Americans have no more than two vowels where the English have three. But many North Americans have also changed the vowel /ɒ/

Table 5.2 Vowels of American English

Height	Tenseness	Front	Central	Back
High	Tense	i (*heed*)		u (*loot*)
	Lax	ɪ (*hid*)		ʊ (*look*)
Mid	Tense	e (*wade*)		o (*coat*)
	Lax	ɛ (*wed*)	ə (*fun, sofa*)	ɔ (*horse*)
Low	Lax	æ (*cat*)		
	Tense	a (*spa*)		ɒ (*caught*)

as in *caught* so that it is pronounced the same as *cot*. For these speakers, all the words we have mentioned in this paragraph have the same vowel, approximately /a/. Are they alike in your own pronunciation?

American English has one more simple vowel that we haven't discussed yet because it is neither front nor back. The vowel /ə/ is considered a **central** vowel. Its height depends a lot on the speaker and the context in the word, but in general it is of mid height. This vowel has the special honor of having its own name, **schwa**. Linguists have traditionally used this symbol only for unstressed vowels, but in contemporary American speech the stressed vowel in words like *fun* does not differ appreciably from the unstressed schwa at the end of *sofa*, so the symbol /ə/ can thriftily be used for both.

Note how in table 5.2 some vowels share the same height and backness. The vowels /e/ and /ɛ/, for example, are both mid front vowels. To distinguish such sounds, linguists refer to an additional property of vowels, their **tenseness**. The vowels /i/, /u/, /e/, /o/, and /a/ are **tense**, while the other vowels are considered lax. An easy way to remember the distinction is that in English, only tense vowels can be stressed at the very end of a word. For instance, there is a word /'de/ (*day*), but not only is there no such word as ×/'dɛ/, but the very idea of such a word would seem strange to most speakers.

Many of the speech sounds of English involve a movement from one vowel position to another. For the sound /aɪ/ of words like *I* and *might*, our articulators start out low, somewhere around the position for /a/, and move toward the high front position of /ɪ/; for the sound /aʊ/ of words like *how* and *now*, we begin near the same position and move toward the high back position of /ʊ/. Vowels that involve significant movements like these are called **diphthongs**. In addition to /aɪ/ and /aʊ/, there is a diphthong /ɔɪ/ in words like *boy* and *soil*.

We noted earlier that vowels are subject to a great deal of variation in English. Perhaps the largest source of this variation is the degree of diphthongization. Pronounce the tense vowels to see the extent to which they are diphthongs for you. Can you feel or see your tongue or jaw move during the vowel sound? To avoid the interfering effects of consonants, pronounce them in words whose consonants are not made with the tongue, such as /h/ or /m/. In Standard English the amount of diphthongization on the high and low vowels is slight. Considerably more diphthongization occurs on the vowels of *raid* and *rode*, which start with a mid vowel and move toward a high vowel. In fact, these are often transcribed /eɪ/ and /oʊ/, respectively, but in this book we keep to the simpler representations /e/ and /o/.

Summary

Consonants can differ from one another in manner and place of articulation and in voicing. The basic characteristics of vowels are the height and backness of the tongue, rounding of the lips, and length or tenseness. Knowing about common features of different sounds helps us to understand a number of types of allomorphy, because sounds that are phonetically similar often behave in similar ways.

Word Elements

Learn the following elements, their meanings and alternate forms.

Element	Gloss	Source	Examples
ag~ac~ig	act, do, drive	L	*agent, navigate, agenda, action, agile, exigent, intransigent, exiguous*
alt	high	L	*altitude, altimeter, altiloquence, altithermal*
ambul	walk	L	*perambulator, ambulatory, amble, somnambulist*
andr	male, man	G	*android, polyandry, androgyny, apandrous*
arch	first, govern	G	*archetype, anarchy, Archaeopteryx, archaeology, oligarchy, archbishop, archive*
av	bird	L	*avian, aviator, avicolous, Aviculidae, avine*
cad~cas~cid	fall	L	*cadence, casual, incidence, coincide, recidivism, incident, Occident*
ced~cess	go, let go	L	*concede, process, cede, secede, antecedent, intercede, excess*

Element	Gloss	Source	Examples
clud~clus	to close	L	*seclude, occlude, recluse, conclude*
doc	teach	L	*doctrine, doctor, docile, docent, document*
doc~dog	opinion	G	*orthodox, doxology, dogma*
ero	physical love	G	*erotic, Eros, autoerogenous, erogenous, erotica*
esth~aesth	feel	G	*anesthetic, synesthesia, aesthetics, kinesthetic*
grad~gred~gress	step, go	L	*gradient, ingredient, regress, retrograde, gradual, ingress, egress*
heli	sun	G	*heliocentric, helium, perihelion, aphelion, heliolatry*
leg~lig	gather, read	L	*elect, legible, selection, elegant, legend, lectern, diligent, eligible*
lic	permit	L	*illicit, licentious, license, scilicet, licet*
ne	new, recent	G	*neo-Fascist, neologism, neonomian, neogamy, neophyte, neoteny, neonatal*
phot~phos	light	G	*photon, phosphor, aphotic, phose, photosynthesis, photosphere, photoprotein*
prac~prag	act, do	G	*pragmatic, practice, practicable, apraxis, practicum*
reg~rig	rule, straight	L	*regular, regent, incorrigible, rex, regal, regimen, regulus, regina, regime, dirigible*
sent~sens	feel	L	*sentient, sensory, sententious, sentinel, sensual, consensus, insensate*
tele	far	G	*telephone, telemetry, telepathy, telesthesia, telekinesis, telegnostic*
ten~tend~tens	stretch, thin	L	*extend, tenuous, tensor, tensile, extenuate, tendon, tend*
trud~trus	thrust	L	*protrude, intrusive, extrude, intrude, abstruse*

Element Study

1. The same gloss, 'man', is frequently given for the elements *anthrop* and *andr*. Compare the words *anthropocentric* and *androcentric*. How do their meanings differ, and what difference between the roots *anthrop* and *andr* does this illustrate?

2. The root *cad~cas~cid* literally means 'fall' in a few words. One example is *deciduous*, which characterizes trees whose leaves fall in the autumn. But typically this root is used more figuratively. Give a one- or two-word gloss for the root in each word below. How are the meanings related to the literal act of falling?

   a. *cadence*
   b. *casual*
   c. *incident*
   d. *occasion*
   e. *recidivism*

3. The meanings of the root *ced* go beyond the simple glosses 'go', 'let go.' Consider variations in the meaning of *ced* (including the alternate spelling *ceed*) in the words below. Using the basic meanings 'go' and 'let go' as a starting point, what differences in meaning do you detect? For example, are there differences in the kind of motion described, or in whether motion in the literal sense is involved?

   a. *accede*   f. *precede*
   b. *cede*   g. *proceed*
   c. *concede*   h. *recede*
   d. *exceed*   i. *secede*
   e. *intercede*   j. *succeed*

4. Two very common roots have the allomorph *ten*. There is *ten* 'stretch', 'thin' and *ten* 'hold'. Look up the following words to determine which of the two roots *ten* is the root in each of these:

   a. *tenant*   h. *tenon*
   b. *tender*   i. *tenor*
   c. *tendril*   j. *tense*
   d. *tendency*   k. *tensor*
   e. *tenement*   l. *tent*
   f. *tenet*   m. *tenuous*
   g. *tennis*

5. After reviewing the word element lists for the preceding chapters, test your knowledge by parsing the words below. Under each element write a one-word gloss indicating meaning or function (e.g., part of speech) and categorize it as a root or tell what kind of affix it is: prefix, suffix, interfix, or superfix. With the aid of a dictionary, construct a brief definition for the entire word while staying as close as possible to the literal meaning of the individual morphs. Important aspects of the meaning that are not expressed by the word parts themselves can be included in parentheses.

a. *amorphous*   e. *incidence*
b. *omniscient*   f. *extenuate*
c. *conducive*   g. *acceptance*
d. *perinatal*   h. *adequate*

Exercises

1. Transcribe the following words using phonetic symbols. For example, for *mention* you would write /ˈmɛnʃən/ or /mɛnʃn̩/.

a. *wounds*   f. *drained*
b. *grounds*   g. *spine*
c. *psychologist* h. *thought*
d. *photograph*   i. *rather*
e. *photography*   j. *doughy*

2. Transcribe passage (a) into IPA using your own dialect, and translate passage (b) into standard English orthography:

a. If life hands you lemons, make lemonade.
b. /ˈdɪfr̩nt stroks fr̩ ˈdɪfr̩nt foks/

3. Render this Early Modern English passage into current English orthography. Then retranscribe it to reflect your own pronunciation. Summarize any differences, listing them by type.

if əɪ proˈfɛːn wɪθ məɪ ʊnˈwʊrðiɪst hand
ðɪs ˈhoːli ʃrəɪn, ðɪ dʒɛntl̩ fəɪn ɪz ðɪs
məɪ lɪps, tuː ˈblʊʃɪŋ ˈpɪlgrɪmz ˈrɛdi stand
tu smuːð ðat rʊf tʊtʃ wɪθ ə ˈtɛndɪr kɪs

4. Describe fully each of the sounds represented by the phonetic symbols. The first is given as an example. For each vowel indicate whether it is

- high, mid, or low
- front, central, or back
- rounded or unrounded
- tense or lax

For each consonant indicate whether it is

- voiced or voiceless
- labial, labiodental, dental, alveolar, postalveolar, palatal, velar, or glottal
- oral stop, fricative, affricate, nasal, or approximant (and if a postalveolar approximant, indicate if lateral or nonlateral)

    a. /ʒ/   voiced postalveolar fricative
    b. /ə/
    c. /dʒ/
    d. /ð/
    e. /e/
    f. /ŋ/
    g. /ɪ/
    h. /ɒ/
    i. /æ/
    j. /ɾ/
    k. /b/
    l. /ʊ/
    m. /h/

5. Give the phonetic symbol represented by each of the following articulatory descriptions, as in the example.

    a. voiceless alveolar fricative—/s/
    b. high back tense rounded vowel
    c. voiceless dental fricative
    d. voiced velar oral stop
    e. low front lax unrounded vowel
    f. alveolar nasal
    g. voiced labiodental fricative
    h. voiceless postalveolar affricate
    i. mid central unrounded vowel
    j. voiceless postalveolar fricative

CHAPTER SIX

Regular Allomorphy; Numeric Elements

Regular Allomorphy in General

In our overview of allomorphy in chapter 4, we discussed a set of variations that simply have to be memorized on a morpheme-by-morpheme or a word-by-word basis. But some allomorphy is **regular**—that is, generally predictable—because it is due to the operation of some simple phonetic principles. Regular allomorphy that applies to all native English words, such as the variation in the pronunciation of the plural morpheme in *cats*, *dogs*, and *finches*, comes to English speakers so naturally that they may be completely unaware of it at a conscious level. But some regular allomorphy is more challenging because it applies only to Latinate vocabulary. Such alternations result from changes due to classical Latin and Greek phonology, and they require study before we moderns can apply them fluently.

Latin Letters and Sounds

Mastering regular allomorphy in Latinate vocabulary is straightforward if we understand two things: what sounds the letters stand for in Latin, and what rules apply to each set of sounds. The bulk of this chapter deals with the rules, but first we consider the letter sounds.

As table 6.1 shows, the great majority of letters were pronounced in classical Latin times the same way they are in English today, for all practical purposes. The letters *c* and *g* always have velar sounds: /k/ and /g/, never ×/s/ or ×/dʒ/. The classical letter–consonant correspondences that seem the strangest to English readers are those for the letters *j* and *v*. In English these represent obstruents, but

Table 6.1 Most Common Pronunciations of the Latin Letters in Classical Latin and in Modern English

Letter	Latin pronunciation	English pronunciation
a	/a/, /aː/	/æ/ *static*, /e/ *stadium*
ae	/ae/	/ɛ/ *Daedalus*, /i/ *Caesar*
au	/aʊ/	/ɒ/ *autumn*
b	/b/	/b/ *bubonic*
c	/k/	/k/ *clinic*, /s/ *cite*
ch	/kʰ/	/k/ *chord*
d	/d/	/d/ *divine*
e	/ɛ/, /eː/	/ɛ/ *epic*, /i/ *femur*
eu	/eu/	/ju/ *euphoria*
f	/f/	/f/ *fission*
g	/g/	/g/ *galaxy*, /dʒ/ *general*
h	/h/	/h/ *hero*
i	/ɪ/, /iː/	/ɪ/ *image*, /aɪ/ *item*
j	/j/	/dʒ/ *joke*
k	/k/	/k/ *kinetic*
l	/l/	/l/ *lily*
m	/m/	/m/ *matrix*
n	/n/, /ŋ/ before velars	/n/ *note*, /ŋ/ *sanctify*
o	/ɔ/, /oː/	/a/ *obvious*, /o/ *oval*
oe	/ɔe/	/ɛ/ *Oedipus*, /i/ *amoeba*
p	/p/	/p/ *paternal*
ph	/pʰ/	/f/ *phone*
qu	/kw/	/kw/ *quantum*
r	/ɾ/	/ɾ/ *rose*
rh	/hɾ/	/ɾ/ *rhythm*
s	/s/	/s/ *sponge*, /z/ *misery*
t	/t/	/t/ *tuba*
th	/tʰ/	/θ/ *thermal*
u	/ʊ/, /uː/	/ə/ *ultimate*, /ju/ *utopia*
v	/w/	/v/ *vacuum*
x	/ks/	/ks/ *sex*, /gz/ *example*, /z/ *xenon*
y	/y/, /yː/	/ɪ/ *hypocrite*, /aɪ/ *hypothesis*
z	/dz/	/z/ *zone*

in classical Latin they were approximants. The vowels have approximately the same value as the corresponding IPA symbol: *a* is a low vowel, *e* and *o* are mid vowels, and *i* and *u* are high vowels. Most sounds in Latin can be pronounced either short or long. For the consonants, a long pronunciation is indicated in the orthography by writing the consonant twice, for example, mitt 'send' has a long consonant. However, long and short vowels are spelled the same. It is good to know in principle that Latin had short and long vowels because a few of the allophony rules care about vowel length. But because the distinction does not affect the spelling and only rarely affects the English pronunciation, we do not mark vowel lengths in this text.

The Greek elements do not pose many additional problems, because they are always romanized—rendered in Latin spellings—before being adopted into English. The only unusual letter sound you will encounter is /y/, a front rounded vowel like the *u* in French or the *ü* in German; in English this Greek sound is pronounced in the same way as the letter *i*.

Although the letters are familiar enough, the pronunciations we are discussing here are essentially those used in classical Rome. These classical pronunciations will help you understand Latin and Greek spellings and allophonic rules, but these pronunciations should not necessarily be used for words of Modern English. Two thousand years of sound changes have resulted in pronunciations that are in some respects different from those of Classical Latin. The most common of these are listed in the last column of table 6.1, but there are additional pronunciations; in particular, most of the vowels are pronounced as /ə/ when unstressed in English. Let your guide be your feeling for the spoken language—or a trusted authority or reference work.

Assimilation

Sometimes a consonant changes its place of articulation to match that of another consonant. This assimilation is almost always **anticipatory** in English and the classical languages: the consonant changes to match the place of articulation of the consonant immediately following it. In short, we say the consonant assimilates in place to the consonant to its right. The most common example involves the nasal consonant /n/. Before a morph beginning with a bilabial consonant this /n/ becomes /m/. This is seen most often when prefixes ending in /n/, such as Latin *con-* 'with', *in-* 'not', *in-* 'in', and Greek *syn-* 'with', are attached to roots that begin with a bilabial consonant:

> *con- + pose → compose*
> *con- + bine → combine*
> *con- + mute → commute*
>
> *in- + possible → impossible*
> *in- + balance → imbalance*
> *in- + mutable → immutable*
>
> *in- + pose → impose*
> *in- + bibe → imbibe*
> *in- + merse → immerse*
>
> *syn- + path + -y → sympathy*
> *syn- + phon + -y → symphony*
> *syn- + bol → symbol*
> *syn- + metr + -y → symmetry*

Although we are discussing the allomorphy rules from the standpoint of Latin and Greek pronunciation, in this chapter we present the words in their anglicized forms, for the convenience of the student of English vocabulary. Although the very ends of some of these words have nonclassical forms, the parts of the words that are involved in the phonological processes are spelled the same way in both languages.

Note that this rule works before <ph> in *symphony* even though the sound of <ph> is /f/ in English—a labiodental, not a bilabial. In classical Greek, <ph> represented a bilabial sound, aspirated /pʰ/, and so the rule applies.

Place assimilation of /n/ is also met with in infixes. Recall from chapter 4 that some roots have an allomorph that contains a nasal infix, <n> or <m>. Although it is pretty much impossible to predict which roots will have a nasal infix, one can at least predict what form it will take when it appears: it is basically a /n/, which can undergo place assimilation. Thus *fund* 'pour', but *cumb* 'lie'.

The assimilation rule can be expressed formally as follows:

Place Assimilation of /n/:

n → m / __ {p, b, m}

This notation is not as daunting as it looks at first glance. The part to the left of the slash mark describes a phonological change, and the part to the right of the slash tells the environment in which that change occurs. The arrow says that the sound to its left, /n/, changes into the sound to its right, /m/. In the environment part of the rule, the low line stands for the sound in question: it says that the /n/ must occur just before any of the sounds in the set {p, b, m}.

The alert reader may wonder why this rule is labeled in such general terms. Why is it called *Place Assimilation* and not simply *Labial Assimilation*? In fact, other types of place are assimilated as well. If /n/ comes before a velar consonant, then the /n/ becomes the velar nasal /ŋ/. But because /ŋ/ is spelled <n> in Latin, the assimilation leaves no mark on the spelling—*congregate, synchronize, tangent* (with nasal infix)—and so we tend to gloss over that part of the rule.

Note that when the /n/ assimilates to a following /m/, the result is the letter sequence <mm>, which actually stands for a long /mː/ in Latin and Greek. Because the /n/ has totally given up its own identity, the process is called a **total assimilation**. Before the other consonants, /n/ is still a separate sound, and has only changed its place of articulation, so by contrast we can call the process **partial assimilation**. Its nasality remains.

Another type of assimilation involves phonation. In many cases, a voiced consonant like /b/ becomes voiceless (i.e., /p/) before a voiceless consonant (often /t/).

Phonation Assimilation

[voiced obstruent] → [voiceless] / __ [voiceless obstruent]
[voiceless obstruent] → [voiced] / __ [nasal]

To take one example, the root *scrib* becomes *scrip* before suffixes that begin with *t*. That is why *prescribe* changes its /b/ to /p/ in *prescription*. Here are a few more examples:

reg + *-tor* → *rector* (cf. *regent*)
frag + *-tion* → *fraction* (cf. *fragile*)
ad- + *tend* → *attend*
sub- + *port* → *support*
leg + *-sis* → *lexis* /-ks-/ (cf. *prolegomenon*)

Note that *g* devoices to *c* /k/ even though words like *regent* are pronounced with /dʒ/ in English. This underscores the fact that we have to consider the Latin pronunciation: *g* was always /g/ in Latin, the voiced counterpart of /k/.

Usually, Phonation Assimilation winds up converting voiced consonants into voiceless ones. But here are some examples in which a voiceless consonant assimilates to a voiced one:

> *doc* + *-ma* → *dogma* (cf. *orthodox*)
> *sec* + *-ment* → *segment* (cf. *secant*)

Some sounds undergo total assimilation before the liquid sounds, /l/ and /r/. The most important cases of this liquid assimilation involve /n/ and /r/:

> **Liquid Assimilation**
>
> $\{n, r\} \rightarrow l / \_\_ l$
> $\{n\} \rightarrow r / \_\_ r$

Here are some examples:

> *con-* + *lude* → *collude*
> *con-* + *rupt* → *corrupt*
> *in-* + *leg* + *-al* → *illegal*
> *in-* + *ration* + *-al* → *irrational*
> *inter-* + *lig* + *-ent* → *intelligent*
> *per-* + *lucid* → *pellucid*
> *coron* + *-la* → *corolla* (cf. *corona*)

Technically /d/ is subject to the same rule of Liquid Assimilation (e.g., *alleviate* from *ad-levi-ate*), but it undergoes total assimilation in so many additional environments as well that it is useful to make a special rule for it:

> **Total Assimilation of /d/**
>
> $d \rightarrow C_1 / \_\_ C_1$ (not /m/ or glides)

The notation C_1 is for matching consonants. That is, whatever consonant follows the /d/, that's what consonant it becomes.

ad- + *liter* + *-ation* → *alliteration*

ad- + *rog* + *-ant* → *arrogant*

ad- + *brevi* + *-ate* → *abbreviate*

ad- + *greg* + *-ate* → *aggregate*

ad- + *pet* + *-ite* → *appetite*

ad- + *cep* + *-t* → *accept*

ad- + *fec* + *-t* → *affect*

ad- + *nota* + *-te* → *annotate*

ad- + *simil* + *-ate* → *assimilate*

In addition, /b/ undergoes total assimilation before velars:

ob- + *cipit* + *-al* → *occipital*

sub- + *ges* + *-t* → *suggest*

It is worth noting again that many of these rules apply, strictly speaking, only to the classical Latin pronunciations. In English *occipital* /ak'sɪpətl̩/, the root *cipit* doesn't begin with a velar, nor do we seem to have total assimilation. The rules become more regular if you think of them applying to Latin first, then think of how the Latin pronunciation of the whole word developed into English pronunciation.

English owes many of its double letters to total assimilations. If you are having difficulty parsing a word that contains a double letter, do not forget to consider the possibility that the first of the pair may have come from a totally different letter that was changed by total assimilation. By far the most frequent cases of total assimilation involve the assimilation of the final consonant of a prefix to the first consonant of a root. What are the basic forms of the prefixes in the following words: *syllogism, irradiate*?

Deletion

A vowel at the end of a morpheme is frequently **deleted** when followed by another vowel. In Greek, that second vowel can be preceded by an /h/, which is often deleted itself. In the following rule formulation, V stands for any vowel, and the symbol Ø ('zero') stands for the absence of a sound.

Vowel Deletion

V → Ø / __ (h) V

This rule works on the final vowel of a fairly large number of prefixes. It also works on the final vowel of the root before a variety of suffixes:

> *anti- + agon + -ize → antagonize*
> *ana- + hode → anode*
> *cata- + hode → cathode*
> *cello + -ist → cellist*
> *America + -an → American*

The Vowel Deletion rule should be distinguished from the spelling rule that leaves off the silent vowel <e> when certain suffixes are attached: *nude~nudist*, and so on. Here we are deleting from morphemes vowels that are actually pronounced in some allomorphs. The final vowel of the prefix *ana-* is pronounced in the word *analyze*; the final vowel of *cello* is pronounced in *cello* itself.

Consonants are also subject to deletion. The consonant /s/ is generally deleted before voiced consonants:

/s/ Deletion

s → Ø / __ [voiced C]

Here are some examples:

> *jus* 'law' + *dic* 'say' + *-ious* → *judicious*
> *bis* 'twice' + *-n-ary* A → *binary*
> *dis- + lig* 'gather' + *-ent* → *diligent*
> *dis- + vulg* 'crowd' → *divulge*

When combining morphemes would bring three consonants together, often one or two of the consonants is deleted. The rules for Cluster Simplification are complicated and do not need to be learned in detail; the important thing is that long runs of consonants may lose one or more consonant.

Cluster Simplification

$C \rightarrow \emptyset / \_\_ s C$

$C \rightarrow \emptyset / C \_\_ C$

among other variants.

sub- + *spic* 'look' + *-ious* → *suspicious*

ex- /ɛks/ + *vade* → *evade*

ex- + *mitt* 'send' + *-ing* → *emitting*

ad- + *scrib* → *ascribe*

ad- + *scend* → *ascend*

amb- 'around' + *put* 'cut' + *-a-te* → *amputate*

con- + *gna* + *-te* → *cognate*

in- + *gnore* → *ignore*

trans- + *jec* + *-tory* → *trajectory*

syn + *ste* + *-mat* → *system*

syn + *stol* + *-ic* → *systolic*

torqu 'twist' + *-ture* → *torture*

fulg 'lightning' + *-men-* + *-ate* → *fulminate*

Cluster Simplification rules are often not applied when the cluster is due to prefixation, but they are quite regular when the prefix is *ex-*. Note how the /s/-Deletion rule applies as well: *ex-vade* → *esvade → *evade*.

Closely related to Cluster Simplification is the rule of Consonant Shortening. When two identical consonants come together, the result is normally a long consonant, which is spelled as two consonants. A long consonant can also result from some of the rules discussed earlier, such as assimilation. However, Latin only permits long consonants between vowels. Consonants are shortened next to another consonant:

Consonant Shortening

$C: \rightarrow C / \{C \_\_ , \_\_ C\}$

The rule has a few additional refinements; in particular, most consonants are also shortened after long vowels. We won't pay too much attention to that part of the rule, because it is too difficult to know when the vowel is long in Latin. It is enough to know that the prefixes that can trigger total assimilation all have short vowels (*ab-*, *ad-*, *con-*, *dis-*, *in-*, *inter-*, *ob-*, *per-*, *sub-*, *syn-*); therefore, resulting long consonants stay long. Examples of actual shortening:

>*ex-* + *spire* → *expire* /ks/, not /ksː/
>*ex-* + *secr* + *-able* → *execrable*
>*ex-* + *secu* + *-tive* → *executive*

   Latin and Greek do not allow certain consonants at the end of the word. One of the more important word-final rules that we took over from Greek is the rule that a word cannot end in a stop. So Greek morphemes that end in stops often lose them, even in English, when used alone or at the end of a word:

Greek Final Stop Deletion

[stop] → Ø / ___ at the end of a word

Many examples involve the suffix -*mat*, but there are a few other examples as well. (An additional loss of a final vowel in some of these examples is not due to Greek phonology but is part of a much later process of naturalizing words to make them conform better to French and English word patterns.)

>*traumat* → *trauma* (cf. *traumatic*)
>*dramat* → *drama* (cf. *dramaturge*)
>*symptomat* → *symptom* (cf. *symptomatology*)
>*themat* → *theme* (cf. *thematic*)
>*schemat* → *scheme* (cf. *schematic*)
>*mastodont* → *mastodon* (cf. *orth-odont-ist*)

Insertion

The opposite of deletion, **insertion,** is also a source of regular allomorphy. Most cases of the insertion of even small elements between or within morphemes are morphological in origin, not phonological. For example, the insertion of *o* between the roots *phil* 'liking' and *soph* 'wisdom' in *philosophy* occurs because that is a morphological element marking classical compounding, not because there is any phonological principle preventing, say, /l/ and /s/ from standing next to each other. But there are occasional examples of phonological insertion, or **epenthesis**. Epenthesis occurs in a number of morphemes when an otherwise awkward combination of consonants would occur, especially at the end of the word. By the rule of Vowel Insertion, a morpheme ending with *r* after another consonant inserts an *e* when it appears at the end of a word.

Vowel Insertion

Ø → e / C __ r at the end of a word

Here are some examples:

> *centr* → *center* (cf. *centrist*)
> *cancr* → *cancer* (cf. *cancroid*)
> *arbitr* → *arbiter* (cf. *arbitration*)
> *ministr* → *minister* (cf. *administrate*)

A less general insertion rule applies only to prefixes. Sometimes one-syllable prefixes ending in a vowel add a /d/ before a root that begins with a vowel.

/d/ Insertion

Ø → d / V __ V after some prefixes

> *re-* + *und* + *-ant* → *redundant*
> *se-* + *i* + *-tion* → *sedition*
> *pro-* + *ig* + *-y* → *prodigy*

This insertion rule may be motivated because otherwise Vowel Deletion would result in a very short prefix—*se-i-tion* would become ×*sition*. Another insertion rule that applies only to prefixes has no such obvious motivation:

/s/ Insertion

Ø → s / b __ {p, t, c} after prefixes

This rule is surprising because all it does is produce big consonant clusters. In some words these clusters are tolerated, but in others they are subjected to the consonant simplification rules:

> ab- + trac + -t → abstract
> ab- + cess → abscess
> ab- + con- + d → abscond
> ob- + tens + -ible → ostensible
> sub- + ten + -tation → sustentation

Practice

Analyze the following words, using the preceding rules to guide your analysis:

> correct
> tiger
> illicit
> Antarctic
> aspect
> intellect

Rhotacism

Rhotacism is the process of turning /s/ into /r/. Latin morphemes with a final /s/ change this to /r/ in words where it appears between two vowels.

> *Rhotacism*
>
> s → r / V __ V

Here are some examples:

> rus + -al → rural (cf. rustic)
> jus + -y → jury (cf. justice)
> mus + -ine → murine (cf. muscle)
> genus + -ic → generic

Vowel Changes

Latin Vowel Weakening occurs when a morpheme appears in a syllable other than the first syllable of a word. It affects only short vowels. It is actually a series of rules, as follows:

Latin /a/ Weakening

a → *e* / [syllable] __

That is, /a/ regularly becomes /e/ when preceded by another syllable in the same word:

> *de-* + *fac* + *-t* → *defect* (cf. *fact*)
> *re-* + *cap* + *-tive* → *receptive* (cf. *captive*)
> *in-* + *apt* → *inept*

Latin /e/ Weakening

e → *i* / [syllable] __ C V

Short /e/ becomes /i/ when it is followed by a single consonant and a vowel. Latin /e/ Weakening affects not only the /e/ that is in the basic allomorph of a morpheme but also the /e/ that comes from Latin /a/ Weakening.

> *de-* + *fac* + *-ient* → *defecient* → *deficient*
> *re-* + *cap* + *-ient* → *recepient* → *recipient*
> *con-* + *ten* + *-ent* → *continent*

Latin Vowel Weakening includes several other minor rules as well. The consonant that follows the vowel can influence the outcome of the weakening. For instance, vowels tend to become /e/ before /r/ (*experiment* not *expiriment*) and /i/ before /ŋ/ (*infringe* from *frang*). When consonants affect the quality of vowels, we speak of **vowel coloring**.

Vowel coloring also occasionally occurs independently of vowel weakening, even in word-initial syllables. This is especially common before /l/:

/l/-Coloring

{*e, o*} → *u* / __ *l* in a closed syllable

Here are some examples:

> *com- + pell + -sive → compulsive* (cf. *compel*)
> *col- + tiv + -ate → cultivate* (cf. *colony*)
> *in- + sal* 'jump' *+ -t → *inselt → insult*
> *ad- + ol + -t → adult*

Note how in the example of *insult*, the /e/ that undergoes this rule came from Latin /a/ Weakening.

Other Consonant Changes

Many Latin suffixes begin with /t/, so it is especially important to understand what changes roots undergo when followed by /t/. We have already seen cases in which suffixes beginning with /t/ trigger Phonation Assimilation (*rec-tor* from *reg*), and /l/-Coloring (*cul-tivate* from *col*), or prevent rules like Rhotacism (*justice* vs. *jury*) and Latin /e/ Weakening (*recep-tive* vs. *recipient*). An additional rule applies when a root ends in a dental stop, /d/ or /t/. Because /d/ in this environment would become /t/ anyway by Phonation Assimilation, we discuss this rule simply as one affecting the contact of /t/ plus /t/.

> *t+t to ss*
>
> *t + t → ss* when roots are combined with suffixes

Here are some examples:

> *pat + -tion → passion* (cf. *patient*)
> *mitt + -tive → *mittive → missive* (cf. *transmitter*)
> *fid + -tion → *fittion → fission* (cf. *pinnatifid*)
> *con- + ced + tion → *concettion → concession* (cf. *concede*)
> *sent + -tu + -al → *senssual → sensual*
> *sent + -t → *senss → sense*
> *dis- + grad + -t → *digratt → *digrass → digress* (cf. *grade*)
> *ex- + lūd + -tive → *elūttive → *elūssive → elusive*

In many cases, Consonant Shortening applies after the change of *tt* to *ss*, so we end up with only a single *s*. This happens whenever another consonant precedes the *ss*, or even a long vowel. Because we are not memorizing whether a root, like *lud* 'play', has a long vowel or not, these shortenings of *ss* may appear unpredictable. When you see a root morph ending in /s/, you should always be alert to the possibility that it is an allomorph of a root that ends in a *t* or *d*, to which a *t*-initial suffix has been added.

Numeral Morphemes; Distinguishing between Latin and Greek Morphemes

The numeral morphemes of Latin and Greek are among the commonest found in English words. Most of them are already familiar to you. Their use often illustrates the tendency to combine Latin morphemes with other Latin morphemes and Greek morphemes with other Greek morphemes. For example, with the root *gon* 'angle' which comes from Greek, we use the Greek numeral morpheme *penta* 'five' in *pentagon* 'a five-sided geometrical figure'. But with the root *later* 'side', which comes from Latin, we use the Latin numeral morpheme *quadr* 'four' in *quadrilateral* 'a four-sided geometrical figure'. Morphemes often occur with others from the same source language simply because the entire word was borrowed from that language. The word *pentagon*, for example, originated in Greek; it wasn't first coined in English from Greek roots. Words that are coined anew in English frequently violate the tendency for a word's morphemes to be monolingual in origin. The word *monolingual* itself is a violation, as it is composed of *mon* 'one' (G) and *lingu* 'tongue' (L). Other examples of this kind of mixing are *neonate* (G, L), *amoral* (G, L), *dysfunction* (G, L) and *posthypnotic* (L, G).

These violations are perfectly valid words, but it is useful to be aware of the strong tendency for words with roots from a given language to contain other morphemes from that language. There are some signs that tell you when a prefix or root morph is Greek rather than Latin. The best clues are the presence in one of the roots of one or more of the following:

- One of the letters that were borrowed into Latin just for spelling Greek words: <y> as in *hyper-, hypo-, myc, cryph, my, onym, pachy*; <z> as in *zo, zyg, zym*.
- An initial <k> as in *kilo, kerat, kin.* (This is an alternative transcription of what is usually spelled <c>.)

- Any of the combinations <rh>, <ph>, <th>, and <ch> (pronounced /k/, not /tʃ/) as in *rhin*; *pher, troph, taph*; *the, esth, sthen, path*; *arch, chrom, chrys*.
- A spelling that represents an initial cluster not pronounceable in English, such as <ps> (*psych, psittac, pseud*), <pt> (*pter, pto, pty*), <pn> (*pneum*), <mn> (*mne*), <x> (*xyl, xen, xer*).

Almost without exception, if a root has one of these characteristics it is Greek in origin and typically combines with other Greek morphemes. Latinate morphs provide a few clues to their origin as well. Generally, a morph in complex scholarly or scientific vocabulary cannot be Greek (and hence is probably Latinate) if it contains

- <f> as in *fer, fa, ferr*
- <j> as in *jus, juven*
- <v> as in *voc, cav, ven, ov, vin, ver, vid*
- <qu> as in *quart, quadr, squam, equ, loqu*

The numeral elements are widely used. They precede the root they modify (or count or order) as in *unicycle* (literally 'one wheel') and *millennium* 'one thousand years'. But most of them are not, strictly speaking, prefixes, because they can occur as the sole root in a word, as in *dual* and *monad*, in which *-al* and *-ad* are suffixes.

The elements listed in table 6.2 are those most commonly used in traditional numeric compounds. Other important variants are Latin *du* 'two' (*dual, duplex*) and Greek *dy* 'two' (*dyad*), *dich* '(split) in two' (*dichotomy*), and *trich* '(split) in three' (*trichotomy*).

In English, ordinal numbers are mostly formed from cardinal numbers by suffixing *-th* (e.g., *tenth*), but some ordinals are irregular (e.g., *third* from *three*) and the words *first* and *second* are totally unrelated to the corresponding cardinal. A very similar situation existed in Latin and Greek. The Latin ordinals are particularly frequent and should be learned by heart: *prim* (*primary, primogeniture*), *secund* (*second*), *terti* (*tertiary*), *quart* (*quart, quarter, quartet*), *quint* (*quintet, quintessence*), *sext* (*sextet, sextuplets*), *septim* (*septimal*), *octav* (*octave*), *non* (*nones, nonagenarian*), *decim* (*decimal, decimate*). For higher numbers, the suffix *-esim* is used, as in *centesimal*. Greek ordinals are not

Table 6.2 Classical Numeric Elements

Meaning	Latin	Greek	Examples
1	un	mon	*uniform, monologue*
2	bi	di	*bisexual, dichloride*
3	tri	tri	*triple, tricycle, triptych*
4	quadr	tetra	*quadrangle, tetrahedron*
5	quinque	penta	*quinquennium, pentagon*
6	sex	hexa	*sextet, hexagon, hexameter*
7	septem	hepta	*semptemvirate, heptagon*
8	octo	octa	*octane, octopus, octahedron*
9	novem	ennea	*November, enneastyle*
10	decem	deca	*decemvirate, decagon, decade*
20	viginti	icosa	*vigintillion, icosahedron*
100	cent	hecaton	*century, hecatomb*
1000	mille	chili	*millennium, chiliasm, chiliarch*
10,000	—	myri	*myriad, myriarch*
½	semi-	hemi-	*semiconductor, hemisphere*
1½	sesqui-	—	*sesquicentennial, sesquipedalian*
both	ambi-	amphi-	*ambidextrous, amphiploid*
few	pauc	olig	*paucity, paucifolious, oligarchy*
many	mult, plur	poly	*multiple, plurality, polygon*
all	omn, tot	pan-~pant-	*omniscient, total, Pantheon, pantomime*

used as widely as the Latin ones, but the first three, *prot* (*prototype, protozoa, protopathic, protoplasm*), *deuter* (*deuterium, Deuteronomy*), and *trit* (*tritium*), are worth learning. Latin also had a series called the distributive numbers. In principle, these were formed by adding the suffix *-n* or *-en* to the basic form of the number, but so many unusual sound changes ensued that it is worthwhile studying these separately. From 'two', these numbers are *bin* (*binary, binaural*), *tern* (*ternary*), *quatern* (*quaternary*), *quin* (*quinate*), *sen, septen, octon, noven*, and *den* (*denarius*).

In English, the basic numbers up to *thousand* are native, but those for *million* and above are constructed with classical morphemes. *Million* itself is based on *mille* and the Italian augmentative suffix *-on*: it is literally a 'big thousand', that is, a thousand thousands. New terms were invented in the modern period for every power of 1,000 above that: *billion, trillion, quadrillion,* etc. The *-illion* was clipped from *million* and reinterpreted as a suffix for indicating large numbers. It is added to the Latin element counting the number of times 1,000 is multiplied by another 1,000. Thus *billion* multiplies 1,000 by 1,000 twice (i.e., 1,000 × 1,000 × 1,000, or 1,000,000,000). An easy way to think of this is that the numeric element counts how many groups of 000 there are in addition to the first group.

Dictionaries are full of terms for very high numbers, but terms higher than *million* are used less commonly than one might expect. One reason is that until quite recently terms like *billion* had different meanings in different English-speaking countries, and so could be a source of massive confusion. Another reason is that scientists, the principal users of huge numbers, prefer to use scientific notation and the International System of Units (SI), both of which obviate the need for special words for large numbers. The SI specifies morphemes that can be prefixed to basic measurement units to refer to much larger or much smaller measurements. For example, three gigawatts are the same as three billion watts.

Summary

Much of the allomorphy seen in word elements of Latin or Greek origin is best understood as the product of phonological rules that apply to the original, classical pronunciation of the elements. Partial assimilation involves a consonant's acquiring some of the phonetic features of the following consonant; in total assimilation, the two consonants merge into one consonant, usually long. The nasal /n/ assimilates place features, obstruents assimilate voice, /n/ and /r/ as-

Table 6.3 Prefixes of the International System of Units

Big numbers		Small numbers	
Number	*SI prefix*	*Number*	*SI prefix*
10^1	*deca-*	10^{-1}	*deci-*
10^2	*hecto-*	10^{-2}	*centi-*
10^3	*kilo-*	10^{-3}	*milli-*
10^6	*mega-*	10^{-6}	*micro-*
10^9	*giga-*	10^{-9}	*nano-*
10^{12}	*tera-*	10^{-12}	*pico-*

similate totally to /l/, and /d/ assimilates to most consonants. Deletion processes may efface a vowel before another vowel or /h/, /s/ before a voiced consonant, a consonant from a large cluster; or stops at the end of Greek words. The shortening of long consonants when not between vowels can also be considered a type of deletion. The less common opposite process, insertion or epenthesis, may insert /e/ between a consonant and /r/ at the end of a word, /d/ between vowels during prefixation, or /s/ before a voiceless stop after the /b/ of a prefix. Rhotacism turns /s/ into /r/ between vowels. Latin Vowel Weakening affects syllables that are not at the start of a word: in general, /a/ becomes /e/, /e/ becomes /i/ in an open syllable. Latin also has vowel colorings, such as mid vowels becoming /u/ before /l/ in closed syllables. The combination of root-final /d/ or /t/ to a suffix that begins with /t/, a common event in Latin, results in /ss/ or /s/.

There is a general, but violable, tendency for roots in the same compound to be drawn from the same language. This rule is easily obeyed for number morphemes, because large sets of numbers have been borrowed from both Latin and Greek. English uses Latin number morphemes to build names for very large numbers, but the current preference is to use scientific notation and the prefixes of the SI.

Word Elements

Element	Gloss	Source	Examples
bell	war	L	*belligerent, antebellum, bellicose, rebellion, bellipotent*
cens	judge	L	*censor, censure, census, censorious, censorate*
cephal	head	G	*encephalitis, microcephaly, acephalous, cephalalgia*
crat~crac	govern	G	*democratic, plutocracy, autocratic, meritocracy, aristocrat*
cur	care	L	*curator, curate, sinecure, procuration*
dem	people	G	*democracy, pandemic, endemic, demiurge, demographic*

Element	Gloss	Source	Examples
fla	blow	L	*inflate, flatus, sufflation, afflatus, flatulent*
loc	place	L	*local, locus, allocate, collocation*
lumen~lumin	light	L	*luminous, lumen, luminary, illuminati*
man	hand	L	*manual, manipulate, emancipate, manumission, manicure*
pl~plec~plic	times, fold, entwine	L	*triple, quadruple. duplex, complicated, explicate, plexus*
son	sound	L	*sonic, sonority, dissonant, assonant, sonnet*

Element Study

1. Guess the meanings of the words below based on the numeral morphemes in this chapter. Then look them up and in a few words explain the connection between the meaning of the numeral morpheme and the meaning of the word it appears in.

   a. *sesquiduple*
   b. *ambiguous*
   c. *monandry*
   d. *omnivore*
   e. *pandemic*
   f. *semitrailer, or semi*
   g. *quinquagenarian*
   h. *octuplet*
   i. *Novena*
   j. *December*

2. Coin adjectives for the following definitions using the numeral morphemes in this chapter and other roots you have learned up to this point. Some of the words you create may be found in the dictionary; others may not. Don't try to capture every bit of the meaning of the definition in the actual morphemes of the term you coin; a prefix and a root or two should be sufficient. Try to restrict yourself to only Latin or only Greek roots within each word.

a. having the head of a human	_____ic
b. having six heads	_____ic
c. occurring every twenty years	_____ial
d. governed by a two-member group	_____ic
e. having a hundred angles	_____al
f. having three gods	_____istic
g. having three letters	_____al
h. having two feet.	_____al

3. Parse and give all glosses and allomorphs you have learned. Primary stresses are marked (´) to aid in pronunciation and recognition of the word.

   a. *héctoliter* (gloss *liter* as 'liter')
   b. *meritócracy* (gloss *merit* as 'deserve')
   c. *tetrálogy*
   d. *primogéniture* (gloss -*iture* as NOUN)
   e. *inflátionary* (*in-* isn't 'not')
   f. *perámbulate* (*per-* isn't *peri-*)

Exercises

1. a. In all but two of the following words, the last letter of the prefix has been assimilated to the first sound of the root. What is the original (i.e., unassimilated) form of the prefix in each word? Use a dictionary to check your answers.

   b. For each word, indicate whether the final consonant of the prefix has been completely assimilated to the initial consonant of the next morph or only partially. In each case say what phonetic characteristics of the final consonant of the prefix have changed as a result of assimilation to the consonant that follows it.

a. *impossible*	i. *annotate*
b. *corrupt*	j. *opposition*
c. *effect*	k. *commit*
d. *infect*	l. *illegible*
e. *suffer*	m. *occlude*
f. *irrelevant*	n. *assimilate*
g. *embolism*	o. *submit*
h. *immemorial*	

2. Analyze the following words using the rules in this chapter to guide your analysis:

   a. *explosion*   c. *expect*
   b. *rectitude*   d. *abscond*

3. The following examples were used in this chapter to illustrate the loss of \<s\> after *ex-*:

   ex- + spire → expire
   ex- + secr + -able → execrable
   ex- + secu + -tive → executive

   Give examples of words in which the roots *spir*, *secr*, and *secu* appear with their initial \<s\>. What is the meaning of each root?

4. What are the meanings of the boldface morphs in these words, which appeared as examples in this chapter? For each word, find another word in which this boldface morpheme occurs. The morph may or may not have a different allomorph.

   a. *redundant*
   b. *immutable*
   c. *convention*
   d. *collude*
   e. *anode*
   f. *nautical*
   g. *cultivate*

5. For each of these words, change the boldface morpheme into one that takes a different allomorph of the prefix. For example, (a) could change by replacing *und* with *lev*, to give *relevant*.

   a. *redundant*
   b. *immutable*
   c. *collude*
   d. *anode*
   e. *syllogism*
   f. *irradiate*
   g. *convention*

6. The word *semester* contains two roots, both of which are heavily disguised, idiosyncratic allomorphs of forms shown in the glossary. (Hint: The first root is a numeral, but it is not *semi-*.) What are the forms and meanings

of these roots as given in the glossary? Use the etymological notes in a dictionary entry for the word *semester* to provide the answer.

7. What do the numeral morphemes in the words *Pentateuch*, *Decalogue*, and *Deuteronomy* count? For example, in the word *tritium*, the *tri* 'three' counts isotopes; tritium is the third isotope of hydrogen. Use the dictionary entry on the origins and definitions of these words for the answer.

CHAPTER SEVEN

Polysemy and Semantic Change

Multiple Meanings and Shifts in Meaning

So far we have been mostly concerned with changes in the form of morphemes. In this chapter we turn to shifts in their meanings. If our goal is to understand a word's meaning by recognizing its components, then mastering **polysemy**— variation in meaning—is just as important as mastering allomorphy, variation in form.

We have already seen many cases of polysemy, as when we had to deal with the multiplicity of meanings for morphemes like *path* 'feel', 'illness'. It is important to understand the difference between polysemy and **homonymy**. In both, the same spelling or pronunciation has two or more different meanings, but in homonymy those meanings are not related except by accident. The homonymous words *ring* 'circular band' and *ring* 'to make a bell sound' are completely unconnected except by the coincidence of sharing a single form. Indeed, in Middle English these two words were not even pronounced the same. Another pair of homonymous morphs encountered in an earlier chapter are *in-* (one of two allomorphs) 'in', 'into' and *in-* 'not'. There are even triplets of homonymous morphs in English, such as *bat* 'club', 'flying mammal', and 'wink'. In this book we list homonyms as separate items in the word element lists and glossary, while polysemy is indicated by giving more than one meaning beside a single form. The focus of this chapter is polysemy, which is much more common than homonymy and a greater challenge to the student of English vocabulary.

One group of morphemes whose variety of meanings we have more or less left our readers to unravel for themselves is the suffixes, which have a kind of rudimentary polysemy. We noted that some suffixes, like *-tion* and *-ary*, mainly dictate the part of speech of the host word. Others, however, contribute more to the meaning of a word. For example, *-oid* signifies not only that the word on which it occurs is an adjective or noun but also that the thing described by the word resembles—usually imperfectly—the thing described in the root. A spheroid resembles a sphere: Astronomers say that planets are typically spheroids rather than spheres, because they are not perfectly round but slightly flattened at the poles. Similarly, a humanoid creature in science fiction resembles a human but is not biologically human. But even this easily definable suffix is polysemous in the sense that it can form words that are either adjectives or nouns, or both: humanoid (A) aliens can be called simply humanoids (N).

Polysemous suffixes are the rule, not the exception, in English. The word *polysemous* itself contains one. Table 7.1 gives an idea of the range of meanings of *-ous*. A list of other *-ous* adjectives would no doubt turn up many other meanings as well. The adjective suffix *-ic* also has a wide range of senses, as shown in table 7.2. Other senses of *-ic* include 'with ROOT', 'connected with ROOT', 'characteristic of ROOT', 'of ROOT', and 'belonging to ROOT'.

Differences in shades of meaning can be difficult to express, but the context in which a word appears helps to narrow down the possibilities, even for unfamiliar words. Use the six examples below to test your ability to gather the meaning of a suffix, as well as to explore differences in pronunciation when a suffix is used to form adjectives, nouns, and verbs. What is the part of speech of the word with the suffix *-ate* in each sentence below? How does the part of speech affect the pronunciation of the suffix?

   a. I **advocate** the abolition of television.
   b. I am an **advocate** of equal rights for women.

Table 7.1 Meanings of the Suffix *-ous*

Word	Meaning	Root
aqueous	'of, relating to, or resembling water'	*aqu*
envious	'feeling or showing envy'	*envy*
gracious	'characterized by grace'	*grat*
libelous	'constituting or including a libel'	*libel*
polysemous	'having many meanings'	*poly, sem*

Table 7.2 Meanings of the Suffix *-ic*

Word	Meaning	Base word
alphabetic	**'of or pertaining to** an alphabet'	*alphabet*
angelic	**'like** an angel'	*angel*
panoramic	**'characterized by** a panorama'	*panorama*
runic	**'consisting of** runes'	*rune*

    c. He will **delegate** authority to his subordinates.

    d. She was a **delegate** to the convention.

    e. Jake was **desolate** when Pat left us.

    f. The enemy will **desolate** the city.

As you can see, adjectives and nouns in *-ate* are generally pronounced /ət/ or /ɪt/, while verbs in *-ate* usually are pronounced /et/. In prefixes and roots, polysemy is no less extensive than in suffixes.

    Historical change can shift meanings so drastically that they are not easy to determine from context. Change in meaning over time is just as frequent and natural as the sound changes studied in chapters 4 and 6. By now you are used to identifying the *fac* of *factor* with with the *fec* of *defect* as allomorphs of the same morpheme, despite the historical change that caused their vowels to differ. In the same way, you need to become aware of the effects of **semantic changes** that cause a morpheme to acquire different meanings over time.

    It doesn't take much imagination to see the relationships between the different meanings in cases like the following:

nom	'law', 'system'
path	'feel', 'illness'
extra-	'outside', 'additional'

But what about the morpheme *cosm*, which can mean 'universe' as in *cosmos* and *microcosm*, or 'adorn' as in *cosmetic*? For *cosm* should we have listed two distinct morphemes, each with a different meaning, even though they have the same form? This clearly is the right approach for the semantically distinct but formally identical prefixes *in-* 'in' and *in-* 'not'. However, we believe it more useful to treat *cosm* as a single polysemous morpheme, because it is relatively easy to reconstruct the historical process that gave rise to this polysemy. In ancient Greek, the word *cosmos* originally meant 'order'. The word came to refer to the world or universe because of its perfect order, at least in the Greek worldview. On a more mundane level, the Greeks applied the word to the aesthetic arrangement of clothing and ornamentation. Another case of polysemy that arose in ancient times is *troch*, which appears in *trochee*, a poetic foot consisting of a long and short syllable, and in *trochoid* 'wheel-like'. The original meaning in both cases was 'run': a trochee is a short and fast poetic foot, and wheels permit fast motion.

Turning now to Latin, consider the root *fac*, which we have glossed as 'do' or 'make'. This meaning is clear enough in words like *factor, fact, effect,* and *efficient*, but now consider *face, facial, deface, efface,* and so on. Are we dealing with a single morpheme *fac* with as broad a range of meanings as 'do', 'make,' and 'face'? In etymological terms, we definitely are. *Face* and *efface* are historically related to *fact* and *effect*. The semantic connection is a series of associations: 'make' → 'form' → 'appearance' → 'face'.

When we are not aware of such historical relationships, we require the relationship of the various meanings of a single morpheme to be fairly transparent. But what is transparent to one person may not be transparent to another. Being able to unravel polysemy may then become a matter of individual imagination or additional knowledge. A highly useful habit in vocabulary study is to gather keys to related meanings from the contexts in which words appear, from your knowledge of history, or from whatever other sources are at your disposal. You should soon be able to create many mental links between new morphemes and the meaning they contribute to the words in which they occur. You will then be able to understand relationships which, although initially unclear, make sense with some extra thought.

Uncovering semantic relationships you were previously unaware of can be satisfying as well as revealing. Take the word *revelation*, for example. The prefix *re-* means 'back' and the root *vel* is the same root that appears in *velum*. In both words, *vel* means 'curtain'. Anatomists see the velum as a type of membranous curtain that hangs down from the hard palate, and a revelation is a pulling back of a curtain. Another colorful example is *depend*, where *de-* means 'from' and *pend* means 'hang', providing a simple but graphic illustration of dependence.

Whether a word is familiar or unfamiliar, chances are that it has undergone fascinating meaning shifts over time.

Reasons for Semantic Change

To understand the kind of semantic change that leads to polysemy, consider first why meaning should change at all.

Errors and Misinterpretation

In certain situations, a speaker may be unable to communicate an idea perfectly. An example is the history of the word *bead*. Originally, *bead* meant 'prayer'. The shift in meaning came from the practice of using a string of beads as a way of keeping track of the sequence of prayers called the rosary. Since counting prayers in this way was connected with counting the beads themselves, the word *bead* shifted to its current meaning. Similarly, the word *since* originally meant 'after', but because effects follow causes in time (as in *Since Jim came, Mary left*), we came to use the word to mean 'because' as well.

Creative Variation

In many realms of language use, creativity is at a premium, and hackneyed phrases or clichés are avoided. Such realms include literature, folk speech, and slang. Language styles like these encourage us to adapt words to new uses as a way of maintaining fresh and lively discourse and displaying our skill with language. Words like *cool, slick*, and *tight*, for example, have been extended to cover not just physical attributes but also aspects of personality, mood, and aesthetics.

Abbreviation

The need to express ourselves quickly and efficiently often leads us to use a single word to carry the burden of a longer phrase of which it is a part. **Ellipsis** or 'dropping out' of the word *doma* 'house' from the longer Greek phrase *cyriacon doma* 'Lord's house' led ultimately to the English word *church*. The same has happened more recently with *microwave (oven)*.

Change in the Thing Named

Sometimes meanings are extended or changed less for linguistic reasons than because the object that the word once described has itself changed. As noted in chapter 3, a ship was once only a vessel for navigating large bodies of water, but later it could be a dirigible—an airship—or vessel for interplanetary travel—a spaceship. Likewise, due to changes in writing technology, the word *pen*, originally 'a writing instrument made from a quill' (from Latin *penna* 'feather'), now has extended its range to include fountain, ballpoint, and felt-tip pens.

The Finite Word Stock

Ultimately, the most important single reason for multiplying the meanings of words is that we find the number of vocabulary items to be small in relation to the infinite variety of the things we have to say. With a limited body of terms at our disposal, we need to discuss things of almost unlimited complexity and bend words to accommodate a wealth of new ideas, events, and entities. We have three choices: make new words, use longer phrases, or extend the duties of existing words. We do all three, but most often it's easier to extend the meaning of a word than to invent a totally new one, and speaking in ever-longer phrases quickly moves from cumbersome to impractical.

Paths in the Development of Meaning

In the simplest cases, it is easy to discern a word's original, basic meaning despite polysemy. For example, table 7.3 shows some developments of meaning for the word *horse* over roughly a thousand years.

In each case when the meaning was extended, the oldest meaning was retained. For example, when we speak of a car as having 300 horses under the hood, that meaning is an extension of the basic meaning of *horse*, '*Equus caballus*', not of the meaning 'four-legged support' or 'cavalry'. We can think of the development of the meanings of *horse* as represented in figure 7.1, where the paths of development are shown by the arrows pointing from the older meaning to the one derived from it.

Table 7.3 Stages in the History of the Word *Horse*

Time period	Meaning
Proto-Germanic times to present	'a member of the animal species *Equus caballus*'
Fifteenth century to present	'four-legged structure on which something is supported (e.g., for sawing)'
Sixteenth century to present	'cavalry soldiers'
Twentieth century to present	'the pulling power of one horse'

For some words, however, an original basic meaning is lost, leaving only extended meanings that are harder to trace to the original sense. This is the case with the word *hysterical*, whose Greek source *hystericos* originally meant 'uterine', which shouldn't be surprising in light of the meanings of its component morphemes, *hyster-* 'womb' and *-ic(al)* A. After time, however—in Greek, Latin, French, and, after it was borrowed, English—this word took on a broad range of other senses, many of which disguise the original one. At one time doctors attributed various severe psychiatric disorders to uterine problems, so the word *hysterical* came to be used to describe such problems. Subsequently people used the word to describe strong emotional reactions even if perfectly normal and transient, such as hysterical anger or laughter. Currently, *hysterical* is often used simply to mean 'very funny', as in a hysterical joke.

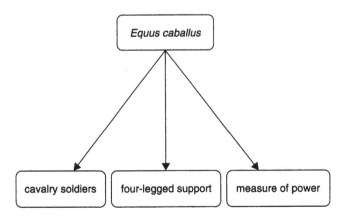

Figure 7.1 Developments of the Meaning of *Horse*

As figure 7.2 shows, the situation with *hysterical* is quite different from that of *horse*. *Hysterical* never meant 'uterine' in English. The gap between this original Greek meaning and the others is quite wide and the relationships among these are vague, if one is not well versed in medical history. All in all, it is impossible to state a single basic meaning for the word *hysterical* today. In addition, it is also hard to contend that the morpheme *hyster* invariably means 'womb'.

For a case like *hysterical*, knowledge of a word's original meaning or its morphemes offers at best only slight assistance. But such unpredictable relationships among the senses of a word are not typical of specialized scholarly, technical, and scientific vocabulary. And when meaning does shift, it tends to happen in a way that can be retraced fairly easily. In fact, many shifts are so obvious that they scarcely have to be mentioned.

Types of Semantic Change

Generally speaking, every semantic change involves an **association** of some kind. The associations between the different meanings of *path*—'feel' and 'illness'—are easy enough to see. Associations tend to fall into three categories. First, the range of things a word refers to can be extended to include an additional set of things that resemble the original set. The resemblance can be based on either form or function. Changes based on resemblance involve **metaphor**, a notion familiar to you from literature or poetry. Using *bright* as a synonym for *intelligent* is a case of metaphoric

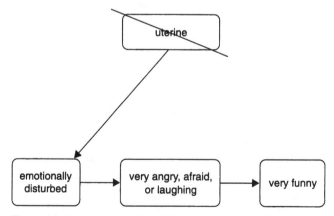

Figure 7.2 Development of the Meanings of *Hysterical*

shift. Another category of associations is based on a different type of connection, often in physical space, time, or the relationship of cause and effect. This type of association is called **metonymy**. When we say we admire Shakespeare, we could literally be referring to the author himself or to his work. Using the term *Shakespeare* to refer to the work of Shakespeare is an example of a metonymic shift.

Metaphor

Metaphor is most often based on resemblance, as when the word *leaf* refers to a page in a book. We can reasonably conjecture that the meaning 'page' is derived from the botanical meaning and not the other way around because books are more recent, and less basic in nature, than leaves of plants. Metaphor is also clearly involved in the extension of meaning in the word *horse* to apply to a four-legged support.

Metaphor can also involve a shift from the concrete (i.e., physical) to the abstract (i.e., intangible or conceptual). A metaphoric shift is apparent if we take apart the word *understand*, which at first literally meant 'stand below'. The figurative usage involved the image of 'holding up' an idea. Compare the colloquial expression *to get behind* meaning 'to support or agree with'. Likewise, the words *comprehend, apprehend,* and *grasp* are all extended metaphorically to express the 'seizing' of something intellectually. Similarly, when we speak of *shelving* an old idea, we are using the metaphor of putting aside some useless physical object (like an out-of-date book) in reference to an idea, an abstract thing.

The **spatial metaphor** is a fundamental method in human language for developing new meanings. Most of the prefixes taught in this course are spatial

Figure 7.3 A Real Horse

Figure 7.4 A Metaphorical Horse

in their basic sense, but in most uses are metaphorically extended to express nonspatial meanings. Table 7.4 provides examples. In each case, the meaning has been extended in at least one way, but generally in a manner that still allows us to see the original meaning as well.

Metaphor is the commonest kind of semantic shift. It is used so frequently that we often have to qualify what we are saying to indicate that we are not speaking metaphorically. When we say something like *I rolled on the floor laughing* we are expected to be speaking metaphorically, and we might try to cancel out this expectation by adding the word *literally* if we wish to communicate that we were actually rolling about. Unfortunately, the term *literally* itself has become extended, so that saying *I literally rolled on the floor laughing* still leaves open the question of whether we are speaking literally or figuratively!

Metonymy

Metonymy is a shift in meaning from some object to something connected with it in some way other than by resemblance. For example, in the 1990s some of

Table 7.4 Metaphoric Extensions of Meaning of Spatial Prefixes

Prefix	Spatial sense	Use in extended sense
de-	'away from'	negative: *desperate* 'lacking hope' (*sper* 'hope') intensive: *declare* 'make totally clear' reverse an action: *de-emphasize* 'reduce emphasis upon'
ex-	'out'	'open, visible': *expose* 'render visible or open' (*pon~pos* 'put') 'not included': *except* 'exclude or bar' (*cep~cap* 'take')
extra-	'outside'	'beyond', 'not': *extraordinary* 'unusual'
ob-	'against'	negative, 'destructive': *obloquy* 'abusive language' (*loqu* 'speak')
per-	'through'	'thorough, strong': *pertinacious* 'holding on thoroughly' (*tin~ten* 'hold')
pre-	'in front of'	'before', 'early': *precocious* 'matured early' (*coc* 'ripen')
sub-	'under'	as part: *subsume* 'take in as member of a larger unit' (*sum* 'take in') 'open or exposed to': *subject* 'bring into sphere of influence' (*jec~jac* 'throw') 'inferior': *subhuman*

our undergraduates referred to their fathers as *the wallet*. Another example is the use of the word *pulp* to refer to a variety of lurid literature, as in *pulp fiction*. In this shift, the material on which the literature was originally printed came to refer to the printed matter itself. Wheat, as its sounds subtly suggest, was named after the word *white*, because of its lightness of color. The connection involved in a metonymic change can be of almost any kind other than resemblance, including such associations as **source ↔ product** and **thing ↔ characteristic** and **person ↔ possession**.

Metonymy can involve the association not only between one object and a completely different object but also between a part of an object and the whole object, or between one type of thing and a more specific type of thing. Two clear examples appear in the sentence *The ranch hands herded a thousand longhorns*, where *hands* must be referring to entire workers and *longhorns* to entire cattle. When we use *plastic* to refer to a credit card, we use one aspect of that object to refer to the entire object. A *bite* of food is usually a serving of several bites of food. This kind of metonymy can be subtle: it may be difficult to decide whether a particular usage is meant figuratively, literally, or perhaps both at once. In *Get your butt over here*, does the word *butt* refer to a body part or a whole person?

Metaphor and Metonymy: Comparisons

A good way to learn the difference between metaphor and metonymy is to compare how the same word functions when used as a metaphor and when used as a metonym. Take the word *head*. Metaphorically, *head* designates a protuberance at one end of things like pins, hammers, beer, and pimples; the top or most important part of something long, like a bed, column, or parade; something roughly spherical, like a head of cabbage; and so on. How about a metonymic use of *head*? When we refer to people or animals as *heads* (*charge ten dollars a head*, *a hundred head of cattle*), that is a type of metonymy associating the whole with the part. When we refer to the obverse side of coins as *heads*, it is not because that side itself looks like a head but because that side is often used for—metonymically associated with—portraits; we still say *heads* even if that side contains something other than a portrait. If we say someone loses his head, we are using *head* as a metonym for self-control, a faculty we associate with literal heads as the seat of rational thought.

Next consider the word *table*. There are several things called *tables* because they somehow resemble the piece of furniture, such as a geological feature (plateau) and a constellation (Mensa). But the word is also used to refer to things associated with a table, such as the food eaten from it (*He sets a good table*) or the people sitting around it (*That table ordered champagne*). To test your ability to distinguish metaphors from metonyms, determine whether *table* is used metaphorically or metonymically in these expressions: *The data are laid out in table 3; That grape makes an excellent table wine.*

Metaphors and metonyms are so frequent in language that it is not unusual for the two to be combined in a single expression. If a person refers to a toilet as a *head*, it is a metaphorical association with the primitive toilets on old sailing vessels. In turn, those heads were so called because they were located at the front, the head, of a ship—a metonymical association. And why was the front of the ship called its head? By metaphorical association with the front part of animals.

In talking about reading the latest news in the *press*, we are again combining metaphors with metonyms. Using the term *press* to refer to a printing press is a result of a metaphor, comparing the modern printing process to Gutenberg's invention, which actually involved using a heavy screw to press the printing block against the paper. Using the name of the means by which a newspaper is printed to refer to the newspaper itself is a metonym. Note also that *the press* has a general meaning, as when one refers to a member of the press. But in talking about what we read in the press, we normally are referring at most to a couple of newspapers. What term would you give to the relationship between the two uses of *press* in the last two sentences?

Outcomes or Results of Semantic Shift

A frequent result of semantic change is **narrowing** (also called **specialization**). Narrowing is the restriction of the meaning of a word to a subset of what it originally denoted. Thus, the word *deer* now refers to a particular animal, but its meaning has narrowed. In Shakespeare's time the word could be used to refer to an animal of any sort ("Mice, and Rats, and such small Deare"). Another example of narrowing is *adder*, which meant 'snake' in Old English and in Middle English but now refers only to a few varieties of snake.

The opposite result of change is also common. In **widening** (also called **generalization**), a word's meaning extends to include cases that go beyond the original ones. The Old French ancestor of the word *arrive* comes from the Latin prefix *ad-* and the root *rip* > *rive* 'shore', as in *river*. (The symbol > means 'becomes'.) This original word, meaning 'to come ashore', widened its reference to the reaching of any destination. The Old English ancestor of Modern English *bird* meant 'young bird', the more general term, applicable to young as well as old, being *fowl*. Only later did *bird* become the general term for any feathered creature, regardless of age.

Not every semantic change results in widening or narrowing. Sometimes one specific meaning ousts another. The word *car* originally meant 'wagon' or 'chariot' but can no longer be used for such vehicles as these but instead is used today mostly for automobiles.

The effects of meaning shift can be relatively value neutral, as in most of the examples we've seen up to this point. But there are also surprising shifts from positive meanings to negative meanings and the reverse. An example of **melioration** (shift from negative to positive) is seen in the word *nice*. Its Latin forebear was *nescius* 'ignorant' (*ne* 'not' + *sci* 'know'). A chain of shifts shows how it improved its lot: 'ignorant' > 'foolish' > 'fussy' > 'proper' > 'pleasant' > 'kind'. Some would say that is losing its positive value and is now almost neutral—'not disagreeable'. The opposite of melioration, **pejoration**, is more common. *Silly* has had a history almost the opposite of *nice*: it originally meant 'blessed'. Pejoration often goes hand in hand with **euphemism**, the process of using a new word to refer to an item or concept that people hesitate to talk about straightforwardly. Once a euphemism is well accepted, the original term becomes even less acceptable, undergoing pejoration. Of course, the euphemism still refers to the same people or objects and so is itself subject to pejoration. For instance, the word *cripple* is now virtually taboo as a noun, being replaced by *handicapped person* or *disabled person*. In turn, some people advocate replacing these words with terms such as *person with a disability*, *handicapable*, and *differently abled*, while other people have strong aversion to some of these euphemisms. Is *disabled* now a pejorative term? In the end, evaluative terms such as *melioration* and *pejoration* are subjective ways of looking at semantic changes, many of which can simultaneously be described by other terms. For instance, *notorious*, which originally meant simply 'widely known' but now means 'widely known for something scandalous', can be described as having undergone a pejorative narrowing.

For the most part, it is whole words and not individual bound morphemes that undergo semantic shifts. When we say, for example, that there has been a widening (at least for a substantial number of speakers of American English) in the meaning of the word *reticent* from 'reluctant to speak' to simply 'reluctant', the morpheme *tac~tec~tic* itself has not altered its meaning 'silent', and this morpheme does not cease to refer to speech in other words, such as *tacit*. Similarly, the word *pretend* originally meant 'stretch forth, assert' and only later came to mean 'falsely claim'. It would be misleading to suggest that the individual morphemes *pre-* and *tend* changed their meaning to include the sense 'false', for only in combination in the word *pretend* is any such sense associated with them.

Applying Principles of Semantic Change to Word Analysis

Ultimately, semantic change can be difficult to precisely describe and explain because so many factors may be involved. It is hard to reconstruct any historical event, especially an invisible event such as a change in a mental state. Even when a meaning change took place in historical times, there is usually a stage where it is not yet clear whether a writer means to be using a word in its older or newer sense.

When a morpheme in a particular word has lost its original sense, you may need to use a certain amount of ingenuity to understand how the gloss you have learned for that morpheme relates to the current meaning of the word as a whole. For example, one has to wonder at first about a verb like *insist*, whose parts mean 'in, into' and 'stand' (*sist* is an extended form of *st~sta*) but whose commonest meanings today are 'strongly demand' and 'strongly assert something'. Rather than simply take a surface interpretation—something like 'stand in'—at face value, we should be prepared to start thinking metaphorically right away, because metaphor is by far the commonest kind of semantic change. Keep in mind that even the native English word *stand* has many different meanings beyond the basic, literal one. Examples in the kind of language you use every day may occur to you, such as those in the sentences *Kim won't stand for it* or *The mayor stands up for the little guy*, or *Pat has to take a stand*. In each of these examples, we can see subtler shadings that include 'tolerate', 'support', 'be steadfast'. We may even want to compare other words containing the element *sist* such as *persist, resist, desist, subsist, persist,* and *exist.* They all have senses that partially overlap with these uses of *stand* and, for that matter, *insist.* In the end, although you certainly won't arrive at a precise etymological reconstruction of the semantic development of *insist,* you will not be surprised to learn that it actually followed a course of shift that can be roughly outlined as follows.

'stand on' (a path) >
'start walking' (on a path)>
'continue walking' >
'continue' doing something despite opposition >
'strongly demand' to do something >
'strongly affirm or assert'

Note that this set of shifts involves several of the processes discussed in this chapter and observable in element lists and elsewhere throughout the book. First is the flexibility of spatial prefixes: Here, *in-* doesn't literally mean 'in' but something similar: 'on'. Second is the process whereby a concrete, physical phenomenon becomes increasingly abstract. One aspect of the action or state of walking—continuing what one is doing—comes via metonymy to be the primary meaning. We also see a narrowing or specialization of meaning to include a resistance to opposition. The next to last step persists today in phrases like *insists on getting his own way.* We see a shift that appears to involve a metonymy between doing something continually and doing something strongly, possibly a matter of connection between cause and effect, because doing almost anything continually requires effort—in other words, doing it 'strongly'. Finally, in phrases like *insists that war is bad for the economy,* we see a subtle shift to a completely mental arena: the insister isn't doing anything but strongly stating an opinion.

Now, this may all seem a bit too much, especially because you already know the word *insist* and are unlikely to ever have to analyze it to understand a sentence. But the same principles illustrated in this case also apply to less familiar words, such as *perspicacity,* which would be glossed as 'through' + 'look' + A + N. In a context like "*Medicine is not a science of souls. Physicians lack the perspicacity to find the world-weary patient's real illness,*" you wouldn't need to do much more than take the literal reading, roughly, 'through looking-ness' and interpret it in some plausible and straightforward—but not simplistic—way. It is likely then that you would arrive at a meaning for *perspicacity* like 'insight', 'vision', or 'deeper wisdom', rather than 'x-ray vision' or some whimsical alternative along these lines. And the accuracy of your interpretation would be supported by a dictionary which defines the word as 'acuteness of perception, discernment, or understanding', all good synonyms for your educated guesses.

Summary

Polysemy is the term for multiple historically or semantically connected meanings in a word or morpheme. It contrasts with homonymy, when unrelated words or morphemes just happen to be spelled or pronounced alike. Polysemy comes about when semantic changes add new meanings without taking away the old one. Changes can arise through misinterpretation but are often the result of a desire to be creative, succinct (through abbreviation or ellipsis), and up to date (when things in the world change). Changes can be challenging to analyze when they occur in long chains. Any given change is the result of some kind of mental association, usually involving metaphor (resemblance) or metonymy (other incidental connection). Changes can also be characterized in terms of their outcomes. Narrowing or specialization happens when the meaning becomes more specific, and widening or generalization is the opposite. Melioration happens when a word takes on more positive connotations, and pejoration is the opposite.

Exercises

1. Many English words begin with Latin spatial prefixes. Table 7.5 indicates (with ×) words combining spatial prefixes with roots *duc* 'lead', *pos* 'place', 'put', *port* 'carry', *jac~jec* 'lay', 'lie', *sist* 'stand', *cap~cep~cip~cup* 'take'. Here are some words combining spatial prefixes with these roots:

   abducent 'drawing apart', said of a muscle when it moves a limb away from the center axis of the body (lit. 'pulling away')
   abduct 'to carry off by force' (lit. 'pull away')
   adduce 'to present or bring forward a point for consideration in a discussion or analysis' (lit. 'draw toward')
   adductor 'a muscle that pulls a body part in the direction of the center axis of the body' (lit. 'that which draws toward')

Table 7.5 Building Words with Latin Spatial Prefixes

Prefix	duc	pos	port	jac~jec	sist	cap~cep~cip~cup
ab-	×			×		
ad-	×	×	×	×	×	×
circum-		×				
con-~co-	×	×	×	×	×	×
de-	×	×	×	×	×	×
dis-		×	×	×		
ex-	×	×	×	×	×	×
in-	×	×	×	×	×	×
inter-				×		×
intro-	×					
ob-		×		×		×
per-					×	×
pre-		×				×
pro-	×	×		×		
re-	×	×	×	×	×	×
se-	×					
sub-		×	×	×	×	×
trans-~tra-	×	×	×	×	×	

apport 'the moving or producing of a physical object by a spiritualist medium (e.g., at a séance) without any apparent physical activity', or 'any object produced in this way' (lit. 'carry toward' or 'bring')

Others include *circumduction, conducive, conduct, comportment, deduce,* and *deduction.*

Choose five interesting or unfamiliar combinations from this list that form words whose meaning has shifted from the literal reading of their glosses. Using an etymological dictionary like the *Oxford English Dictionary*, investigate the range of meanings the words have had over time and identify the semantic shifts involved. For example, look for words combining *sub-* and *sist* or *tra-* and *ject*. Determine their principal meanings at various times and identify the semantic shifts they have undergone. Don't forget that allomorphy, especially partial or total assimilation, may disguise some morphemes in certain combinations.

2. Table 7.6 indicates (with '×') English words combining Greek spatial prefixes with roots *leg~log* 'study', 'speak', 'pick', *pher~phor* 'carry', *the* 'put',

Table 7.6 Building Words with Greek Spatial Prefixes

Root	pher~phor	the	leg~log	tom~tm	bol~bl	sta~ste
Prefixes						
ana-	×	×	×	×	×	×
anti-		×				
apo-		×				×
cata-	×	×			×	×
dia-	×	×	×	×	×	×
ec-		×				×
en-				×	×	
epi-	×	×	×	×	×	×
hyper-					×	×
hypo-		×				
meso-		×				
meta-	×	×			×	×
para-		×			×	
peri-	×				×	
pro-		×	×		×	×
pros-		×				
syn-		×	×		×	

tom~tm 'cut', *bol~bl* 'throw', *sta* 'stand', 'state'. Here are some words combining Greek spatial prefixes with these roots:

anaphoric (grammatical term) 'referring to a preceding word or phrase' (lit. 'carrying back')

analogy 'similarity of properties, ratios, etc.' (lit. '(the act of) studying back')

anathema 'something banned or cursed' (lit. 'thing put back')

Others include *diathesis, epitome, epilog, anabolic, prosthetic,* and *synthesis.*

    Choose five interesting or unfamiliar combinations from this list that form words whose meaning has shifted from the literal reading of their glosses. Using an etymological dictionary like the *Oxford English Dictionary*, investigate the range of meanings the words have had over time, and identify the semantic shifts involved. For example, look for words combining *hypo-* and *sta* or *syn-* and *log*. Determine their principal meanings at various times and identify the semantic shifts they have undergone. Don't forget that allomorphy, especially partial or total assimilation, may disguise some morphemes in certain combinations.

3. The following is a pair of cognate morphemes in which both the formal resemblance and the relation of meaning is problematic, at least without some special knowledge: *graph* 'write' as in *calligraphy* and *crab* as in *fiddler crab*. Should *graph* and *crab* be considered allomorphs of the same morpheme if we can state a rule of allomorphy which relates the <g> and <ph> of *graph* and the <c> and <b> of *crab*? Where would you draw the line, and why?

4. Which of the two meanings given for each of the words below is earlier? What knowledge about semantic shift or other factors leads you to this conclusion? (Use an etymological dictionary like the *Oxford English Dictionary* to check your answer.)

    a. *text* 'weave' as in *textile* or *text* 'writing' as in *textual*
    b. *ex-* as in *expose, extend* or *ex-* as in *ex-wife, ex-doctor*
    c. *divine* 'godly' or *divine* 'wonderful'

5. Following the example of *insist* from the last section of this chapter, detail the major developments along the paths (such as metaphor or metonymy) and outcomes (such as narrowing or widening) of semantic shift involved in the history of the word *inaugurate* from its beginnings in ancient Rome to the present. Be sure to propose a plausible path for every step you can.

    'take omens from the flight of birds' >
    'consecrate by taking omens from the flight of birds' >
    'consecrate an installation into office by taking omens from the flight of birds' >
    'install in office'

6. Each of the following words has undergone either a metaphoric or metonymic shift in meaning. Identify the type of shift from the earlier meaning (on the left of the arrow) to the current meaning that you feel is most plausible. You may use a dictionary as an aid if you like. Explain your answer in a sentence or two. Some meaning shifts cannot be confirmed by the historical record or cannot be neatly classified as metaphor or metonymy. If you believe that there is more than one plausible answer in a particular case, give and explain both.

    a. *vermicelli* 'small or thin worms' > 'a kind of thin macaroni not unlike spaghetti'
    b. *redeye* (2 words) 'an eye that is red' > 'a minnow that has red eyes'
    c. *seminary* 'a place where seeds are sprouted and nurtured' > 'school of religion'

    d. *convince* 'to physically overcome' > 'to intellectually persuade'

    e. *urbane* 'pertaining to cities; urban' > 'sophisticated'

    f. *muscle* 'a little mouse' > 'an organ such as the biceps'

    g. *sandwich* (capitalized) 'earl said to have dined on finger food rather than leave the gambling table' > 'food consisting of two slices of bread and a filling'

7. Political discussion has introduced a number of changes into our vocabulary. Nowadays the estate tax is often referred to as a death tax; antiabortion people refer to their position as pro-life, and so on. How do such examples compare to the types of change discussed in this chapter?

CHAPTER EIGHT

Usage and Variation

Many Englishes

Up to now, we have been considering English to be a language. That seems eminently reasonable, yet in a sense it is inaccurate. What goes by the single name *English* is not a single language. Instead, it is a large set of varieties from different parts of the globe, used in a wide assortment of social situations.

Earlier chapters have mentioned variation in style. Some usages are more appropriate for formal contexts than for informal ones, while usages out of place in formal contexts may be perfectly fine in informal ones. Still, this doesn't begin to capture the range and complexity of variation actually observed in speech. Doctors, farmers, social workers, bakers, biologists, carpenters, philosophers, exterminators, psychologists, actors, educators, lawyers, gardeners, and physicists all either work with a set of special terms or use more general terms in special ways. A major goal of this book is to provide access to such specialized vocabularies and, in particular, to the words associated with more formal and scholarly styles.

At the same time, we need to consider whether formal styles deserve a privileged status over other styles. Recent innovations in our language come from many places on the social and professional spectrum. Consider the diversity of the origins of the words *latte, regifting, infotainment,* and *bling.* Clearly, English speakers are looking not just to one source for models to follow in their speech. We have already seen that our rich and varied linguistic past includes constant changes to suit new conditions. Obviously, this is still going on. The users responsible for this constant reshaping include the most and least educated speakers, from communities all over the country and the world.

Our focus continues to be words, but let us keep in mind that variation involves not only vocabulary but also pronunciation, spelling, and other aspects of language.

Roots of Variation and Change

Chapter 2 illustrated profound effects on the language due to **external** forces, including war, invasion, geography, migration, commerce, and both social and technological change. Likewise, **internal** factors, including phonetic and semantic changes, have led to major and minor differences in pronunciation, meaning, word formation, and language use, as described in chapters 5 through 7. Occasionally changes may unify a language; in the Old English period King Alfred the Great is credited with a number of reforms that made the dialect of his court the literary standard for all of England. However, internal and external forces more often have the opposite effect. They create new, divergent varieties. Ultimately these varieties may develop into different languages that are incomprehensible to each other's speakers. Of course, that is exactly what happened with the West Germanic tongue that was the source of both Modern German and Modern English.

Seeds of Dialectal Division

The truth is that English has never been a single, unified speech form. In northern and southwestern England to this day, there are rural English folk whose speech is nearly incomprehensible to Americans and often quite difficult to understand even for speakers from other parts of England. Elsewhere in Britain, too, distinct types of English survive and in some cases thrive among the modern Scots, Irish, and Welsh. Beyond the British Isles, new varieties of English have sprung up in Australia, New Zealand, the United States, and South Africa.

Further from the heart of the world settled by English speakers, even more linguistic differentiation has occurred. In the former British colonies of India, Sri Lanka, Nigeria, Singapore, and many others, contact with local languages and other factors have created what have been referred to as **new Englishes**. The English used in these countries has official status and is taught in schools at various grade levels. It serves as an important language of mass communication and business, functioning in these nations as a **lingua franca**, a common language for groups that share no other language. Such local English was once modeled on the speech and writing of the educated upper classes of England, but today the population at large in these countries often speaks a rather un-British kind of English. In English-speaking countries of Asia and Africa, where national ties with Britain have weakened since independence, the model for English is increasingly a local one. As a result, these national varieties are moving ever further from their historical roots in England. In time, they may come to differ as much from our English as Dutch and German differ from each other today. In a sense, then, the very status of English as a world language contains the seeds for its eventual diversification and division.

Where Do Standards Come From?

A **standard language** is a set of linguistic norms established by some generally accepted political or social authority. In the extreme case, a standard may be shaped by the practice of a single respected speaker or writer or group of speakers or writers. In many countries, the standard is whatever is spoken by the ruling classes in the capital city. The situation is not too different in England, where the language of London and environs has been setting the standard since the late Middle Ages. In the United States, on the other hand, Washington itself is not particularly influential. The standard is sometimes said to be set by the broadcast media. But it is more accurate to say that the media follow a standard that has already been set, primarily by educated speakers in the Northeast.

Some standards are based on a variety used in religious scripture, such as the Arabic found in the Qur'ān. On occasion, the authority is a grammarian's or lexicographer's description. For English this was the case with the dictionary of Samuel Johnson, who aimed to exhaustively enumerate the words and meanings of the language of the well educated in England. His American counterpart, Noah Webster, sought to promote national unity and independence by recording the vocabulary of the new American variety of English.

Standards are quite often based on the language of those in a society who are judged most powerful. This makes some sense, because using the language established by an authority typically lends the user some of the symbolic or actual social status of that authority. Still, there is something perverse about one segment of society holding a special claim on the language of society as a whole.

Another important force in creating a standard language is printing. Books demand a certain amount of consistency, notably in spelling but also in other facets of a language. In England at the end of the fifteenth century, the introduction of printing led to many decisions that crossed lines of regional linguistic variation in Britain. Even today we are living with some of the results of the decisions made back then.

Speaking versus Writing

We distinguish between spoken and written standards, for these are not the same. All of us normally acquire the spoken language of our community before receiving any formal education. But in school we are introduced to a new standard—a literary one. After many years of immersion in the new standard in school, we may come to write quite differently from the way we speak. This is true even if our community speaks the standard language, and it is truer still if our community does not.

Spoken varieties continue to change even when a written language or accepted literary form doesn't budge. Writing is generally conservative, as we can see from the number of letters no longer pronounced in the word *knight*. Over time, writing tries to comes into line with speech. Some languages—for example, Spanish, Norwegian, and Russian—have reformed their spelling to eliminate inconsistencies. English has also undergone such reforms, but inconsistencies remain pervasive. The sequence <ough> is famously pronounced differently in each of the following words: *rough, bough, through, thought, trough, though,* and *hiccough*. The sound /ʃ/ can be spelled as in *fish, motion, passion, sugar,* and *facial*. Such inconsistencies are often bemoaned, but at the same time there is resistance to such modest innovations as *lite* and *thru* for *light* and *through*.

Changing Standards

We need only compare the literary usages of Shakespeare's time with our own to see that standards themselves can and must change. Such flexibility can strengthen a standard language. To the extent that the standard has vitality and wide usage, it may serve to unite a nation, facilitate communication, and therefore serve the common good. But this is not to say that the only valid language is a standard one, even though some "experts" behave as if that is the case. Let us explore some cases where the standard language is actually inappropriate.

Where the Standard Fails

A standard serves many purposes, but it is by no means the appropriate medium for all communication. After Latin had evolved into the distinct Romance languages, it remained the written and spoken standard for members of the European priestly and scholarly community. Yet they, like their associates and neighbors, spoke local Old French, Old Spanish, and Old Italian varieties in many nonofficial contexts. Today, although government, business, and other authorities support the use of a single written standard, large numbers of people in France, Italy, and Germany grow up speaking a distinct regional variety of their languages. Regional dialects are often sources of great pride, often bolstered by rich oral traditions and sometimes a written literature. Although the level of literacy in the standard is very high in these countries and all students study it in school, regional varieties are still often preferred for talk between relatives and friends, traditional folk customs, and a range of other activities.

You may even find yourself in a situation where using Standard American English of the type taught in school or used in literature is clearly not the best way to communicate. In the streets of Brooklyn, where one of the authors of this book grew up, insisting on speaking a national educated standard—for example, a typical college professor's pronunciation, word choice, and syntax—could result in being shunned (or worse) by associates and mistrusted by strangers. This is not so much because speaking Standard English would have hampered his ability to communicate as because it may have been socially inappropriate. Brooklyn is, of course, hardly unique in this respect.

Most of us generally speak like the people we grew up with unless we have modified our language for particular purposes. Many actors, of course, are adept at speaking in different accents. Archibald Leach, who grew up speaking the working-class accent of Bristol, England, changed his accent along with his name, and did it so successfully that Cary Grant became known as the emblematic debonair American.

Can Our Tung Be Cleane and Pure?

Some experts can be quite tolerant of regional dialects yet very protective of the standard language that they command. Since the time of the earliest English standard, there have been those who have seen fit to criticize certain differences in usage as corruptions, barbarisms, and marks of intellectual, even moral, decline. In England in the sixteenth century Sir John Cheke responded to those who used lots of words borrowed from French, Latin, and other foreign sources by writing, "I am of this opinion that our own tung should be written cleane and pure, vnmixt and vnmangeled with borowing of other tunges." Perhaps he should have reconsidered his own choice of words before writing, because the words *opinion, mix, mangle,* and *pure* are themselves borrowed.

Gripes about innovative usages have come from many quarters, ranging from some of our most distinguished authors to national governments. Jonathan Swift despised the use of *rep* for *reputation* that was common in his day and condemned the practice of clipping words in general. An author writing in 1872 labeled the word *belittle* "incurably vulgar." Fowler and Fowler[1] took the position that Americanisms should be treated as "foreign words" in British English. Straining to give American English its due, these authors concluded, "The English and the American language and literature are both good things; but they are better apart than mixed." French law imposes fines for using foreign words in the media when a French equivalent exists.

What unites these attempts to control linguistic change is their failure. No language has ever really been frozen, and there is no good reason to expect that any ever will. Few prescriptivists seem to understand this fact, and many seem unaware that essentially all their linguistic battles are lost over time. Extraordinary efforts were made to convince speakers to never split an infinitive, and yet the previous phrase will not strike most readers as being odd, despite the fact that the infinitive *to split* has the adverb *never* interrupting it. In school we are taught to use the subjunctive in contrary-to-fact expressions like *as if he were the devil himself.* Yet *as if he was the devil himself* is at least as common. Another example is the use of *hopefully* as a sentence modifier, as in *Hopefully it will rain today.* Critics see this use as illogical, because *hopeful* as an adjective should modify a word referring to

---

1. H. W. Fowler and F. G. Fowler, *The King's English,* 3rd ed. (Oxford: Clarendon Press, 1931). The second edition (1908) is available at http://www.bartleby.com/.

a person, as in *we are hopeful.* The fact that no person is referred to in *Hopefully it will rain today* may still raise powerful objections among purists, but without much effect on the rest of the linguistic community as far as we can tell.

A common justification used by purists is the desire to uphold clarity and precision in language. This is no doubt sometimes well founded, but often it is just a flimsy, pseudoscholarly excuse for preferring the old to the new. In none of the three new but highly criticized developments cited in the paragraph above does clarity seem to suffer.

Logic is another type of justification offered for resisting language change. Samuel Taylor Coleridge equated rules of grammar with rules of logic. But this couldn't be right. Experts want us to say *It is I* rather than *It is me*, allegedly because the word *is* (due to its equational meaning) logically takes the same case, nominative, on both sides. But this is not logic; it was merely a rule of Latin. In French, it is the opposite. It is totally ungrammatical to say ˣ*C'est je* (literally 'It's I'), with the pronoun in the nominative case. The correct thing to say is *C'est moi* (literally 'It's me'), with the pronoun in an objective case. What is grammatically correct does not always coincide with what strikes experts as logical.

We do not mean to imply that purists are totally unjustified in their attempts to preserve the language. In many instances, their love for the language and for clarity point up features that deserve to be savored rather than forgotten or taken for granted. But there is something wrong with the belief, however sincere, that without continuing efforts to preserve the language in its present state it will disintegrate over time. The history of language change offers ample reassurances.

Correctness Is Relative

The real problem with prescriptivism arises when it is put forth as an absolute. Some experts act as if there is only one standard—theirs. This is so far from the truth that it is silly. The varieties of English that they habitually ignore (regional dialects, ethnic dialects, local variants) are just as valid, useful, and appropriate in their contexts as standard formal English is in its contexts. Consider this analogy. We all go by different names at different times. Our friends know us by a first name or by a nickname. Our family may know us by a different nickname. In other settings, our first name may not be appropriate, and our last name will be used. There is nothing wrong with this. Language use in general follows the same principle: a usage appropriate in some situations may be wildly out of place in others.

Language serves a multitude of needs determined both by our nature and our environment. As long as it remains flexible it remains vital. If the primary purpose of speech and writing is the expression and communication of thought, we can evaluate any particular language or variety of language on the basis of its usefulness for these purposes. This is what we are really asking when we question whether it is "right" to use *lite* or *light, irregardless* or *regardless, hopefully* or *I hope that,* /æsk/ or /æks/ *for ask,* or *contact your senator.* Because no choice in these pairs is inherently superior to its partner, the question must be, which is more effective for communication on a particular occasion?

When we find ourselves in a new community of any kind we should be sensitive to the norms of that community and learn at least some of its language if we want to understand and be understood without difficulty. In a sense, we must all become adept in multiple varieties of language just as an international traveler may have to learn different languages to function effectively in different lands.

But surely it is possible to learn and apply the rules of standard formal English without imposing them on other dialects. And surely it is possible to master the rules of Standard English without concluding that there is anything wrong with nonstandard dialects. Imposing homogeneity risks robbing the language of its expressive resources and robbing some speakers of the pride that they take in their speech. This, to us, is the real danger in prescriptivism.

Word Choice and Clarity of Communication

Because this book is concerned with expanding vocabulary, we ought to address some of the deeper purposes of word study. Gaining access to the vocabulary of a scholarly or specialist group gives us some of the power of that group. Becoming familiar with a group's specialized language is one step toward membership in that group. While not all scholars and specialists intend to exclude the rest of us, we can all remember occasions when specialized vocabulary was used not to communicate effectively but to mystify and bedazzle us, perhaps to make us feel like outsiders. English legal language, for example, has caused centuries of confusion and consternation to the average citizen. In recent years, legislators in many locales have passed laws that require legal documents to be written in "plain English" so that nonlawyers can take a more active role in matters that may significantly affect their lives.

Control over advanced vocabulary includes recognizing the danger that it can be used to obfuscate or disguise rather than clarify meaning. An enhanced vocabulary brings the ability to decode the sometimes unnecessarily altiloquent, arcane words of the initiated. We are certainly better off with this knowledge than without it. Otherwise, to learn from your physician that you are suffering from *otitis externa* may appear more significant, perhaps even more upsetting, than hearing that you have a simple inflammation of the outer ear. Similarly, we don't want to be too impressed, put off, or confused by the use of a phrase like *longitudinal extent* for the more straightforward *length.* Other kinds of examples include the empty phrases known as bureaucratese (e.g., *We explored a comprehensive set of options before the finalization process*) and euphemistic circumlocutions (e.g., *vertically challenged* to mean 'short').

This is not to belittle the technical use of language but only the pretentious use of it. In fact, technical terminology serves a very important function in every discipline as a means of communicating both precisely and unambiguously. And multiple stylistic levels of vocabulary may in fact allow even the nonspecialist to manipulate not merely different connotations, such as degrees of formality, but also fine distinctions in denotational meaning that often accompany different word choices. In both cases, the clear transmission of ideas may require a choice of specific terms that one might not use in ordinary conversation.

The use of a special vocabulary in writing is also necessary at times. Written language suffers certain disadvantages as compared to speech. For example, it lacks the devices of intonation, pauses, and other subtleties that spoken language affords, not to mention the expressiveness that face and body movement provide in face-to-face interaction. Compared to speech, written language has limited ways of expressing emphasis, emotion, and other important aspects of communication. Speech usually affords immediate feedback from the listener, so that one can quickly detect and correct miscommunication, whereas mistakes in writing often endure. So choosing the right word can be more critical to writing than to speech.

Ultimately, an enhanced and enlarged vocabulary, like any part of the complex phenomenon called language, is a multipurpose tool. Like a hammer, it can be used either to build or to injure. The individual is responsible for the use to which it is put.

Word Elements

Element	Gloss	Source	Examples
aden	gland	G	*adenoids, adenoma, adenomyoma, adenopathy*
alg	pain	G	*analgesic, neuralgia, nostalgic, algolagnia, algogenic*
aur	ear	L	*aural, auricle, aurilave, auris, auristillae*
axill	armpit	L	*axillary, axilla, axillar, cervicoaxillary*
caud~cod	tail	L	*caudate, coda, caudal, longicaudate, caudiform, caudad*
cervic	neck	L	*cervix, cervical, cervicoaxillary, cervicodynia*
cut	skin	L	*cuticle, subcutaneous, cutis, cuticula*
dermat~derm	skin	G	*hypodermic, dermatitis, taxidermy, dermopterous, pachyderm*
galact	milk	G	*galaxy, galactic*
gastr	stomach	G	*gastrointestinal, gastropod, gastritis, gastronome, gastrula*
gravid	pregnant	L	*gravid, gravidity, prima gravida, multigravida*
hem~haem~em	blood	G	*hemoglobin, anemia, hemostat, hematology, hematoma, hemophilia*
hepat	liver	G	*hepatitis, hepatoma, hepatolysis, hepatotomy*
hist	body tissue	G	*histology, histanoxia, histoma, histogenesis, histoteliosis*
hyster	womb, neurotic disorder	G	*hysterectomy, hysteria, hysterolysis, hysteropathy, hysterics, hysterical*

Element	Gloss	Source	Examples
-ia	land, state, medical condition	G, L	*utopia, pneumonia, Albania, neuralgia, exophthalmia*
-itis	inflammation	G	*hepatitis, neuritis, endocarditis, phlebitis, pleuritis*
lab	lip	L	*labial, labret, labiomental, labiocervical, labiomancy*
lacrim~lachrym	tear	L	*lacrimase, lachrymose, lacrimatory, lachrymator*
lact	milk	L	*lactose, lactation, lactiferous, lactein*
laryng	voice box	G	*larynx, laryngitis, laryngectomy, laryngophony*
mamm	breast	L	*mammary, mammal, mammogram, mammoplasty, mammae*
nas~nar	nose	L	*nasal, nares, narial, nasturtium, nasopharynx, nariform*
nephr	kidney	G	*nephritis, epinephrine, nephrostomy, nephron, nephrocele*
-oma	tumor, growth	G	*carcinoma, glaucoma, melanoma, fibroma*
op	see	G	*optics, autopsy, biopsy, isometropia, myopic*
ophthalm	eye	G	*ophthalmology, exophthalmic*
os~or	mouth	L	*osculate, oral, oratory, osculant, oscitation, oracle*
oss~os	bone	L	*ossify, os, osseous, ossuary*
oste	bone	G	*osteoporosis, osteomyelitis*
phleb	vein	G	*phlebitis, phlebostasis, phlebotomy, phlebosclerosis*

Element	Gloss	Source	Examples
phob	fear	G	phobia, Russophobia, claustrophobia, agoraphobia, hydrophobia
phylac	guard	G	prophylactic, anaphylaxis, phylacteries, phylaxin
pne~pneum	breathe, lung	G	pneumonia, apnea, dyspnea, pneumatic, pneumothorax
pulm~pulmon	lung	L	pulmonary, pulmolith, pulmometer
rhin	nose	G	rhinoceros, rhinitis, oxyrhine, rhinoplasty
sarc	flesh	G	sarcophagus, sarcoma, sarcopoietic, sarcosome
scler	hard	G	arteriosclerosis, sclera, sclerosant, sclerokeratitis
sep	putrid, infected	G	antiseptic, sepsometer, septicemia, sepsis
stom~stomat	mouth	G	stoma, colostomy, stomatitis, stomach, anastomosis, cyclostome
thromb	clot	G	thrombosis, prothrombin, thrombus, thrombocyte, thromboembolism
vas	vessel, duct	L	vasectomy, vas, vasodilator, vascular
ven	vein	L	intravenous, vena, venose, venomotor, venostasis

Element Study

1. Your surgeon offers you a choice between a *nephrotomy, nephrectomy,* and *nephrostomy.* What is the difference?

2. Note that *sarcasm* contains the root for 'flesh'. What is the connection between the literal and figurative meanings?

3. Here are some disease names derived from the Greek. The prefix *dys-* normally means 'bad', 'improper'. Based on their structure, what sorts of disorder do you think they involve?

   a. *dysemia*
   b. *dysphemia*
   c. *dyspepsia*
   d. *dyspnea*
   e. *dystopia*

4. Here are descriptions of some diseases whose names are derived from Greek. What do you think they are called?

   a. inflammation of the liver
   b. inflammation of the stomach
   c. inflammation of the larynx
   d. inflammation of a gland
   e. inflammation of the nose

5. The words below from the field of medicine contain a number of morphemes you have not yet encountered. With the help of an unabridged dictionary or, better yet, a large dictionary of medical terms plus a glossary or dictionary of roots,[2] briefly define, parse, and gloss each term. For example:

nephr	*o*	*lith*	*o*	*tom*	*-y*
'kidney'		'stone'		'cut'	N

   nephrolithotomy: 'removal of kidney stones'

a. *leukocytotaxis*		g. *endosteoma*
b. *achromotrichia*		h. *lithotroph*
c. *brachymetacarpia*		i. *paraplegia*
d. *aphonogelia*		j. *hemostasis*
e. *retrocalcaneobursitis*		k. *chromaffinoblastoma*
f. *antixerophthalmic*		l. *paronychia*

---

2. *Dorland's Illustrated Medical Dictionary* is one of several good larger medical dictionaries generally available. If you cannot find a particular term in the dictionary you use, you may still find portions of it or similar words that will allow you to make an educated guess at the meaning of your word. For example, with *antixerophthalmic*, you might only find *xerophthalmic* or *xerophthalmia*, which should suggest that *antixerophthalmic* means 'against xerophthalmia'.

Exercises

1. Some people draw a distinction between the vowels /a/ and /ɒ/, and others do not. Determine whether you make this distinction in your own speech. A good test for this is to pronounce word pairs like *cot~caught, Don~Dawn,* and *knotty~naughty* and see if there is any difference. Then, survey eight to ten people from different parts of the United States or Canada to see if they distinguish such words. Paying attention to the geographical backgrounds of the individuals as far as you can ascertain them, can you make any generalization about who makes the distinction? Besides the speaker's geographical background, is there any other factor that seems to play a role in the pronunciation of this word?

2. Look up dictionary[3] entries for the following words, paying attention to any variation in spelling and pronunciation given as well as to notes on etymology or word history and standard versus nonstandard usage. Describe, explain, and evaluate the indications of variation and any usage arguments in light of the discussion found in this and earlier chapters as well as your own knowledge of variation in their pronunciation and spelling and your sense of usage. You may have to consult multiple dictionaries or, perhaps, compare the entries in British and American dictionaries.

a. *hopefully*	k. *prodigious*
b. *irregardless*	l. *process*
c. *either*	m. *fair*
d. *ask*	n. *host*
e. *which*	o. *disinterested*
f. *nuclear*	p. *every*
g. *shall, will*	q. *cohort*
h. *ain't*	r. *convince*
i. *anxious*	s. *balding*
j. *hectic*	t. *contact* (v)

3. Pick a trendy expression (at the time of printing, "awesome," "cool," and "totally" are good choices, but you are the best judge of what's currently a good choice) and examine its use in different contexts, written and oral.

   For written contexts, choose different types of publications that you can consult online. Among these might be national newspapers, alterna-

---

3. Useful sources include *The American Heritage Dictionary of the English Language* (3rd and 4th eds.) and *The Columbia Guide to Standard American English* (1993). Online editions of both titles are available at http://bartleby.com/.

tive newspapers, and blogs. Compare the number of times the expression you are studying comes up per 1,000 words (or per 10,000 words, or whatever).

For oral contexts, select a variety of contexts that you have easy access to: television, class lectures, and informal conversations, for example. Listen for the expression you've chosen, and keep track of how many times it comes up per minute, or per fifteen-minute period, or whatever.

What do your data show? Is the frequency of occurrence different? If the expression occurs in several of the different contexts you studied, does it function differently? Does the expression mean something different in the different contexts?

CHAPTER NINE

Latin and Greek Morphology

Colleges and high schools used to place a far greater emphasis on Latin and Greek than they do now. In Europe, some universities used to require that doctoral dissertations be written in Latin. Times have changed, and the special status once accorded to classical languages is now given to other subjects, including modern languages. But the classical languages remain our most important source of new words, as shown by additions like *megavitamin, telecommute,* and *cyclotron.*

As shown by allomorphy in the morpheme sets at the ends of our chapters, the shapes of Latin and Greek morphemes found in English often change from word to word. The vast majority of these changes that are not attributable to English phonetics go back to changes required by the inflectional and derivational systems of Latin and Greek. The aim of this chapter is to introduce the aspects of Latin and Greek morphology that are responsible for the majority of these changes. Learning these should make English words easier to parse.

Noun Inflection

In Chapter 3, we were introduced to inflectional morphology. Inflection is used in Latin, Greek, and English to tell us such things as the number of nouns. Inflection is almost always indicated by adding endings to stems. Thus to the English stem *book-* we may add the plural ending *-s* to form *books.* For the singular, *book,* we add nothing, though many other languages do. In short, we can say that English words inflect for number, contrasting singular and plural. There is also a rudimentary inflection for case, to indicate the genitive form (*book's, books'*).

Latin and Greek are more challenging. Like English, they inflect for number, contrasting singular and plural. They also inflect for case, but quite a bit more enthusiastically than English does: whereas English nouns have just two forms in the singular and two in the plural, a Latin noun can appear with up to five different endings in the singular and four in the plural. For example, the word for 'bull' may appear in a Latin sentence in any of the forms *taurus, taurī, taurō, taurum,* or *taure,* and in the plural as *taurī, taurōrum, taurīs,* or *taurōs.*

Whenever English borrows a Latin or Greek noun whole—without stripping off its endings—it virtually always borrows the word in the nominative case. The nominative case is the one used for the subject of a sentence: ***Taurus*** *vidit agricolam* '**The bull** sees the farmer'. It is also the form used when citing, or talking about, a word. If someone asked you what the Latin word for 'bull' is, you would answer *taurus,* rather than picking one of the other case-inflected forms like *taurum.* The fact that English borrows nouns in the nominative case is a great boon to us, because it means that we don't need to master the other cases in this course. You will appreciate this free pass all the more when you consider that different nouns form their case endings differently; the genitive singular, for example, can be expressed by any of five different endings, depending on which word it is used with.

However, the nominative case is not devoid of complications of its own. Different words form the singular and plural with different inflectional endings. This fact is relevant to our study of English, because a fair number of scholarly words in English use the Latin nominative plural form for their plural. Fortunately, the correct plural form for a Latin or Greek word can often be guessed with a high degree of accuracy, as table 9.1 shows.

Table 9.1 Nominative Plural Endings in Latin and Greek

Singular	Plural	Example
-a	*-ae*	*alumna*
-es	*-es*	*species*
-is	*-es*	*crisis*
-on	*-a*	*criterion*
-um	*-a*	*memorandum*
-us	*-i*	*alumnus*
-us	*-us*	*hiatus*

In general, a particular plural ending regularly replaces a particular singular ending. Because *scapula* ends in an *-a* in the singular, you can infer that the plural is *scapulae*. But what about a word like *apparatus*? Table 9.1 shows that there are two possible plural endings for words that end in *-us*. Most such words take *-i* in the plural, so people often guess that the plural of *apparatus* is ×*apparati*. Unfortunately that turns out to be the wrong guess: *apparatus* is actually one of the minority of words that take *-us* in the plural, so the correct answer is *apparatus*. It is always wise to check your guess in a good dictionary.

Other Latin and Greek words that are sometimes used with the Latin or Greek plural shown in table 9.1 are *antenna, larva, hippopotamus, radius, sarcophagus, syllabus, basis, analysis, series, cranium, memorandum, millennium, symposium, phenomenon, polyhedron,* and *polyhedra.*

Memorizing table 9.1 will go a long way toward allowing you to handle Latin and Greek plurals, but there is still one important class of nouns to talk about. These are words that have *-s* in the singular and *-es* in the plural. In a few words this works in a straightforward way: *stirps*, plural *stirpes*. But usually some complications arise. In Latin, as we have seen, /ks/ is spelled *x*, so we get words like *appendix*, plural *appendices*. These words are very straightforward from a phonological point of view, but this additional spelling rule makes the singular and plural look more different from each other when written than when pronounced.

Very often, though, some additional changes happen in the pronunciation as well. Some of these changes occur because of phonological rules that were studied in chapter 6. Consider for example *larynx*, plural *larynges*. If we work backward from the plural form, we can see that the stem is *laryng-*. Adding *-s* to that stem, to form the singular, would give ×*laryngs*. But the rule Phonation Assimilation would lead us to expect the /g/ to devoice to /k/ before the voiceless consonant /s/. That plus the spelling rule for *x* gets us the to the expected singular spelling.

Another example of a word where a phonological rule comes into play is *index*, plural *indices*. If we start off with a stem form *indec-*, the singular form is immediately understandable. Adding the plural ending *-es* to the stem would give a plural ×*indeces*, but applying the rule of Latin /e/ Weakening takes us the rest of the way. Recall that this rule does not apply in a closed syllable, and so the singular form retains the stem vowel /e/.

A final case we might mention are words where Cluster Simplification comes into play. We might expect the singular of *glandes* to be ×*glants*, but Cluster Simplification reduces that to *glans*. Cluster Simplification is particularly common in Latin and Greek at the end of words, with many stem consonants being lost in the nominative singular.

The rules we have mentioned here account in whole or part for a great number of instances where the singular and plural don't quite match, but there are other times when it is best for the student to simply memorize the plural. Such a study pays off not just because the Latin or Greek plurals are sometimes used in English but also because the plural form tends to have the more basic stem, which is commonly used in building new words. If you knew only the singular forms *appendix* and *larynx*, you might have a hard time deciding how to add *-itis* to make the medical name for an inflammation of those organs: ˣ*appendixitis*? ˣ*laryncitis*? But knowing the plural forms *appendices* and *larynges* immediately leads to the correct derivation: remove the plural ending and add the suffix to get *appendicitis* and *laryngitis*. Similarly, the irregular plural *genera* ties in better with derivatives like *generic* than does the singular form *genus*.

You are now in a position to understand a great deal about how plurals work in words borrowed from Latin and Greek. Just remain aware that there are several exceptions; it is never a bad idea to consult a dictionary before using a Latin plural ending on a word you are not confident about. A blind use of table 9.1 can lead to strange plurals like ˣ*octopi* from *octopus* or ˣ*pentaga* from *pentagon*. Although such overgeneralizations find their way into print often enough, many of your readers and listeners would be sure to object to them.

A final note of caution is that Latin plurals often mark a word as being scholarly or technical. Sometimes that is appropriate; sometimes it is taken to be annoyingly pedantic. When in doubt, it is always best to take your cue from listening to your intended audience. As our distance from classical culture continues to widen, we expect that fewer words will occur with Latin and Greek endings.

Derivation

The main theme of this entire book has been the derivational patterns of Latin and Greek, but this may be a good time to consolidate some information about how complex words are formed in those languages and, by extension, in the more scholarly vocabulary of English.

Nouns

The kernel of all lexical words is the root, which almost always takes the form of a simple syllable—for example, *oss* 'bone', *caud* 'tail', *hom* 'human', *ped* 'foot'. Some roots can form words by attaching inflectional endings directly to the root. For example, from the root *caud* comes the noun *cauda* 'tail'. There are also several suffixes that can be inserted between the root and the inflectional endings to make nouns. Table 9.2 lists some of the more common of these. All the words given as examples have been borrowed into English with little or no change, so we leave the translations as an exercise for the reader. We do, however, occasionally note in parentheses the root or base form the example word was derived from.

Occasionally one can discern some semantic content in the suffix. Among those listed in table 9.2, *-arium* designates a place; *-tor* designates a person or

Table 9.2 Noun-forming Suffixes

Nominative singular	Examples
Latin	
-arium	*librarium, sanctuarium, dispensarium, aquarium*
-ia	*miseria, constantia, agentia, scientia, abundantia*
-la	*molecula* (*mole* 'mass'), *capsula* (*caps* 'box')
-lum	*granulum* (*grano-*)
-lus	*alveolus* (*alveo-* 'hollow'), *circulus* (*circo-*)
-mentum	*tormentum* (*torqu*), *mōmentum* (*mov*), *complementum*
-monia	*acrimonia, alimonia, hegemonia*
-monium	*matrimonium, patrimonium*
-tas (stem -tat-)	*gravitas, fidelitas, sobrietas, aequalitas*
-tio (stem -tion-)	*electio* (*leg*), *fissio* (*fid*), *captio* (*cap*), *illuminatio* (*luc*)
-tor	*actor* (*ag*), *successor* (*ced*), *tractor* (*trah*)
-tura	*lectura* (*leg*), *fissura* (*fid*), *captura* (*cap*), *pictura* (*pig*), *natura* (*gena* 'birth')
-tus (plural -tus)	*adventus* (*ven*), *rictus* (*rig* 'gape'), *coitus* (*i*)
Greek	
-ma (stem -mat-)	*pragma* (*prac*), *schema, thema, epigramma* (*graph*)
-sis	*praxis* (*prac*), *analysis, stasis*
-tor	*rhetor* 'orator', *chiropractor* (*prac* 'do')

thing that does something; and the suffixes that begin with /l/ are diminutives: they often name something that is smaller than usual.

Adjectives

Adjectives also are formed by adding at least one suffix to the root, as shown in table 9.3. Adjectives take various forms in the Latin and Greek nominative singular. They are here listed in their masculine form, but that detail is unimportant, because adjectives are rarely borrowed into English without dropping the inflectional ending or replacing it with a silent <e>.

The clearest semantics can be found here with -(*i*)*or*, which forms comparative adjectives. The suffixes -*ilis* and -*bilis*, when applied to a verbal root, often describe things that are readily affected or produced by the state or activity named by the root; for example, a *fragilis* thing (English *fragile*) is something easily or readily broken. Quite often, though, the most accurate thing we can say about suffixes like these is simply that they form adjectives.

Verbs

Like nouns and adjectives, verbs are formed from roots by the addition of a suffix. In the simplest cases, this is a single vowel, which may get lost or replaced by silent <e> when borrowed by English. For example, the root *err* 'wander' adds -*a*- to form a verb. This -*a*- shows up in many derivatives such as *erratic* and *inerrant*, but it was discarded in the simple loanword *err*.

Table 9.3 Adjective-forming Suffixes

Suffix	Examples
-acos	cardiacos
-alis	regalis (reges 'kings')
-bilis	capabilis, tangibilis, affabilis
-icos	polemicos, anarchicos
-ilis	facilis, fragilis; puerilis (puer 'boy')
-(i)or	inferior, superior, posterior, junior
-osus	verbosus (verbum 'word'), bellicosus (bellum 'war')
-tivus	captivus, fugitivus

Often other elements are added as well. The nasal infix that we have often mentioned was originally one way of making a verb from a root. And a few words add the suffix -*sc*-, which often has the meaning 'begin to', as in *candesce*- 'begin to glow' (cf. English *incandescent*). Several verbs add a -*ta*- or -*ita*-, which originally was meant to intensify the meaning of the verb. For example, English *agitator* comes from the same root as *actor* (*ag*).

Beyond these basic facts, the most important thing to know about verbs is how they form participles. A **participle** is a derived form of a verb that can be used as an adjective or as noun. The **present participle** stem in Latin ends in -*ent*-, although the *e* is deleted after an *a*. Thus we get the present participle stems *docent*-, *agent*-, *sapient*-, and *sentient*-, but *errant*-. As you can see from these examples, present participles are borrowed into English in their stem form, without any inflectional ending. When present participles are used as nouns, they commonly denote a doer: an agent is one who acts on another's behalf. To make slightly more abstract nouns, -*ia* is often added to the participial stem in Latin, as in *agentia*, *sapientia*, and *sentientia*. These are usually borrowed into English with -*ce* or -*cy* in place of the Latin -*tia*.

The **perfect participle** is the other highly important participle in Latin. It indicates that the noun the participle modifies is in the state indicated by the verb meaning. It often has a passive feeling, as opposed to the active feeling of the present participle. For example, the perfect participle stem of *dissolv*- 'loosen, break up' is *dissolut*-, which can be translated as 'loosened, broken up', or, meta- phorically, 'morally lax'. Something that breaks things up, actively acting on other objects, may be denoted by the present participle *dissolvent*-; something that has been passively broken up is *dissolut*-.

The forms of the perfect participle differ quite a bit from verb to verb. It is usually formed by adding -*t*- to the root, or after an added *a*; thus from the root *doc* comes the perfect participle stem *doct*-; from *fac* comes *fact*-; from *err-a*- comes *errat*-. Some of the phonological rules discussed in chapter 6 may apply. Especially common is Phonation Assimilation: the root *ag* forms the perfect participle stem *act*-. The rule *t*+*t*-to-*ss* also applies very frequently, sometimes with Cluster Simplification. Thus the root *sent*, which forms the present participle *sentient*-, forms the perfect participle *sens*-. One can think of this as a derivation: *sent-t* > *senss* > *sens*. There are additional rules and irregularities that make it hard to predict exactly what form the present participle will take, but its stem always ends in a <t> or an <s>. When perfect participles are used in English, a silent <e> is often added to the end of the word.

English uses quite a few Latin perfect participles in their original, adjectival, meaning. Thus the English adjective *dissolute* corresponds closely to the Latin perfect participle meaning of *dissolut-*. But perfect participles are even more commonly used as nouns or verbs, by the derivational process of conversion. Thus English *fact* is always used as a noun, and *act* is used as a noun or a verb.

From an etymological standpoint, this use of the perfect participle as a noun or verb can be quite confusing, because, as we have already seen, Latin had a suffix *-tus* that could form nouns and a suffix *-ta-* that could form verbs. Since all these forms, just like the perfect participle suffix, tend to be reduced in English to a simple <t>, how can we tell them apart from the perfect participle? How do we know whether the English noun *act* comes from the Latin noun *actus* or the Latin perfect participle *act-*? The simple answer is that these sources often cannot easily be told apart, and because the meanings are so similar, it is not very important that we do so. Unless a specific derivation is readily obvious—for example, you have found a reliable etymology in a dictionary—it is usually quite good enough to say that an English adjective, noun, or verb that agrees in form with a Latin perfect participle *is* a Latin perfect participle.

There is one additional reason that the Latin perfect participle is important. In Latin, many derivational suffixes begin with a /t/, just like the one that forms perfect participles. For almost all verbs, the same phonological changes that apply to the perfect participle apply when these other suffixes are used. For example, the root *ag* gives the perfect participle *act-* as well as the adjective *activ-* and the nouns *actor* and *action-*. All these forms have *c*, just like the perfect participle. The perfect participle *dissolut-* is similar to the noun *dissolution-* and the adjective *dissolutiv-*. All these words are used in English. Therefore if you learn the perfect participle of a Latin verb, you will also know the base form of many other important derivatives that are heavily used in English.

Latin has other participles that are not used nearly as often as the two we have just discussed. One worth knowing about is the **gerundive**. This participle denotes the attitude that the named activity ought to be done. For example, the *agenda* are things that ought to be done at a meeting; a *memorandum* is something that ought to be remembered. The gerundive is very similar in form to the present participle, except that it has *d* instead of *t*. Not rarely, gerundives appear in English with the Latin suffix *-um*, plural *-a*, in which case they denote things, as opposed to people. Perfect participles show up with these endings as well. For example, the English words *errata* and *data* were originally Latin plural perfect participles.

Summary

Latin and Greek inflectional endings are found on many words that have been borrowed into English without any adaptation. Such words are mostly nouns, which are borrowed in the nominative case; some of these use the original Latin ending to express the plural. The correct plural to use with Latin nouns can frequently be predicted from the ending of the singular. For other words, the plural cannot be correctly formed unless one knows the stem, which appears in most derivative words.

Most Greek and Latin words are formed by adding derivational suffixes to roots, to form noun, adjective, or verb stems, as well as present, perfect, and gerundive participles.

Word Elements

Element	Gloss	Source	Examples
ac	sharp	L	*acid, acrid, acerbic, acuity, exacerbate*
acr	height, tip	G	*acrophobia, acromegaly*
agr	field	G, L	*agriculture, agrostology, agronomy*
alb	white	L	*albumen, albino, albescent, albedo, albumin*
aster~astr	star	G	*asteroid, asterism, astral, asteriated*
aud	hear	L	*auditory, subaudition, audit, audiology*
auto~tauto	self	G	*autonomy, tautology, autolysis, automaton, tautonym, tautophony, autodidact*
bath~bathy	depth	G	*bathysphere, bathos, bathyal, bathochrome*

Element	Gloss	Source	Examples
bene~bon	good	L	*benediction, bonus, benefactive, bonhomie, debonair*
brach~brachy	short	G	*brachylogy, brachydactylic, brachycephalic*
carn~car	flesh	L	*carnal, carnelion, carnivorous, incarnation, carrion*
cli	lean, lie	G, L	*client, recline, proclivity, clinograph, declivity, cline*
cred	believe	L	*credo, credendum, incredulous*
cryph~cryp	hide	G	*crypt, apocrypha, cryptogenic, cryptogamic, cryptonym*
damn~demn	loss, harm	L	*indemnity, indemnify, damnable, condemn*
dic	say	L	*dictate, dictum, interdict, juridical, malediction, benediction, jurisdiction*
do	give	G	*dosology, epidote, anecdote*
do~da~di	give	L	*edit, donate, data, addition, donor, condone, dative, tradition, perdition*
dol	suffer	L	*condolences, dolorific, condole, indolent*
flu~fluc~fluv	flow	L	*fluid, fluctuate, fluvial, confluence, effluvium, flux, influence*
gloss~glott	tongue	G	*gloss, polyglot, glottis, epiglottis, glossolalia, bugloss, glottal, glossary, diglossia*
gno	know	G	*agnostic, diagnostic, prognosticate, gnosis, gnostic*
gno~no~gni	know	L	*cognition, ignoramus, ignorant, notion, notorious*
gyn~gynec	woman	G	*gynecology, polygyny, gynecocracy, androgyne*
hes~her	to stick	L	*adhesive, coherent, hesitate, cohesive, inhere*
hydr~hydat	water	G	*dehydrate, hydatid, hydrography, hydrolysis*
jus	law	L	*justice, jury, adjure, abjure, adjudicate, jurisprudence, juridical*
lith~lit	stone	G	*megalith, albolite, lithotripter, neolithic, dendrolite, lithotomy*

Element	Gloss	Source	Examples
mega~megal	great, million	G	*megalith, megaton, megalomania, megabyte*
misc~mix	mix	L	*miscellany, mixture, miscegenation, permixture, commixture, promiscuous*
nihil~nil	nothing	L	*annihilate, nil, nihilism, nihil obstat*
ocul	eye	L	*ocular, monocle, oculomotor*
pen~pun	punish	L	*penal, punitive, impunity, penology*
ple	full, many	L	*replenish, plenty, plethora, plenary, replete*
pon~pos	place, put	L	*postpone, propose, impone, interpose, postiche, apposite*
pug~pugn	fist, fight	L	*pugilist, pugnacious, impugn, oppugn, repugnance*
tac	arrange	G	*tactic, syntax, hypotactic, taxonomy, taxidermy, taxon, taxis*
tach~tachy	fast	G	*tachometer, tachygraphy, tachylite, tachistoscope*
terr	earth	L	*extraterrestrial, terra cotta, Mediterranean, terre-verte, Terran, terra incognita, inter, disinter*
vac~van	empty	L	*vacuum, vanish, vacuity, evacuate, evanescent, vanity*
ver	turn	L	*convert, converge, verge, divergence, extroversion, converse, inverse, adverse, obverse, perversity*
viv~vit	live	L	*vivid, vital, convivial, vita, curriculum vitae, viva, vivacious, viviparous, vitamin*

Element Study

1. There is a simple phonetic rule of thumb for distinguishing the root *ver* 'turn' from the root *ver* 'true'. Put words with *ver* 'turn' in one column and words with *ver* 'true' in another. Then determine what it is about adjacent sounds that will almost always tell you which root is which. Finally, explain what makes *verdict* an exception to this rule.

   aver, inversion, perverse, revert, veracity, veritable, versatile, converge

2. The following words from the fields of biology and medicine contain several morphemes you have not yet encountered. With the help of an unabridged dictionary and specialized dictionaries of biological and medical terms and using a glossary or dictionary of roots,[1] briefly define, parse, and gloss each term.

   a. *tectospondylic*
   b. *endolymphangial*
   c. *Pithecanthropus*
   d. *insessorial*

3. Parse, gloss, and give allomorphs for the following words.

   a. *vivíparous*
   b. *occasion*
   c. *supplicant*
   d. *dolorífic*
   e. *eclécticism* (root isn't 'law')
   f. *ássonance*

4. Find the word in the list below which best matches the dictionary definition given. Do not refer to a dictionary at first; you may do so when you are finished. Some of the words are decoys. Use no word more than once. Work from definition to word. Avoid multiple answers, but if you can't decide between two choices, give both and explain the problem for a chance at partial credit.

   1. *heteronomous*
   2. *licentious*
   3. *polity*
   4. *telegamic*
   5. *probophily*
   6. *autocratic*
   7. *atmesis*
   8. *peristaltic*
   9. *parhomologous*
   10. *delectation*
   11. *inculpatory*
   12. *theurgy*
   13. *homotronic*
   14. *malocclusion*
   15. *gradiometric*
   16. *apandrous*
   17. *paratomy*
   18. *perigonium*
   19. *mesophilic*
   20. *dolorifuge*
   21. *parergon*
   22. *anatopism*
   23. *thearchy*
   24. *parachromoparous*
   25. *appetent*
   26. *hypidiomorphic*
   27. *toparch*
   28. *syntrurgious*
   29. *illicitness*
   30. *metachronism*
   31. *alegonymy*
   32. *homeostasis*

---

1. *Dictionary of Word Roots and Combining Forms* by Donald J. Borror (Palo Alto, Calif.: Mayfield, 1960) is recommended.

a. _____ Marked by the absence of legal or moral constraints.

b. _____ Improper closure of the teeth so that the cusps do not fit together.

c. _____ Possessing functionless male organs.

d. _____ Having only some constituents with distinct crystalline form (said, e.g., of a rock).

e. _____ Civil order.

f. _____ Desiring eagerly.

g. _____ Thriving in an intermediate environment (e.g., of moderate temperature).

h. _____ A subordinate activity or work.

i. _____ A sac surrounding the reproductive organs in certain species.

j. _____ Reproduction by fission along a special division zone.

k. _____ The tendency in an organism to maintain a stable internal condition.

l. _____ A human act, process, power, or state of supernatural efficacy or origin.

m. _____ An error in a temporal sequence placing an event after its real date.

n. _____ A minor ruler or prince.

o. _____ Of or pertaining to involvement or implication in a charge of misconduct.

p. _____ Subject to external controls.

q. _____ Something that banishes or mitigates grief.

5. Fill in the blanks in each string of morphemes and other elements, then write out the complete word formed.

a. _____   *tic*   _____   *-ia*   =   _____
   'putrid'   A   'BLOOD'   'condition'   =   'illness resulting from toxins in the blood'

(Use the allomorph of the morpheme meaning 'blood' which lacks an initial consonant.)

b. _____*n*_____   =   _____
   'lung'   'inflammation'   =   'alternative term for *pneumonia*'

(Do not use *pne~pneum* for 'lung'.)

c. _____ s   = _____
   'important point'   [singular] = 'pivotal point in an argument or
                                     discussion'
   (Apply a spelling rule.)

d. ____ _____ = _____
   'gland' 'tumor' = 'tumor with glandular structure'

e. *sine*____*e*   = _____
   'without' 'care' = 'paid job requiring no work'

6. Gloss the boldface morphemes in the space provided.

   a. rhinolaryngology   'study of disease of _____ & _____'
   b. lactation   'production of _____'
   c. cervix uteri   '_____ of _____'

Exercises

1. Based on what you've learned in this chapter and the meanings of the
   roots, some of which you can find in the appendix and others in a dictionary, parse the following Latin and Greek expressions. Then give a short
   definition that reflects, at least in part, the meanings of the individual
   morphemes.

   a. Latin perfect participles: *desideratum, (terra) incognita, errata, invicta*
   b. Latin present participles: *parent, recumbent, errant*
   c. Latin gerundives: *addendum, explicandum, memorandum, corrigen-
      dum, referendum, agenda, pudenda, disputandum, disputanda*
   d. Greek: *schema, stigmata*

2. The following terms from the field of botany contain several morphemes
   you have not yet encountered.[2] Note that some consist of two words: the
   first for the genus and the second for the species. Most botanical terms
   have endings taken from Latin. With the help of a large dictionary and a
   specialized dictionary of botanical terms and a glossary or dictionary of
   roots, briefly define, parse, and gloss each term. For example:

---

2. The use of Latin in botany is described in considerable detail by William T. Stearn in *Botanical
Latin*, 4th ed. (Portland, Ore.: Timber Press, 1992). This book also has a useful glossary.

Calochortus pulchellus: 'yellow globe tulip', a plant with delicate yellow flowers. Its bulbs are considered a delicacy in India.

cal (o)	*chort*	*us*	*pulch*	*ell*	*us*
'beautiful'	'feeding place, garden'	N [singular]	'beautiful'	[diminutive]	A [singular]

You can see from this example that the connection between the meaning of the morphemes and the characteristics of the thing being described can be quite a distant or tenuous one.

a. *rhizocorm*
b. *filiformis*
c. *procumbens*
d. *Oryza angustifolia*
e. *caulocarpous*
f. *Leucospermum*
g. *involutus*
h. *pleniflorus*

3. The following words and phrases are taken from the field of law. Using an unabridged dictionary or a legal dictionary (e.g., *Webster's Third New International Dictionary* or *Black's Law Dictionary*[3]), your knowledge of Latin morphology, and a glossary, briefly define, parse, and gloss each term.

a. *probation*
b. *logomachy*
c. *jurisdiction*
d. *impignoration*
e. *defenestration*
f. *mortuus sine prole*

---

3. Bryan A. Garner, ed., 7th ed. (St. Paul, Minn.: West Group, 1999).

CHAPTER TEN

The Prehistory of English and the Other Indo-European Languages

The Discovery of the Deeper Linguistic Past of English and Related Languages

The origins of the different languages of the world have intrigued human beings throughout history. The story of the Tower of Babel in the Hebrew Bible expresses a widespread feeling that the diversity of languages is a remarkable state that needs to be explained: why aren't we all still speaking the original language of the first humans?

As we have seen in previous chapters, linguists now understand that change is a normal and universal characteristic of language. And given the fact that change is certain, it is also certain that the languages of different groups of people will diverge if those people are not in close contact with each other. But it is a large step from understanding divergence as a linguistic generality to understanding the specifics of how the current languages of the world diverged from common ancestors. Research into both the generalizations and the specific details of language history is the concern of **historical linguistics**.

The current tradition of scientific inquiry into historical linguistics began in the eighteenth century, when scholars proposed that Hungarian and Finnish, until then considered quite separate languages, were in fact related through descent from a single hypothetical ancestor, which is now known as Proto-Finno-Ugric. In a 1786 address, the British jurist Sir William Jones hypothesized that most of the other languages of Europe and the ancient Indian language Sanskrit were part of another such family of related languages. Jones, who worked in India during the British colonial period, was one of the first Europeans ever to intensively study Sanskrit, which functions as the ecclesiastical language of

Hinduism, much as Latin did in Roman Catholicism. He proposed that Sanskrit, Latin, and Greek might have "sprung from some common source," which itself might no longer be spoken.

Jones's address kicked off a boom of historical linguistic scholarship in the nineteenth century. These investigations clearly established the existence of the family of languages that came to be identified as *Indo-European*, so called because speakers of those languages occupied, at the dawn of the Western historical period, much of the Eurasian land mass stretching from the Indian subcontinent to the western boundaries of Europe.

The Indo-European Languages

Divergent dialects arose as the Indo-Europeans migrated to far-flung areas of Europe and Asia and became isolated from each other. These dialects gave rise to the individual subgroups of the Indo-European family. There are perhaps thirteen branches of Indo-European. Eight branches have languages that are still spoken; a sampling of those languages is listed below:

> **Germanic.** English, German, Dutch, Yiddish (West Germanic); Norwegian, Swedish, Danish, Icelandic (North Germanic or Scandinavian)
> **Italic.** Latin, with its descendants, the **Romance** languages: French, Italian, Spanish, Portuguese, Romanian
> **Hellenic.** Greek
> **Celtic.** Gaelic, Irish, Welsh, Breton

Table 10.1 Cognate Words in Latin, Greek, and Sanskrit

Meaning	Latin	Greek	Sanskrit[a]
'creeps'	serpit	herpei	/sərpəti/
'family'	genus	genos	/ɟənəs/
'ten'	decem	deca	/dəʃə/
'three'	tres	treis	/trəjəs/

[a]Sanskrit is transcribed in IPA symbols. /ɟ/ is a voiced palatal stop, similar to /dʒ/.

Balto-Slavic

    Baltic. Lithuanian, Latvian

    Slavic. Russian, Ukrainian, Czech, Polish, Serbian, Croatian, Bosnian, Bulgarian

Indo-Iranian

    Indic. Sanskrit and its descendants: Hindi, Bengali, Urdu, Romany (Gypsy), Punjabi, Gujarati

    Iranian. Farsi (Persian), Pashto

Armenian

Albanian

Some branches of the Indo-European family that are known from written records but have no living descendant languages include Tocharian in Western China and Anatolian in Turkey; the latter includes Hittite. Most of the groups represented by living languages once also contained additional languages that have since died out (e.g., Gothic, from the Germanic branch).

From Proto-Indo-European to Germanic

One of the most important discoveries about the relationship of the Indo-European languages, and an important factor in the establishment of linguistics as a scientific study with a reliable methodology, was the elucidation of the sound correspondence usually called *Grimm's law*. This was named for Jakob Grimm, who was one of the two brothers who collected the famous folktales. In the early 1820s, he put the finishing touches on some observations about Germanic first noted by Rasmus Rask. As you can see from the word-initial consonants in table 10.2, English (viz. Germanic) words that descended from the original Indo-European language, Proto-Indo-European (PIE), usually have different obstruents than do the words of the same meaning in other Indo-European languages. Grimm's law showed, however, that underneath these differences there was regularity. For example, if a word begins with /f/ in English, the Latin word for the same meaning regularly begins with a /p/. This led to the hypothesis that Proto-Indo-European had a consonant which, by sound changes in Germanic or Italic or both, became /f/ in one branch and /p/ in the other.

Table 10.2 Some Obstruent Correspondences and
Reconstructed PIE

English	Latin	Greek	Sanskrit	PIE
/f/	/p/	/p/	/p/	*/p/
father	pater	patēr	/pita:/	*p
/θ/	/t/	/t/	/t/	*/t/
three	trēs	treis	/trəjəs/	*t
/h/	/k/	/k/	/ʃ/	*/kʲ/
hundred	centum	hecaton	/ʃətəm/	*ḱ
/(h)w/	/kw/	/p/	/k/	*/kʷ/
where	quis	pou	/kvə/	*kʷ
/t/	/d/	/d/	/d/	*/d/
ten	decem	deca	/dəʃə/	*d
/k/	/g/	/g/	/ɟ/	*/gʲ/
kin	genus	genos	/ɟənəs/	*ǵ
/kw/	/w/	/b/	/g/	*/gʷ/
quick	vīvus	bios	—	*gʷ
/b/	/f/	/pʰ/	/bʰ/	*/bʰ/
be	fuit	phῡei	/bʰəvəti/	*bh
/d/	/f/	/tʰ/	/dʰ/	*/dʰ/
do	facit	thes	/dʰa:tu/	*dh
/g/	/h/	/kʰ/	/ɦ/	*/gʲʰ/
gold	helvus	chloē	ɦaris	*ǵh

Note: All words cited in a particular row have the same roots, but not always
exactly the same meaning, as the English word. /ʲ/ means preceding velar is
palatalized—pronounced closer to the hard palate, as in English *cute, geek.* /ʷ/
means preceding velar is labialized—pronounced with rounded lips, similar to
English *quote, guano.*

The discovery of **recurrent sound correspondences** helped put historical
linguistics on a firm scientific basis. A prescientific way to show that languages
are related was to simply point out how similar they look to each other. But all
words in all languages resemble each other to some degree, so it is hard to tell
when resemblance is merely coincidental. In contrast, it is not at all likely that
pairs of languages would have a large number of words that have recurrent
sound correspondences, so they constitute good and convincing evidence that
languages are related to each other.

Historical linguists often take the further step of guessing what the original
sound was that led, for example, to /f/ in English but to /p/ in Latin. This is

known as **reconstruction**. Reconstructions are usually preceded by an asterisk (*) to show that the form is based on inference, and is not actually found in any written record. Proto-Indo-European was spoken before the invention of writing, and so the only things we can say about the language are necessarily reconstructions.

The last column in table 10.2 gives the commonly accepted reconstructions for the PIE consonants under consideration. They are given twice; first in the IPA we are already familiar with, and then in the more traditional notation developed in the nineteenth century. Reconstructions are based, when possible, on changes that experience tells us are most likely to occur in languages. For example, palatalized *k̑* /kʲ/ is reconstructed because that is the sound that would most likely change to an velar oral stop in some languages (Latin, Greek) and to a palatal affricate in others (Sanskrit). The reason that the change is so likely is that /kʲ/ is intermediate between those two sounds articulatorily.

The particular correspondences involved in Grimm's law can be most easily understood as the result of a sound shift in Proto-Germanic that regularly affected the phonation and manner of articulation of the stop consonants without substantially changing their place of articulation. Thus, we can see a shift in which

1. The **voiceless** stops changed their manner of articulation from that of stops to that of the similar fricatives:

   /p/ > /f/
   /t/ > /θ/
   /kʲ/ > /x/, which later > /h/ in English
   /kʷ/ > /xʷ/, which later > /hw/, now usually /w/ in English

2. The unaspirated **voiced** oral stops lost their voicing:

   /d/ > /t/
   /gʲ/ > /k/
   /gʷ/ > /kw/

3. The **breathy** aspirated stops lost their aspiration to become simple (unaspirated) voiced stops:

   /bʰ/ > /b/
   /dʰ/ > /d/
   /gʲʰ/ > /g/

If /dʰ/ > /d/ and /d/ > /t/ and /t/ > /θ/, why didn't all three of these dental sounds eventually become /θ/? And one might ask the same question for the other points of articulation. The answer is that these changes must have happened in the order of enumeration (1–3), so that, for example, by the time /d/ changed to /t/, /t/ had already changed to /θ/ and that particular sound change had stopped operating. This makes Grimm's law a **chain shift** of sounds, not unlike the Great Vowel Shift, which was discussed in chapter 2.

The Nature of Proto-Indo-European

Sounds

Based on the sort of evidence we have just considered in connection with Grimm's law, linguists have reconstructed the consonants of Proto-Indo-European as shown in table 10.3.

As you might expect from an enterprise as difficult as figuring out what a long-extinct language sounded like, there are many controversies and unanswered questions. Consequently, you need not be intimidated about pronouncing these sounds correctly in class: you can always tell your teacher that you subscribe to a different theory. The pronunciation of three of the fricatives is so conten-

Table 10.3 The Consonants of Proto-Indo-European

	Labial	Dental	Palatal	Velar	Labiovelar
Obstruents					
Oral stops					
Voiceless	/p/ p	/t/ t	/kʲ/ k̂	/k/ k	/kʷ/ kʷ
Voiced	/b/ b	/d/ d	/gʲ/ ĝ	/g/ g	/gʷ/ gʷ
Aspirated	/bʰ/ bh	/dʰ/ dh	/gʲʰ/ ĝh	/gʰ/ gh	/gʷʰ/ gʷh
Fricative		/s/ s			
Sonorants					
Nasal	/m/ m	/n/ n			
Approximant		/r/ r	/j/ y	/w/ w	
Lateral		/l/ l			

Note: Letters in italics show one common way of writing the sounds. Accompanying IPA transcriptions are approximate.

tious that we did not even hazard a guess as to where to put them in the chart. Most often, writers prefer to simply assign them numbers, such as H_1, H_2, and H_3. They are known as **laryngeals**, for no good reason; they probably have no particular relation with the larynx. In the discussion below, we notate them as H_e, H_a, and H_o, because they have left traces as those subscripted vowels in daughter languages.

Proto-Indo-European had five vowels, both long and short, much like Latin; they are transcribed *a, e, i, o, u*, with macrons when long: *ā*, etc. In addition, the sonorants and laryngeals often were used as <u>syllabic consonants,</u> that is, in place of a vowel. For example, the word for 'liver' was *yekʷr̥* /jekʷr̥/, with the *r* serving as the vowel of the second syllable, much as in the familiar American pronunciation *butter* /'bətr̥/. It is traditional to draw a circle under syllabic consonants. When the laryngeals were used as syllabic consonants, they show up as vowels in the daughter languages. In Greek, for example, H_e becomes /e/, H_a becomes /a/, and H_o becomes /o/. Because laryngeals so often show up as vowels, another common way of transcribing them is as *ə*.

Laryngeals have two interesting effects on vowels. One is **laryngeal vowel coloring.** When H_a appears next to an *e*, the pronunciation of the *e* becomes /a/; for example, $H_a egro$- 'field' gives us Latin *agr*- as in *agriculture*. Similarly, when H_o stands next to an *e*, the latter becomes /o/: $H_o ekʷ$- 'eye' ends up as Latin *oc*- as in *oculist*. The other effect is **laryngeal lengthening:** when a laryngeal comes after a vowel or syllabic consonant in the same syllable, the effect in daughter languages is for the laryngeal to disappear but for the preceding sound to be lengthened; for example, *pleH_e*- 'fill' ends up as Latin *plē*- as in *plenary*. One reason why it is good to keep these effects in mind is because they account for a lot of differences between reference works. For example, what one authority transcribes as *bhāǵos* 'beech', another may transcribe as *bheH_aǵos* (or *bheH_2ǵos*)—which would be pronounced the same way, after laryngeal vowel coloring and laryngeal lengthening take effect.

Grammar

In addition to the sounds of words, it is possible to reconstruct a great deal else about Proto-Indo-European. Much of its morphology has been reconstructed. It had heavily inflected nouns and verbs, like its descendants Latin and Greek, but more so. Proto-Indo-European seems to have had at least eight cases. Instead of distinguishing only singular and plural number, Proto-Indo-European had a third category, the dual, which was used when there were exactly two things; for example, one *H$_e$ékwos* 'horse', two *H$_e$ékwoH$_e$*, three or more *H$_e$ékwōs*. To add to the complication, different words often expressed the same cases and numbers with different inflectional endings. Adjectives had to be inflected for the same case and number as the noun they modified, and also had to agree with their gender—a mostly arbitrary three-way contrast that we call masculine, feminine, and neuter, but which in fact had little to do with natural sex.

Some of the sources of irregular allomorphy that we discussed in chapter 4 have their origin in grammar rules that were more regular in Proto-Indo-European. For instance, the nasal infix in some allomorphs of roots like *frang* 'break' made verbs transitive. This is why it appears in the present participle, which can take a direct object in Latin, more often than in the perfect participle, which usually can't. But in Latin, there are many exceptions to the rule; for example, the perfect participle of *jung-* 'join' is *junct-* instead of $^×$*juct*. Such irregularities arose through analogy after the true function of the nasal infix became obscure. Presumably, the original purpose of things like the nasal infix were still understood during Proto-Indo-European times, and so they functioned as part of the grammar rather than as inexplicable irregular allomorphy.

Ablaut was also more regular in Proto-Indo-European. The interchange of *e*, *o*, and zero that we discussed in chapter 4 was pervasive throughout the whole vocabulary and followed rules, which are now imperfectly understood. For example, a verbal root would normally take the *e* grade when it appeared in a simple present tense, an *o* grade in certain past tenses, and a zero grade if it appeared in certain adjectival forms.

The Indo-European World

Indo-European was the first large language family with which Western scientists were able to practice **linguistic archaeology**. Vocabulary shared by disparate branches of the Indo-European diaspora shows that they once shared a substantial lexical and cultural base. By comparing words in the descendant languages and extrapolating from the regular correspondences observed in words like those noted above, linguists have been able to infer a great deal about the Indo-European language and the Indo-Europeans themselves as they lived five or six thousand years ago. The following aspects of the physical and conceptual universe are just a few of those represented by the Indo-European morphemes that have been reconstructed. Traditional transcription is used here; a useful exercise would be to read the Proto-Indo-European words aloud, using the phonetic values suggested in the previous section. English words in italics are based ultimately on these words; translations are added only when not obvious from the English derivatives.

Names for things in the physical environment include *$snoyg^who$s* (*snow*), *$\acute{g}hyem$-* 'winter' (*hiemal, hibernate*); the plants *$bhaH_a\acute{g}os$* (*beech*), *$bherH\acute{g}$-* (*birch*) or 'ash', *$ghr̥sdh$-* 'barley'; and the animals *$r̥tkos$* 'bear' (*arctic*), *$wl̥k^wos$* (*wolf, lupine*), *$bhibhrus$* (*beaver*), *$\acute{k}as$-* (*hare*), *$mūs$* (*mouse*), *$H_e\acute{k}wos$* 'horse' (*equine*), *g^woH_ous* 'cow' (*cow, bovine, bucolic*), *$uksēn$* (ox), H_oowis 'sheep' (*ewe, ovine*), *$suHs$* (*swine, sow*), *$\acute{k}wōn$* 'dog' (*hound, canine*), *H_oor-* 'eagle' (*erne, ornithology*), *$\acute{g}hans$-* (*goose, anserine*), *$gerH_a$-* (*crane*), and *$bhey$-* (*bee*). The overall pattern of such vocabulary suggests that the Proto-Indo-Europeans lived in temperate woodlands, neither too hot for snow nor too cold for the attested flora and fauna.

The Proto-Indo-Europeans knew of *$\acute{g}hol$-* (*gold*), *$H_aar\acute{g}n̥tom$* 'silver' (*argentine*), and *H_aayos* 'bronze' (*aeneous*), but apparently not iron. They had the *g^wiH-* 'bow' and *$isus$* 'arrow', as well as the *naH_aus* 'ship' (*navy*), which they would H_ereH_e (*row*), but apparently had no sails. Various words like *$H_amel\acute{g}$-* (*to milk*) and *$H_ong^wn̥$* 'butter' (*unguent*) demonstrate knowledge of husbandry; *suH_e* (*sow*), *H_aarH_o-* 'plow' (*arable*), and *g^werH_a-* (*quern*) demonstrate that they had agriculture. They must also have known how to *H_awebh-* (*weave*) *$wl̥HnaH_a$* (*wool*). Perhaps most important, they had the *k^wek^wlos* (*wheel*) and *$H_aa\acute{k}s$-* (*axle*). Some of these activities and culture items were not invented until around 4000 BC, which suggests the Proto-Indo-Europeans must not have left their homeland before then. A popular theory proposes that all these details from linguistic archeology are most compatible with what traditional archeology has learned about the kurgan culture that was situated in eastern Ukraine around that time. Conceivably the use of the horse and the wheel—hence war chariots—gave this culture the military edge to eventually spread through so much of Europe and southwestern Asia.

The Proto-Indo-Europeans appear to have worshipped at least one god, called *dyēws pH_atēr*, that is, *Father Zeus*, the Roman *Jupiter*. They were patrilocal and patriarchal. The *demspotis* 'master of the house' (*despot*) would *wedh-* 'carry off' a woman to live in his *domHos* 'house' (*domicile*). This led eventually to an extended family, whose members would live together in a *woiḱos* 'village' (*vicinity*).

Changes Leading to Latin and Greek

As the Proto-Indo-European speakers spread out through Europe and Asia, the descendant languages underwent many independent changes, such as Grimm's law in Germanic. Most significant for our purposes are those that occurred in Latin and Greek. A few of the most important of these are listed below.

Greek

Proto-Indo-European vowels are well preserved, with only two important changes. Long and short *u moved forward in the mouth, becoming *y*. Thus *mūs* 'mouse' > *mȳs* (the root *my* is used in English in the metaphorical sense 'muscle'). The other important vowel change is that long *ā became *ē*. Thus *mātēr* 'mother' > *mētēr* (*metropolis*).

Most of the oral stops did not undergo anything as comprehensive as Grimm's law. But as you can see from table 10.2, the PIE breathy-voiced aspirates became voiceless aspirates.

The labialized oral stops (*kʷ, *gʷ, *gʷh) ordinarily became labials in Greek: *p, b, ph*. These are the changes shown in table 10.2. There are also conditioned changes: The labialized stops become dentals (*t, d, th*) before front vowels. Thus *kʷetwores* 'four' > *tessares*.

Word-initial *s became /h/. Thus *septm̥ > *hepta*.

Laryngeals (*H_e, *H_a, *H_o) either disappeared, perhaps leaving behind traces in the form of laryngeal vowel coloring or laryngeal lengthening (e.g. *deH_o-* 'give' > *dō-*), or they turned into the corresponding vowels *e, a,* and *o* (e.g., *dhH̥_emn̥ > *thema*, *pH̥_atēr* > *patēr*).

Syllabic consonants like *r̥ or *m̥ did not remain such in Greek. Instead, Greek usually added an *a* next to the consonant. Thus *$\hat{k}r̥d$- 'heart' > *card*-. Often the syllabic nasals *$m̥$ and *$n̥$ simply became *a*: *$H_onH_omn̥$ > *onoma* 'name'.

The glide /w/ normally disappeared: *$widesyā$ > *ideā*.

Latin

Much of the regular allomorphy described in chapter 6 is due to changes that happened in the descent of Latin from Proto-Indo-European. In particular, Rhotacism, despite its Greek-derived name, is distinctively Latin: *$swesōr$ 'sister' > *sorōr*-. So is the change of *t+t* to *ss*.

Latin vowels preserved the Proto-Indo-European state of affairs pretty well in the first syllable, but in subsequent syllables the distinctively Latin vowel weakenings often make it difficult to tell what the original vowel was.

As can be seen from table 10.2, most of the oral stops are very similar to the original Proto-Indo-European ones—except that *g^w became the glide /w/—until we get to the breathy aspirated consonants. The single most useful rule to learn is that these usually became *f* in Latin.

Laryngeals either disappeared, behaving as in Greek, or they turned into the vowel *a*. Latin did not get different vowels for the three different laryngeals (e.g., *$dhH̥_e$- > *fa*- as in *fac* 'do'; *$pH̥_atēr$ > *pater*).

Syllabic consonants added a vowel next to the consonant. Thus *$\hat{k}r̥d$- 'heart' > *cord*-, *$H_onoH_omn̥$ > *nōmen* 'name'; see table 10.4 for details.

Relevance to the Study of English Words

We have been concentrating on how native English, Greek, and Latin words have changed since Proto-Indo-European times, but for us as students of English vocabulary, the bigger news is that there has been a remarkable amount of stability over the past six thousand years. Many Proto-Indo-European sounds have not changed at all in one or more of the three languages we are focusing on, and of those that have changed, many of the changes are minimal or show regular correspondences between the languages. The similarities and correspondences can help us to associate Latin and Greek morphemes with each other and with native English words. To use this knowledge as a key to

Table 10.4 Consonant Correspondences for PIE, Greek, Latin, and English

PIE	Greek	Latin	English
*p	p	p	f (v)
*t	t	t	th
*ḱ, k	c	c	h (gh)
*kʷ	p, t, c	qu	wh
*b	b	b	p
*d	d	d	t
*ǵ, g	g	g	c, k (ch)
*gʷ	b, d (g)	v (gu)	qu
*bh	ph	f (b)	b (v)
*dh	th	f (d)	d
*ǵh, gh	ch	h (g)	g (y)
*gʷh	ph, th (ch)	f (v)	w
*s	h, s	s, r	s
*Hₑ	e, —	a, —	a, —
*Hₐ	a, —	a, —	a, —
*Hₒ	o, —	a, —	a, —
*m	m	m	m
*m̥	a	em	um
*n	n	n	n
*n̥	a	en	un
*l	l	l	l
*l̥	al (la)	ul	ul
*r	r	r	r
*r̥	ar (ra)	or	ur
*w	— (h)	v	w
*y	z (h)	j	y

recognizing and learning a new Latin or Greek morpheme, you can guess at its possible English cognates by applying the expected sound correspondences. This can be done even more easily using the *American Heritage Dictionary* (4th edition), which lists Proto-Indo-European roots and their major English, Greek, and Latin descendants.

The correspondences in table 10.4 are valid for most initial consonants and many medial and final consonants. The alternants enclosed in parentheses are for reference only and need not be memorized.

Word Elements

Element	Gloss	Source	Examples
al	other	L	*alias, alibi, alter*
all~allel	other	G	*allomorph, allele, allopathy, allelocatalytic*
card	heart	G	*cardiac, electrocardiogram, endocardium*
cord	heart	L	*cordial, misericord, accord*
cruc	cross, important point	L	*crucify, crucial, crux, cruciform, crucible, cruciate, excruciating*
dec	acceptable	L	*decent, decorum, decorous, decorist, decor*
ed~es	eat	L	*edible, obese, comestible, edacious, esurient, esculent*
fa	speak	L	*famous, ineffable*
fer	carry	L	*transfer, fertile, differ, refer*
fratr	brother	L	*fraternity, fratricide, fraternal*
ge	earth	G	*geology, perigee, apogee, geode, georgic, epigeal*
gemin	twin	L	*Gemini, bigeminal, trigeminus, gemellus, geminate*
ger	old person	G	*geriatric, gerontogeous, gerontomorphosis, gerontology*
graph~gramm	write	G	*telegraph, telegram, tetragrammaton, pantograph, graphite, epigram, diagram, digraph*
juven~jun	young	L	*juvenile, rejuvenate, junior*

Element	Gloss	Source	Examples
lat	carry	L	*translate, ablation, collate, illation, superlative, dilatory, prolate, elate, prelate*
lig	tie	L	*ligament, oblige, ligate, ligature, alligation, colligate, religion*
lign	wood	L	*ligneous, lignify, lignite, lignescent*
loqu~locu	speak	L	*soliloquy, elocution, circumlocution, interlocutor, obloquy, grandiloquence, colloquium, colloquial*
magn	great, large	L	*magnify, magnanimous, magniloquent, magnum, magnitude*
matr	mother	L	*maternal, matrilineal, dura mater, material, matrix*
metr	mother, uterus	G	*metritis, metrorrhagia, metropolis, endometrium*
myc	fungus	G	*mycology, streptomycin, mycosis*
noct	night	L	*nocturnal, equinox, nocturn, noctule*
nomen~nomin	name	L	*nominate, nomenclature, nominal*
nyct	night	G	*nyctophobia, nyctitropism*
onom~onomat~onym	name	G	*onomatopoeia, pseudonym, patronymic, onomastic, synonym, antonym, eponym*
orth	straight, correct	G	*orthopedic, orthodox, orthographic, orthogonal, anorthite, orthotic*

Element	Gloss	Source	Examples
pale~palae	old	G	*paleolithic, paleontology, paleoclimatic, paleobotany*
patr	father, country	L, G	*paternal, expatriate, perpetrate, patron, repatriate, sympatric, patriarchal, patrilocal, patron*
ped	foot	L	*pedal, centipede, expedite*
ped~paed	child, teach	G	*pediatric, encyclopedia, pedology, pedodontia, pedophilia, orthopedic, pedagogy, paedomorphism, paedogenic*
pha~phe	speak	G	*aphasia, euphemism, blaspheme, phatic, emphasis, dysphasia*
pher~phor	carry	G	*metaphor, peripheral, pheromone, phosphor, electrophoresis, hemapheresis, euphoria*
phyll	leaf	G	*chlorophyll, phyllotaxis, heterophyllous, phylloid, phyllophagous*
phyt	plant	G	*phytogenic, thallophyte, phytoplankton, neophyte*
pod~pus	foot	G	*podiatry, platypus, cephalopod, octopus*
pom	fruit	L	*pomegranate, pomade, pome, pomiferous, pomology, pomaceous*
pred	preying	L	*predator, depredation, predacious, predatory*
rhiz	root	G	*rhizome, mycorrhiza, rhizopod, rhizophagous*

Element	Gloss	Source	Examples
sal~sil	jump	L	*salient, resilience, salacious, saltitory, saltation, saltigrade*
salv~salu	safe, greet	L	*salvation, salubrious, salutary, salvable, salubrity, salutatorian, salute, salvo*
soror	sister	L	*sorority, sororial, sororicide, sororate*
spor	scatter, seed	G	*diaspora, sporozoan, sporadic, sporogenesis, sporophyll, sporophore, sporophyte*
the	put	G	*epithet, thesis, prosthesis, antithesis, diathesis, parenthetical, thetic, anathema*
uxor	wife	L	*uxorial, uxoricide, uxorious, uxorilocal*
val	strong	L	*valor, valid, valence, convalesce, prevalent, valetudinarian*
voc	call, voice	L	*vocation, vociferous, invoke, vocative, convoke, evoke, revoke*

Element Study

1. With the help of dictionaries and a book of roots,[1] parse, gloss, and simply define the following electronics terms:

   a. *rheostat*
   b. *electrode*
   c. *anhysteresis*
   d. *fluorescent*
   e. *resistance*
   f. *impedance*
   g. *potentiometer*
   h. *superheterodyne*
   i. *commutator*
   j. *insulation*

2. Parse, gloss, and give allomorphs and brief dictionary definitions for the following words:

   a. *effluent*
   b. *quìncenténnial*
   c. *ìnterlócutor*

Exercises

1. The members of each of the following pairs of words or boldface morphemes share a single Proto-Indo-European source. In each pair one has been borrowed into English from Latin, French, or Greek while the other is an inherited, native Germanic word. On the basis of your knowledge of consonant correspondences, circle the word in each pair that is borrowed.

   a. *sediment, sitter*   f. *spume, foam*
   b. *float, pluvial*   g. *erode, rat*
   c. *cram, agora*   h. *farina, barn*
   d. *fantasy, beacon*   i. *eaten, edible*
   e. *dough, figure*   j. *vehicle, wain*

---

1. E.g., Donald J. Borror, *Dictionary of Word Roots and Combining Forms, Compiled from the Greek, Latin and Other Languages, with Special Reference to Biological and Scientific Terms* (Palo Alto, Calif.: Mayfield, 1960).

2. Fill in the blanks using your knowledge of Grimm's law by providing the Greek and Latin root forms and their cognates in modern English. In your answers give the correspondences to the PIE consonants shown in **boldface** type. Leave the cells marked —— empty. Some meanings are intentionally left blank to avoid giving away the answer.

PIE	Greek	Latin	English word	PIE root meaning
a. *dheu	——	——	_ew	'flow'
b. *bheH$_a$	_a, _e	_a	_an	'speak'
c. *bend	——	——	_en	'protruding point'
d. *bher	_er, _or	_er	_ear	'carry'
e. *pet	_ _er	——	_ea_er	'fly'
f. *ten	_on	_en(d)	_in	'stretch'
g. *k̑erd	_ard	_ord	_eart	
h. *bhu	_yt	——	_e	'plant, grow'
i. *k̑er	_ran	_orn	_orn	'head'
j. *H$_a$eug	au_	au_	e_e	'increase'
k. *gel	——	_el	_ool	
l. *peH$_a$u	_ed	_auc	_ew	'little'
m. *terH$_a$	——	_rans	_rough	'cross over'
n. *kan	——	_an	_en	'sing'
o. *paH$_a$	——	_an 'bread'	_ood	
p. *sweH$_a$d	he_	sua_	swee_	'pleasant'
q. *treud	——	_rud 'push'	_rea_	'squeeze'
r. *dheH$_e$	_e	_ac 'make'	_o	'put, set'

CHAPTER ELEVEN

Later Changes: From Latin to French to English

In most of the previous chapters of this book and in all the Word Elements lists, we have been considering Latin and Greek elements from the point of view of how they were spelled and pronounced in classical Roman times. We have done so because that is the best way to account for the spelling and the allophonic changes undergone by the morphemes used in the technical and scientific vocabulary of English. Because the great bulk of the learned vocabulary was borrowed from the classical languages using the original Latin spelling, for all practical purposes English has incorporated much of the phonology and morphology of Latin into this higher vocabulary.

Nevertheless, classical Latin is not the end of the story. All languages change, even Latin. In this chapter, we consider some of the ways in which changes that Latin underwent since its classical period have made an impact on English vocabulary.

Learned Borrowings

When words or morphemes are borrowed directly from the written Latin language, they are known as learned, or scholarly, borrowings. Learned borrowings present the fewest changes from classical Latin usage, but even they are by no means unchanged from the language of Cicero. When used in English, Latin words and word elements may have different semantics, spelling, pronunciation, and endings.

Semantics

We have already covered changes in semantics in chapter 7. Of the many reasons that words and elements change their meaning over time, one that has been particularly important in the case of borrowings from Latin is the need to increase the word stock. Scholars and scientists have shown no reluctance to borrow Latin words in only their most technical meanings, or even to assign them meanings they never had in classical times. For example, in classical Latin, *continent-* meant 'continuous' or 'uninterrupted'. It could be applied to all sorts of objects, including land, in which case it meant 'mainland', as opposed to an island. The idea of reserving the word to apply specifically to one of the seven great landmasses of the world is a seventeenth-century invention that would have seemed quite foreign to the Romans.

Spelling

Spelling is the aspect of our words that has changed the least since Roman times. This is not so much because spelling is inherently stable but because many English scholars from the sixteenth century on have been actively concerned that words of Latin extraction should be spelled as if they were still Latin. There are, however, a few prominent cases where modern spelling departs from the classical norm. The ancient Romans did not distinguish uppercase from lowercase letters, nor did they distinguish the vowel *i* from the consonant *j* or the vowel *u* from the consonant *v*. These very useful distinctions were introduced in modern times, and we doubt that even the most classically inclined scholar believes that we should go back to spelling the Latin loanword *junior* as IVNIOR.

One important change in classical Latin spelling, however, is still a bit controversial. Classical Latin had two diphthongs, *ae* and *oe*, that eventually came to be pronounced the same as the letter *e*. It became so common to confuse these three forms that eventually people tended to give up and just write *e* in all cases. Nowadays there is some hesitation about just how far to restore the classical spelling. By far the most common treatment is to spell such words with a simple *e*, so that Latin *haesitation-* became *hesitation* and *poenal-* became *penal*. On the other hand, the rule is to retain the diphthongal spelling in proper names like *Caesar* and *Oedipus*; in the plural ending *-ae* as in *alumnae*; and in highly technical scientific terms like *paedomorphosis* or *coelacanth*. In between is a broad gray area. Is it *encyclopaedia* or *encyclopedia*? *Aesthete* or *esthete*? *Foetus* or *fetus*? Usage varies, with the United States often leading the way in abandoning the classical digraphs in favor of the simpler single *e*.

Pronunciation

The third area of change in learned loans was in pronunciation. Classicists have been less successful in getting people to pronounce Latin loanwords in a classical way than in getting them to spell them classically. Actually, until about a hundred years ago, even scholars tended to pronounce Latin—not just Latin loanwords in English but actual Latin text—according to a fairly complicated set of rules that were far removed from the pronunciation of ancient Rome. Many changes in the pronunciation of Latin words have a surprisingly long history. For example, *j* and *v*, which were approximants in classical Latin (/j/ and /w/) but are obstruents in English (/dʒ/ and /v/), are pronounced as obstruents in all the Romance languages—evidence of a sound change that must have occurred throughout Latin-speaking Europe before the Middle Ages. You also may have noticed that Latin *c* and *g*, which were always velar /k/ and /g/ in classical Latin, are often pronounced /s/ and /dʒ/ in English. To be more precise, these letters are pronounced more toward the front of the mouth before the front vowels *e* and *i*. It turns out that the Romance languages have this rule too, though the outcomes vary from language to language; this coronalization (usually called palatalization) must also be a very old, though postclassical, sound change.

These changes entered English because English-speaking scholars were imitating the pronunciation of other European scholars—mostly from France—for whom these changes occurred throughout their language. French scholars pronounced the root *civ-* 'citizen' as /siv/ instead of classical /kiːw/ because "/w/ > /v/" and "/k/ > /s/ before /i/" were regular sound changes in French. English speakers pronounced *civ-* as /siv/ because they learned how to pronounce Latin words from the French. English speakers did not change /w/ to /v/ in native words like *wind*, nor did they change /k/ to /s/ in words like *kiss*.

Other changes in the pronunciation of Latin borrowings are entirely the work of English speakers. Many of the vowels are pronounced quite differently from anything heard in ancient Rome. The most noteworthy change is that many of the vowels were lengthened and subsequently raised and diphthongized, or both, during the Great Vowel Shift (chapter 2). As a consequence, Latin *a*, *e*, and *i* are often pronounced /e/, /i/, and /aɪ/ in English.

These pronunciations are by now hundreds of years old and well established in English. It is difficult to imagine that zealous reformers will ever convince English speakers to restore classical Latin pronunciations on any great scale, turning familiar words like *circus* into ancient forms like /kɪrkʊs/. However, we have noticed people undoing the Great Vowel Shift in several words and phrases like *re* (formerly /ri/, now mostly /re/), *per diem* (older /daɪəm/, now mostly /diəm/), and in *-i* plurals as in *stimuli* and *fungi* (older /aɪ/, now often /i/). Even people who don't speak Latin seem to understand that the Great Vowel Shift is unique to English, and they seek to supply more authentic-sounding pronunciations to words they perceive as foreign in origin.

Endings

Many Latin and Greek words have been borrowed whole, in their original citation form. The many nouns we saw in chapter 9 that take Latin plurals retain their Latin singular endings as well, as do many more words that take normal English plurals, like *camera, bonus,* and *senator.*

The more general pattern, however, is for words to change or drop their endings when they are borrowed into English. There seem to be at least two motivations for this. The first is that Latin endings carry many functions that endings do not carry in English. For example, *citabar* means 'I was being cited'. It must have seemed more natural to get rid of that complexity by stripping off the ending entirely. By borrowing simply the stem *cit-* and adding only a silent *e*, English has ended up with a word that can be used like any native English word, with no unnecessary inflectional apparatus.

The second reason for discarding or changing the Latin endings has to do with sound change. In French, many unstressed final syllables were lost or turned into *e*. This, naturally, got rid of most inflectional endings. Because Latin words that were inherited by French as a daughter language had reduced or lost their inflectional endings, it must have been natural to think of applying the same changes to words when they were borrowed by scholars directly from Latin.

As in many other matters dealing with Latinity, French precedent strongly influenced English usage. In most, though by no means all, Latin words borrowed into English, endings are discarded or replaced by silent *-e.* Very often we ended up with Latin words that are in their stem form. Words like *legislature, contradict, natal, nation, omnipotent,* and *procure* never appear in such guises in Latin, but such shortened, endless words are the norm for Latin borrowings in English as well as in French.

The rest of the learned borrowing is normally spelled like the original Latin word. The very end of many words, however, have been adjusted to agree with common Old French sound changes. Many words whose stem ends in a vowel plus /l/ in Latin drop that vowel and add final *e* in French; this becomes a rule in English as well. Thus *tabula, corpusculum, circulus,* and the suffix *-abilis* become *table, corpuscle, circle,* and *-able* in English; the full stem is visible in derivatives like *tabular.* The adjective-forming suffix *-os-*, as in *bellicose,* more often appears in the Old French form *-ous,* as in *laborious.* Another common alteration changes the root *-fic-* 'make' to *-fy* at the end of the word, as in *petrify* (cf. *petrification*). More examples of this sort can be found. It is not, of course, surprising that changes occurred in Latin words during the millennium or so that they were passed down through French. What is more interesting is the huge number of words that come down to us with a French ending but with the rest of the word looking perfectly like a Latin word. Of course, in almost all cases the full Latin stem is there because it is a learned borrowing, or restoration, on the part of scholars. Apparently these scholars felt that there was so much precedent to dropping the Latin endings and tinkering with the occasional suffix that little would be gained by insisting that the end of the word appear in its original Latin form as well.

Borrowings from Popular French

In contrast to the learned borrowings we discussed in the previous section, many words that English borrowed from French don't look very much like the Latin words they descended from. For example, we saw in chapter 1 that the word *chief,* which was borrowed from Old French, descended from the Latin morpheme *cap.* Similarly, *friar* is not spelled like its ancestor *frater,* and *voyage* is not spelled like *viaticum.*

In general, no attempt is made to spell words in a Latin fashion if they are not perceived as Latin words. This can happen if the original word was never written down in classical Latin texts. If *language* ever existed as a Latin word, something like **linguaticum,* it was no doubt coined long after the classical Latin period. Other words may date back to classical times but were not used in the standard literary style of Latin and so were never or only rarely written down. Such words are said to descend from popular Latin, which is often called Vulgar Latin. For example, English borrowed the word *river* from Old French, but the classical Latin words for 'river' were *amnis* and *flumen*. The word *river* must have come from a Vulgar Latin word like **riparia*.

Perhaps a more important reason why people didn't respell words like *voyage*, *chief*, and *friar* in a Latin fashion is because these words just don't seem like Latin. They had changed so much in the thousand years or so since the classical Latin period that their original Latin roots were unrecognizable. Words that descend naturally from Latin into French, accumulating changes over the centuries, without being affected by scholarly knowledge of Latin, are called popular French words. When they are borrowed into English, their relationship to the Latin morphemes we have been studying in this book may be irregular or flat-out obscure.

It would be a massive undertaking to explain all the changes that took place between Latin and Old French, but to give you a taste for their extent, here is a brief summary of some of the highlights.

Deletions

French usually preserved, in one form or another, the beginning of the word and the stressed syllable. Other syllables were often deleted.

> *periculósum* > *perilous, parlous*
> *rotúndum* > *round*
> *cadéntiam* > *chance*
> *focárium* > *foyer*
> *ratiónem* > *reason*

Coronalizations

In addition to the coronalizations we mentioned as being reflected even in scholarly loans, several more types affected popular words. One famous change turned *c* /k/ into *ch* /tʃ/ before *a*. Various other changes also produced palatal or postalveolar sounds:

> *cap-* > **chief**
> *cantum* > **chant**

gaudium > joy
judicem > judge
diurnalem > journal
cambiat > change
fructum > fruit
legalem > loyal

Diphthongizations

Most Latin vowels underwent some change or another in the course of the development of Old French. Perhaps the set of changes most characteristic of Old French were the **diphthongizations**: simple vowels turning into diphthongs. Many of these subsequently turned back into simple vowels, so often the most explicit evidence for the diphthongization is in the spelling, which still has two vowel letters.

fidem > faith
manutenet > maintain
pictum > paint
sanctum > saint
punctum > point

Word Elements

Element	Gloss	Source	Examples
al	wing	L	*aliform, ala, alar, alary, alate, alula, aliped, aliferous*
api	bee	L	*apiary, apiculture, apian, apiarist*
arachn	spider	G	*arachnid, arachnoid, arachnean, arachnodactyly, arachnophobia*
bov	cow	L	*bovine, bovate, bovid, Ovibos*
bu~bou	cow	G	*boustrophedon, butyric, bucolic, bulimia*
chir	hand	G	*chiropractor, chiropodist, enchiridion, chiromancy, Chiroptera*

Element	Gloss	Source	Examples
clam~claim	call out	L	clamor, reclaim, clamant, declaim, acclaim, conclamation, clamorous
clav	key	L	clavier, conclave, enclave, clavichord, clavicle, autoclave, claviger, exclave
col~cul	inhabit, grow	L	colony, cultivate, culture, arboricole, horticulture, saxicole, arenicolous
curs~curr	run	L	cursor, current, discursive, excursive, curriculum, incursion, precursor, cursory
dendr~dry	tree	G	rhododendron, dryad, dendrochronology, dendrite, philodendron, dendriform
dent	tooth	L	dental, edentate, dentition, trident
dyn	power	G	dynamo, dyne, dynasty, aerodyne, dynamic
en~oen	wine	G	enology, oenophile, oenomel, oenotherapy
ev	age	L	medieval, coeval, primeval, longevity
formic	ant	L	formic, formicary, formicivorous
herp~herpet	to creep, reptile	G	herpes, herpetology, herpetism
hor	hour	G	horology, horoscope, horologe, horologer, horometry
ichthy	fish	G	ichthyology, Ichthyornis, ichthyosis, ichthyism, Ichthyopsida
lu~lv	dissolve	L	dissolve, solution, solvent, dissolute
ly	loosen	G	analysis, electrolyte, lyotropic, electrolysis, dialysis, electrolyte
mal	bad	L	malefactor, malicious, maleficent, malaprop, malice, malign, malevolent
mant~manc	prophesy	G	necromancy, mantic, chiromantic, praying mantis, ceromancy

Element	Gloss	Source	Examples
mun	public service, gift	L	municipal, remunerate, munificent, commune, immune, communicate
nau	boat	G	nautical, Argonaut, astronaut, nautilus, nausea
nav	boat	L	naval, navigate, nave, navicular
null	nothing	L	null, annul, nullify, nullity
odont	tooth	G	periodontal, mastodon, odontoid, orthodonture
oo	egg	G	oocyte, oogamous, oology, oolite
orn~ornith	bird	G	ornithology, ornithomancy, ornithosis, notornis
ov	egg	L	ovum, oval, ovary, ovate, ovoid, ovule, ovulate
ox~oxy	sharp	G	oxymoron, oxalic, oxygen, oxycephaly, paroxysm, oxytone, oxyacetylene, amphioxus
phag	eat	G	sarcophagus, bacteriophage, anthropophagy, phagocyte, dysphagia
pithec	ape	G	Australopithecus, Pithecanthropus, pithecan, pithecological, Dryopithecus
plac	please	L	placate, placid, placebo, placable
plac	flat	G	placoid, placenta
pter	wing	G	pterodactyl, helicopter, archaeopteryx, pteridophyte, pteridology, apterous
rog	ask	L	interrogate, supererogatory, rogatory, surrogate, abrogate, prerogative, subrogate
sen	old (person)	L	senility, senescent, senator, senectitude, senopia
serp	to creep, snake	L	serpent, serpentine, serpigo, serpolet, Serpula
som~somat	body	G	psychosomatic, chromosome, soma, somatic, somatogenic, somatotype, acrosome

Element	Gloss	Source	Examples
soph	wise	G	*sophisticated, philosophy, sophist, sophomore, theosophy, sophistry, gastrosoph*
strat	stretch, level, layer	L	*prostrate, stratum, stratify, stratigraphy, stratus, substrate*
tel~tele	end, complete	G	*telic, teleology, teleorganic, telencephalon, telesis, teleostome, telephase*
trop	to turn	G	*heliotrope, trope, tropism, entropy, phototropic, anatropous, tropotaxis*
verm	worm	L	*vermicelli, vermiform, vermouth, vermicular, vermifuge*
vin	wine	L	*vinegar, vino, vinaceous, viniculture*
xyl	wood	G	*xylophone, xylem, xyloid, xylograph, xylose, xylophagous*

Element Study

1. Here are some phobias using elements from our morpheme sets or roots that you may recognize. What do you think they mean? For a good educated guess, use both your knowledge of morphemes and your knowledge of conditions that affect humans.

   a. *aerophobia*
   b. *algophobia*
   c. *autophobia*
   d. *cryophobia*
   e. *dysmorphophobia*
   f. *gamophobia*
   g. *iatrophobia*
   h. *nyctophobia*
   i. *phobophobia*
   j. *scopophobia*

2. What would be appropriate terms for the following phobias and manias?

   a. abnormal fear of depths
   b. abnormal fear of spiders
   c. abnormal fear of dogs
   d. abnormal fear of animals
   e. abnormal fear of snakes
   f. obsession with males
   g. obsession with wine
   h. obsession with cutting (said of overeager surgeons)
   i. obsession with solitude
   j. obsession with foreign things

3. Use the literal meanings of the word elements to express what these doctors specialize in.

   a. orthodontist
   b. periodontist
   c. chiropodist
   d. gerontologist
   e. ophthalmologist

4. Parse and gloss the following words, using their definitions as guides to associating their analyzed and actual current meanings.

   a. *mýriapod* 'arthropod with long, segmented body'
   b. *senópia* 'changes in lenticular elasticity, due to sclerosis, at a stage following presbyopia'
   c. *ichthyósis* 'skin disorder characterized by rough, dry skin with plate-like hardenings'
   d. *complacency* 'smugness' (*com-* is intensive)
   e. *communion* 1. 'a Christian religious denomination'; 2. 'the Eucharist'
   f. *coeval* 'isochronous' (*-al* = ADJECTIVE)
   g. *altíloquent* 'sesquipedalian'
   h. *entropy* 'total measure of energy (specifically, in the universe) not available for work'

5. The following words are taken from the field of philosophy. Using an unabridged dictionary and a glossary of morphemes, briefly define, parse, and gloss each term.

   a. *empiriological*
   b. *monothelitism*
   c. *encratism*
   d. *theophany*
   e. *metempsychosis*
   f. *panentheism*

6. Find the word in the list below which best matches each dictionary definition given. Don't use a regular dictionary but refer to Borror's *Dictionary of Word Roots and Combining Forms* to identify unfamiliar morphemes. Some of the words are decoys. Use no word more than once. Work from definition to word. Avoid multiple answers, but if you can't decide between two choices, give both choices and explain the problem.

1. dynotrusion	11. inculpatory	21. ambiplasty
2. Cynodontia	12. pantocrator	22. epipodium
3. degramic	13. homeoregion	23. symplectic
4. metastasis	14. anthobrach	24. theurgy
5. hypergamy	15. ectropion	25. illative
6. androgynous	16. ergatogyne	26. anthophyte
7. tmesis	17. nephropathy	27. epiphonema
8. peristaltic	18. telegenic	28. epiphilious
9. protuse	19. epiopticon	
10. delectation	20. mastobrach	

a. __15__ An abnormal turning out of a part of the body (e.g., of an eyelid).

b. __25__ Pertaining to the grammatical case denoting movement into a place or thing.

c. __23__ Relating to or being an intergrowth of two different minerals.

d. __5__ Marriage into a higher social class or caste.

e. __2__ A division of Triassic Therapsida comprising a number of small carnivorous reptiles often with cusps on the teeth resembling those of certain mammals.

f. __26__ A flowering plant.

g. __12__ The omnipotent lord of the universe.

h. __24__ An occult art by which one may evoke or utilize the aid of divine and beneficent spirits.

i. __16__ A wingless queen ant resembling a worker.

j. __27__ A summary argument concluding a discourse.

k. __22__ A lateral ridge or fold along either side of the foot of various gastropods.

l. __7__ The separation of the parts of a compound word by intervening words (e.g., of *another* in *a whole nother thing*).

Exercises

1. Using the meanings of Latin and Greek morphemes you've learned or can find in a glossary, and the information on typical changes in the forms of words in Romance illustrated in this chapter, give the English word borrowed from French that comes from the Latin word shown. The first two items are completed as examples. You may use a dictionary to confirm your answers.

	Latin	*French > English*
a.	*tractum*	____*trait*____
b.	*musculum*	___*muscle*___
c.	*diversitatem*	_____
d.	*lacte*	*café au* _____
e.	*planum*	_____
f.	*magister*	_____
g.	*catena*	_____

2. Based on your knowledge of sound changes in the development from Latin to French as well as plausible semantic changes, find ten Latin–French pairs (i.e., doublet words or morphemes). Ignore parts in parentheses. Many of the words are decoys.

solid	*cadence*	*journey*
fancy	*employ*	*char(coal)*
fang	*involve*	*calm*
wide	*choir*	*implic(ate)*
capit(al)	*contin(ent)*	*chance*
capt(ure)	*chorus*	*rouse*
clam(or)	*rouge*	*contain*
couch	*fantasy*	*isle*
emblem	*ruby*	*view*
chase	*joint*	*insul(ate)*
junct(ion)	*claim*	*video*

Elements to Glosses

Element	Gloss	Chapter	Source
a-~an-	not, without	3, 4	G
-a	[feminine]		L, G
-a	[plural]	9	L, G
ab-~abs-	from, away	3, 6	L
-able~-ible~-ble	A	3, 11	L
abs-~ab-	from, away	3, 6	L
ac	sharp	9	L
-ac	A	9	G
acanth	spine, thorn		G
acet (< *ac* 'sharp')	vinegar		L
-acl~-acul (< -*l* diminutive)	little	9	L
-acle~-acule (< -*l* diminutive)	little	9	L
acou	hear		G
acr	height, tip	9	G
ad-	to, toward	3, 6	L
-ad	group		G
adelph	brother		G
aden	gland	8	G
adep~adip	fat		L
-ae	[plural]	9	L
aer	air		G
aesth~esth	feel	5	G
aeti~eti	source, cause		G
ag~ig	act, do, drive	5	L
agog	to lead		G
agon	struggle, contest		G
agr	field	9	L

Element	Gloss	Chapter	Source
-al~-ial	A	9	L
al	other	10	L
al	wing	11	L
al~ol~ul	nurture, grow	4	L
alb	white	9	L
alg	pain	8	G
all~allel	other	10	G
alt (< *al* 'grow')	high	5	L
am~im	love	4	L
ambi-	both		L
ambul	walk, go	5	L
amphi-	both		G
ampl	large		L
-an~-ian	A		L
an-~a-	not, without	3, 4	G
ana-	up, again, back	3, 6	G
-ance	N	3, 4	L
-and~-end	N [gerundive]	9	L
andr	male, man	5	G
anem	wind		G
angi	(blood) vessel		G
angin	painful spasm		L
anim	soul, mind, spirit, (nonplant) life	2	L
ann~enn	year	4	L
-ant	A, N [present participle]	3, 9	L
ante-~anti-	before	3	L
anth	flower		G
anthrop	human	1	G
anti-	against, opposite		G
anti-~ante-	before	3	L
apec~apic	tip		L
api	bee	11	L
apo-	away from, off	3	G
apt~ept	fit, capable	4	L
aqu	water		L
-ar	A		L
ar~ard	dry, burn		L
arachn	spider	11	G
arbitr	judge		L

Element	Gloss	Chapter	Source
arbor	tree		L
arch	first, govern	5	G
ard~ar	burn, dry		L
-arium	place	9	L
arthr	joint		G
-ary	A, N	3	L
aster~astr	star	9	G
-ate	N, A, V	3, 7	L
aud	hear	9	L
aug	increase		L, G
aur	ear	8	L
austr	south		L
auto~tauto	self	9	G
av	bird	5	L
axill	armpit	8	L
bar~bary	heavy		G
bas	bottom, low		L
bath~bathy	depth	9	G
batrach	frog		G
batt	beat		L
beat	blessed		L
bell	war	6	L
bene~bon	good, well	9	L
bi	two	6	L
bi	life	1	G
bib	drink		L
bibli	book, Bible		G
bin	two (each)	6	L
blast	bud, embryonic		G
bl~bol	throw, extend	4	G
-ble~-able~-ible	A	3, 11	L
blephar	eyelid		G
bol~bl	throw, extend	4	G
bon~bene	good	9	L
bou~bu	cow	11	G
bov	cow	11	L
brachi	arm		G
brach~brachy	short	9	G
brev	short		L

Element	Gloss	Chapter	Source
bu~bou	cow	11	G
bucc	cheek		L
burs	pouch, purse		L
cac	bad	1	G
cad~cas~cid	fall	5	L
calc	heel		L
calc	limestone		L
calcul	pebble, count		L
call~cal	beautiful		G
can~cen	sing, intone		L
can	dog		L
cancr	crab, cancer		L
cand	shine, glow		L
cap~caput~capit	head		L
cap~cep~cip~cup	take, contain	4	L
capr	goat		L
caps	box		L
car~carn	flesh	9	L
carcin	cancer		G
card	heart	10	G
carn~car	flesh	9	L
cas~cad~cid	fall	5	L
cata-	down, backwards	3	G
caud~cod	tail	8	L
caus~cauter	burn		G
cau~cav	warn, beware		L
cav	hollow		L
ced~cess	go, let go	5	L
cens	judge, assess	6	L
cent	hundred	6	L
centr	center		L
cep~cap~cip~cup	take, contain	4	L
cephal	head	6	G
cer~corn	horn, head		L
cer~ker~cran	head		G
cer~cri~cre	separate	4	L
cere~cre	grow, produce		L
cervic	neck	8	L
chili	thousand	6	G

Element	Gloss	Chapter	Source
chir	hand	11	G
chondr	cartilage		G
chrom	color	1	G
chron	time	1	G
chrys	gold		G
chthon	earth		G
cid~cad~cas	fall	L	5
cid~cis	cut, kill	4	L
cili	eyelash, eyelid		L
cin	ashes		L
cin~kin	move		G
cip~cap~cep~cup	take, contain	4	L
circum-	around		L
cis-	on this side of		L
cis~cid	cut, kill	4	L
cit	move, arouse		L
clam	call out	11	L
clar	clear, bright		L
clav	key, locked	11	L
-cl~-cul (< -l diminutive)	little	9	L
cli	lean, lie, bed	9	L, G
clud~clus	close (v)	5	L
co-~con-~com-	with, together	3	L
coc	cook, ripen		L
cod~caud	tail	8	L
col	inhabit, grow	11	L
coll	glue		G
coll	neck		L
com-~con-	with, together	3	L
con	cone		G
con-~com-~co-	with, together	3	L
contra-~counter-	against, facing	3	L
copr	dung, feces		G
cor	pupil (of eye)		G
cord	heart	10	L
corn	horn		L
coron	crown		L
corp~corpor	body, flesh	2, 3	L
cortec	covering		L
cosm	universe, adorn, order	1	G

Element	Gloss	Chapter	Source
cost	rib, side		L
counter-~contra-	against, facing	3	L
cra	mixture		G
crac~crat	govern	6	G
cran~cer~ker	head		G
crat~crac	govern	6	G
cre~cere	produce, grow		L
cre~cri~cer	separate	4	L
cred	believe	9	L
cri	judge, separate	4	G
cri~cre~cer	separate	4	L
crin	hair		L
cruc	cross, important point	10	L
cry~crym	cold, freeze		G
cryph~cryp	secret, hidden	9	G
cub~cumb	lie down, remain	4	L
-cule~-cle (< -*l* diminutive)	little	9	L
culp	fault	2	L
cumb~cub	lie down, remain	4	L
cumul	heap		L
cup	desire		L
cup~cap~cep~cip	take, contain	4	L
cur	care	6	L
curs~curr	run	11	L
cuss	shake, strike		L
cut	skin	8	L
cyan	blue		G
cyn	dog		G
cyt	cell		G
da~do~di	give	9	L
dactyl	finger		G
damn~demn	loss, harm	9	L
de-	reverse, from	3, 7	L
de~div	god, augury	4	L
deb	owe		L
dec	acceptable	10	L
deca	ten	6	G
decem	ten	6	L
decim~deci-	tenth	6	L

Element	Gloss	Chapter	Source
dem	people	6	G
demn~damn	loss, harm	9	L
den	ten (each)	6	L
dendr~dry	tree	11	G
dent	tooth	11	L
dermat~derm	skin	8	G
deuter	second	6	G
di~da~do	give	9	L
di~dy	two	6	G
dia-	through	3	G
diabol (*dia-* + *bol*)	devil		G
dic	say, point	9	L
dich (< *di*)	(split in) two	6	G
digit	finger, toe, number		L
dign	worthy, fitting		L
dipl	double	6	G
dis-~di-	apart, reversed		L
div~de	god, augury	4	L
do	give	9	G
do~da~di	give	9	L
doc	teach	5	L
doc~dog	opinion	5	G
dol	suffer	9	L
dom	house, master		L
dom	house		G
dorm	sleep		L
dors	back (N)		L
drom	run, course		G
duc	to lead	2	L
dulc	sweet		L
dur	hard, lasting		L
dy~di	two	6	G
dyn	power	11	G
dys-	bad		G
e-~ex-	out	3, 6, 7	L
ec-	out	3	G
ec~oec	home		G
eccles	church		G
ecto-	outside	3	G

Element	Gloss	Chapter	Source
-ectomy (*ec-* + *tom* + *-y*)	cut out		G
ed~es	eat	10	L
ego	self, I		L
eid~id	see		G
-ell (< *-l* diminutive)	little	9	L
em	take, buy		L
em~hem~haem	blood	8	G
-eme	[abstract unit]	4	G
eme	vomit		G
en-	in	3	G
-ence	N	3, 4	L
encephal (*en-* + *cephal*)	brain		G
-end~-and	N [gerundive]	9	L
endo-	inside	3	G
enn~ann	year	4	L
ennea	nine	6	G
ent (< *es* + *-nt*)	be		L
-ent	A, N [present participle]	3, 9	L
enter (< *en* 'in')	intestine		G
entom (*en-* + *tom*)	insect		G
eo	dawn, early		G
epi-	on, over	3	G
episi	vulva		G
ept~apt	fit, capable	4	L
equ	horse		L
equ~iqu	even, level	4	L
erg~urg~org	work	4	G
ero	physical love	5	G
err	wander, do wrong	9	L
eryth~erythr	red		G
es~ess	be, basic		L
-esc~-sc	begin	9	L
-esim	-th (ordinal number)	6	L
eso-	inward		G
ess~es	be, basic		L
esth~aesth	feel	5	G
eth	behavior, custom		G
ethn	nation		G

Element	Gloss	Chapter	Source
eti~aeti	source, cause		G
etym	true		G
eu-	good	5	G
ev	age	11	L
ex-~e-	out	3, 6, 7	L
exo- (< *ec*-)	outside		G
exter-~extern- (< *ex*-)	outside		L
extra- (< *ex*-)	outside	3, 7	L
fa	speak	10	L
fac~fec~fic	do, make	4	L
fan~phan~phen	appear		G
febr	fever		L
fec~fac~fic	do, make	4	L
fel	cat		L
felic	happy		L
fer	carry	10	L
ferr	iron		L
fic~fec~fac	do, make	4	L
fid	trust		L
fid~fiss	split, divided		L
fil	thread, line		L
fil	offspring		L
fin	end, boundary		L
fiss~fid	split, divided		L
fla	blow	6	L
flor	flower		L
flu~fluc~fluv	flow, river	9	L
formic	ant	11	L
foss	dig		L
frag~frang~fring	break	4	L
fran~fren (< *phren*)	mad		L
frang~frag~fring	break	4	L
fratr	brother	10	L
fren~fran (< *phren*)	mad		L
fring~frag~frang	break	4	L
fru~frug~fruc	fruit, produce		L
frutic	shrub		L
fug	flee	2	L

Element	Gloss	Chapter	Source
fund	base, bottom		L
fund~fus	pour, melt, blend	4	L
furc	fork		L
fus~fund	pour, melt, blend	4	L
galact	milk	8	G
gam	marry, unite	1	G
gastr	stomach	8	G
ge	earth	10	G
gel~glac	cold, ice		L
gemin	twin	10	L
gen	knee		L
gen~gn~na	birth, type, origin	4	L
gen~gon	birth	4	G
ger	old person	10	G
ges~ger	carry, do		L
giga	giant, billion	6	G
gingiv	gums		L
glac~gel	ice, cold		L
gli~gle	stick		G
glob~glomer	ball		L
gloss~glott	tongue, speech	9	G
gluc~glyc	sweet		L
glut	glue		L
glyc~gluc	sweet		G
gn~gen~na	birth, type, origin	4	L
gno	know	9	G
gno~no~gni	know	9	L
gon	angle		G
gon~gen	birth	4	G
grad~gred~gress	step, go	5	L
gran	grain		L
graph~gramm	write	10	G
grat	goodwill, thankful, pleased, kind	2	L
grav	heavy		L
gravid (< *grav* 'heavy')	pregnant	8	G
gred~grad~gress	step, go	5	L
greg	social group, gather	2	L
gress~grad~gred	step, go	5	L

Element	Gloss	Chapter	Source
gust	taste		L
gyn~gynec	woman, female	9	G
gyr	circle, spin		G
haem~hem~em	blood	8	G
hagi	holy		G
hal	salt		G
hecaton	hundred	6	G
hedon	pleasure		G
hedr	seat, face of a solid		G
heli	sun	5	G
helic	spiral		G
helminth	worm		G
hem~haem~em	blood	8	G
hemer	day		G
hemi-	half	6	G
hepat	liver	8	G
hepta	seven	6	G
her~hes	to stick, hold back	9	L
herp~herpet	to creep, reptile	11	G
hes~her	to stick, hold back	9	L
hetero-	other, different	3	G
hexa	six	6	G
hier	holy		G
hipp	horse		G
hist	body tissue	8	G
hod~od	path		G
hol	whole		G
hom	human	2	L
homeo-	similar		G
homo-	same	3	G
hor	hour	11	G
hum	earth, low		L
hydr~hydat	water	9	G
hyper-	over, above		G
hypn	sleep, trance		G
hypo-	under, below, partial	3	G
hyps	height		G
hyster	womb, neurotic disorder	8	G

Element	Gloss	Chapter	Source
i	go		L
-i	[plural]		L
-i-	[empty interfix]	3	L
-ia	land, state, medical condition	8	G, L
-ial~-al	A	9	L
-ian~-an	A		L
iatr	heal	1	G
-ible~-able~-ble	A	3, 11	L
-ic	A, N	3	G, L
ichthy	fish	11	G
-icl~-icul (< -l diminutive)	little	9	L
icon	image		G
icosa	twenty	6	G
id~eid	see		G
-id	A		L
idi	personal	1	G
ig~ag	act, do, drive	5	L
ign	fire		L
-il	A	4, 9	L
-ill (< -l diminutive)	little	9	L
im~am	love	4	L
in-	not	3	L
in-	in, into	3	L
-in	A		L
infra-	below, after	3	L
inguin	groin		L
insul	island		L
inter-	between, among	3	L
intra-	within	3	L
intro-	inwards		L
iqu~equ	even, level	4	L
-ise	V		G
-ism	N		G
iso-	equal	3	G
-ist	N		G
-itis	inflammation	8	G
-ity	N	3	L
-ium~-um	thing [singular]	9	L
-ive~-tive	A, N	3, 4, 6	L

Element	Gloss	Chapter	Source
-ix~-trix	woman		L
-ize	v	3	G
jac~jec	throw, lay		L
jug~jung~junc	join		L
jun~juven	young	10	L
jus~jur	law, judge	9	L
juven~jun	young	10	L
ker~cer~cran	head		G
kerat	horn, hard, cornea		G
kilo-	thousand	6	G
kin~cin	move		G
-l [diminutive]	little	9	L
lab	lip	8	L
lachrym~lacrim	tear /tir/	8	L
lacrim~lachrym	tear /tir/	8	L
lact	milk	8	L
lagni	lust		G
lal	babble, talk		G
lamin	layer, blade		L
lapar	abdominal wall		G
lapid	stone		L
laryng	voice box	8	G
lat	carry	10	L
lat	wide, broad		L
later	side		L
latri	worship		G
lav	wash		L
leg	law, deputize	2	L
leg~lex~log	speak, study	1	G
leg~lig	gather, read	5	L
len	soft, gentle		L
-lent	A		L
leo~leon	lion		L
lep~lepr	scaly		G
leuc~leuk	white, clear		G
lev	light, rise		L
lex~leg~log	word, speak	1	G

Element	Gloss	Chapter	Source
liber	free		L
libr	book		L
libr	balance, weigh	2	L
lic	permit, unrestrained	5	L
lic~linqu	leave		L
lig	tie, bind	10	L
lig~leg	gather	5	L
lign	wood	10	L
lim~limen~limin	threshold, border, shore		L
lin	flax		L
lingu	tongue		L
lip	fat		G
liqu	fluid		L
lit~lith	stone	9	L
liter	letter	2	L
lith~lit	stone	9	G
loc	place	6	L
locu~loqu	speak	10	L
log~leg~lex	speak, study	1	G
loqu~locu	speak	10	L
lu~lv	dissolve	11	L
luc~lumen~lumin	light		L
lud	play		L
lumb	lower back, loins		L
lumen~lumin~luc	light	6	L
lun	moon, madness		L
ly	loosen	11	G
-ma	thing [singular]	9	G
mac	spot, stain		L
mach	batttle		G
macr	large	1	G
magn	great, large	10	L
mal~male	bad	11	L
mamm	breast	8	L
man	remain		L
man	hand, handle	6	L
mand (*man* 'hand' + *d~da* 'give')	order		L
mani	intense desire		G
mant~manc	prophesy	11	G

Element	Gloss	Chapter	Source
mar	sea		L
mascul	male		L
mast	breast		G
math	learn, study		G
matr	mother	10	L
maxill	upper jaw		L
med	middle		L
mega~megal	great, million	9	G
mel	honey		G
mel~melan	black		G
mell	honey		L
memor	remember		L
men~min	projéct, threaten		L
men~mon	think, mind	4	L
mens	moon, month		L
-ment	N	9	L
mer	share		L
mer	part		G
merg~mers	sink, dip		L
meso-	middle	3	G
meta-	beyond	3	G
metr	mother, uterus	10	G
micr	small	1	G
mille	thousand	6	L
milli-	thousandth	6	L
mim	copy		G
min	little		L
min~men	projéct, threaten		L
mis	hate	1	G
misc~mix	mix	9	L
mitt~miss	send	3, 4	L
mne	remember	4	G
mo	move	4	L
mod	moderate, manner		L
mon	one	6	G
mon~men	remind, think	4	L
-mony	N	9	L
mor	manner, custom		L
mor	die		L
morb	disease		L

Element	Gloss	Chapter	Source
morph	shape, form	1	G
mov~mo	move	4	L
muc	sticky		L
mult	many	6	L
mun	public service, gift	11	L
mus~mur	mouse, muscle		L
mut	change, exchange		L
my	muscle		G
myc	fungus	10	G
myel	spinal cord, bone marrow		G
myri	countless, ten thousand	6	G
myrmec	ant		G
na~gen~gn	birth, source, tribe	4	L
nan	dwarf		G
nano-	billionth	6	G
nar~nas	nose	8	L
narc	sleep		G
nas~nar	nose	8	L
nat	swim		L
nau	boat	11	G
nav	boat	11	L
-nd~-and~-end	N [gerundive]	9	L
ne	new, recent	5	G
nec~noc~nic~nox	harm	4	L
nec~necr	die	4	G
nect~nex	tie		L
nephr	kidney	8	G
neur	nerve		G
nex~next	tie		L
nic~nec~noc~nox	harm	4	L
nigr	black		L
nihil~nil	nothing	9	L
no~gno~gni	know	9	L
noc~nec~nic~nox	harm	4	L
noct	night	10	L
nod	knot		L
nom	law, system	1	G
nomen~nomin	name	10	L

Element	Gloss	Chapter	Source
non	ninth	6	L
nov	new	2	L
novem	nine	6	L
noven	nine (each)	6	L
nox~noc~nec~nic	harm	4	L
-nt	A, N [present participle]	3, 9	L
nub	marry		L
nuc	nut		L
null	nothing	11	L
nunci	message		L
nutri	feed		L
nyct	night	10	G
-o-	[empty interfix]	3	G
ob-	toward, against	3	L
octa	eight	6	G
octav	eighth	6	L
octo	eight	6	L
octon	eight (each)	6	L
ocul	eye	9	L
od	song		G
od~hod	path		G
od~ol	smell		L
odont	tooth	11	G
odyn	pain		G
oen~en	wine	11	G
-oid (A, N)	resembling	3	G
ol~al	nurture, grow	4	L
ol~od	smell		L
-ol (< -l diminutive)	little	9	L
ole	oil		L
olig	few	6	G
-oma	tumor, growth	8	G
omn	all	2, 6	L
-on	N [singular] thing	9	G
onc	mass, tumor		G
onom~onomat~onym	name	10	G
ont (< -nt participle)	be		G
oo	egg	11	G
op	see	8	G

Element	Gloss	Chapter	Source
ophthalm	eye	8	G
ophi~ophid	snake		G
or	speak formally, pray		L
or	rise		L
orb	circle		L
orch~orchid	testicle, orchid		G
org~erg~urg	work	4	G
orn~ornith	bird	11	G
orth	straight, correct	10	G
-ory	A, N	3	L
-os	N [masculine singular]		G
os~or	mouth, opening	8	L
os~oss	bone	8	L
-ose~-ous	A		L
osm	push		G
oss~os	bone	8	L
oste	bone	8	G
ot	ear		G
-ous~-ose	A	3	L
ov	egg	11	L
ox~oxy	sharp	11	G
pac	agree, peace		L
pachy	thick		G
paed~ped	child, teach	10	G
pale~palae	old	10	G
palin	again		G
pall	pale		L
palp	feel, touch		L
pan-~pant-	all	6	G
par	equal		L
par	give birth to	2	L
para-	beside, nearly	3	G
path	feel, illness	1	G
patr	father, country	10	G, L
pauc	few	6	L
pecc	sin		L
pector	chest		L
pecu	wealth, property		L
ped	foot	10	L

Element	Gloss	Chapter	Source
ped~paed	child, teach	10	G
pell~puls	push		L
pen	lack, shortage		L
pen~paen	almost		L
pen~pun	punish	9	L
pend~pond	hang, weigh	4	L
penn~pinn	feather		L
penta	five	6	G
pept~peps	digest		G
per-	through, thorough	3	L
peri-	around, near	3	G
pet	seek, go to	2	L
petr	rock	1	G
pha~phe	speak	10	G
phag	eat	11	G
phall	penis		G
phan~phen~fan	show, appear		G
pharyng	throat		G
phe~pha	speak	10	G
phen~phan~fan	show, appear		G
pher~phor	carry	10	G
phil	liking, tendency	1	G
phleb	vein	8	G
phob	fear	8	G
phon	sound	1	G
phor~pher	carry	10	G
phot~phos	light	5	G
phras	speech		G
phren	diaphragm, mind		G
phyl	tribe, class, race		G
phylac	guard	8	G
phyll	leaf	10	G
phys	nature		G
phyt	plant	10	G
pig~pic	paint		L
pil	hair		L
pinn~penn	feather		L
pisc	fish		L
pithec	ape	11	G
pl~plec~plic	fold, entwine, times	6	L

Element	Gloss	Chapter	Source
plac	please	11	L
plac	flat	11	G
plag~plagi	oblique, slanting		G
plas	form, mold		G
plat~platy	flat, broad		G
plaud~plod	clap, accept		L
ple	full, many	9	L
pleb	common people		L
plec~pl~plic	times, fold, entwine	6	L
pleg~plex	strike, stroke		G
plic~pl~plec	times, fold, entwine	6	L
plod~plaud	clap		L
plur	many, more	6	L
plut	wealth		G
pluvi	rain		L
pne~pneum	breathe, lung	8	G
po	drink		L
pod~pus	foot	10	G
poe~poei	make		G
pol	community	1	G
poli	gray (matter of brain/ spinal cord)		G
poly	many	6	G
pom	fruit, apple	10	L
pon~pos	place, put	9	L
pond~pend	hang, weigh	4	L
por	passage, opening		L
port	carry		L
pos~pon	place, put	9	L
poss~pot	able, powerful	2	L
post-	after, behind	3	L
pot	able, powerful	2	L
potam	river		G
prac	act, do	5	G
prae-~pre-	before		L
pre-	before	3	L
prec	entreat, pray		L
pred	preying	10	L
prehend~prehens	take, seize		L
presby	old		G

Element	Gloss	Chapter	Source
preter-	go by, beyond		L
prim	first	6	L
pro-	forward, for	3	L, G
prob	good, test	2	L
proct	anus		G
prol	offspring		L
prot	first	6	G
proxim	near		L
pseud	false	1	G
psittac	parrot		G
psor	itch		G
psych	mind	1	G
pter	wing, feather	11	G
pto	fall		G
pty	spit		G
pu~putr	rot, decay		L
pub	mature		L
pug~pung	poke, fight		L
pugn (< *pug*)	fist, fight	9	L
pulm~pulmon	lung	8	L
pun~pen	punish	9	L
punct (< *pug*)	point		L
pur~purg	clean		L
pus~pod	foot	10	G
putr~pu	rot, decay		L
py	rot, decay		G
pyg	buttocks		G
pyr	fire	1	G
quadr	four	6	L
quart	fourth	6	L
quatern	four (each)	6	L
quin	five (each)	6	L
quinque	five	6	L
quint	fifth	6	L
rach	spine, vertebrae		G
radi	spoke, ray		L
radic	root, basic		L
ram	branch		L

Element	Gloss	Chapter	Source
rap	seize		L
re-~red-	again, back	3, 4, 6	L
reg~rig	rule, straight	5	L
ren	kidney		L
ret	net		L
retro-	reverse, back		L
rhin	nose	8	G
rhiz	root	10	G
rid~ris	laugh		L
rig~reg	rule, straight	5	L
robus~robor	strong		L
rog	ask	11	L
rrh~rrhag	flow		G
rub~ruf	red		L
sacr~sanc~secr	holy	4	L
sal	salt		L
sal~sil	jump	10	L
salv~salu	safe, greet, healthy	10	L
sanguin	blood		L
sap	taste, perceive		L
sapr	rotten		G
sarc	flesh	8	G
sat	sufficient		L
saur	lizard		G
-sc~-esc	begin	9	L
scand~scend~scans~scal	climb, steps		L
scat	dung, feces		G
scend~scand~scans~scal	climb, steps		L
schiz~schis	split, divide		G
sci (< sec)	know, discern	2	L
sci~ski	shadow		G
scind~sciss (< sec)	split		L
scler	hard	8	G
scop~scep~skep	view, see		G
scrib~scrip	write		L
se-~sed-	apart	3, 6	L
seb	fat, sebum		L
sec	cut, split	2	L

Element	Gloss	Chapter	Source
secu~sequ	follow		L
sed~sid~sess	sit		L
seism	shake		G
sem	sign, meaning		G
semen~semin	seed	4	L
semi-	half	6	L
sen	old (person)	11	L
sen	six (each)	6	L
sent~sens	feel	5	L
sep	putrid, infected	8	G
septem	seven	6	L
septen	seven (each)	6	L
septim	seventh	6	L
sequ~secu	follow		L
ser	fluid, serum		L
serp	to creep, snake	11	L
serr	saw		L
serv	work for		L
sesqui-	one and a half	6	L
sess~sed~sid	sit		L
sex	six	6	L
sext	sixth	6	L
sicc	dry		L
sid~sed~sess	sit		L
sil~sal	jump	10	L
sim	one		L
-sis	N	3	L
sist (< *st*)	stand		L
ski~sci	shadow		G
sol	alone, single		L
sol	sun		L
solv~solu (< *lu~lv*)	loosen, unbind		L
som~somat	body	11	G
somn	sleep	2	L
son	sound	6	L
sop~sopor	sleep		L
soph	wise	11	G
soror	sister	10	L
spas	convulsion		G

Element	Gloss	Chapter	Source
spec~spic	look, see	4	L
spel	cave		G
sperm (< *spor*)	seed		G
sphing~sphinc	bind tight		G
sphygm	pulse		G
spir	breathe		L
spondyl	backbone, vertebra		G
spor	scatter, seed	10	G
squam	scale		L
sta~ste	stand, state	4	G
sta~ste~sti~st	stand, state	4	L
steat~stear	fat		G
steg~teg	cover, roof		G
stell	star		L
sten	narrow		G
steth	chest		G
sthen	strong		G
sti~sta~ste~st	stand, state	4	L
still	drop, drip		L
stom~stomat	mouth, opening	8	G
strat	stretch, level, layer	11	L
stru~struc	build, pile up		L
styl	pillar, stylus		G
sub-	under, inferior	3, 6, 7	L
succ	juice, sap		L
sud	sweat		L
super-	above, excessive	3	L
supra-	above, greater		L
syn-	with, together	3, 6	G
-t	[perfect participle]	9	L
tac	silent		L
tac	arrange, order	9	G
tach~tachy	fast	9	G
tag~teg~tig~tang~ting	touch	4	L
taph	tomb, grave		G
taur	bull		L
tauto~auto	self	9	G
teg~steg	cover, roof		G
teg~tag~tig~tang~ting	touch	4	L

Element	Gloss	Chapter	Source
tel~tele	end, complete	11	G
tele	far	5	G
tempor	time	3	L
ten~tend~tens	stretch, thin	5	L
ten~tin	hold, maintain	4	L
tend~tens~ten	stretch, thin	5	L
tera-	trillion		G
terat	monster		G
terg	back (N)		L
tern	three (each)	6	L
terr	earth	9	L
terti	third	6	L
tetra~tessara	four	6	G
thalass	sea		G
thanat	death		G
thaum~thaumat	miracle		G
the	put, place	10	G
the	god	1	G
therm	heat, temperature		G
thromb	clot	8	G
-tic~-ic	A		G, L
tig~ting~tag~teg~tang	touch	4	L
-tion~-ion	N	3	L
-tive~-ive	A, N	2, 3, 6	L
tom~tm	cut	4	G
ton	tension, pitch		G
top	place	1	G
torqu~tors	twist, drill		L
tot	whole, all	6	L
tox	poison		L
tra-~trans-	across, through	3, 6	L
trac	pull		L
trans-~tra-	across, through	3, 6	L
trem	shake		L
tri	three	6	L
tri	three	6	G
trich (< *tri*)	three (parts)	6	G
trich	hair		G
trit	third	6	G
-trix~-ix	woman		L

Element	Gloss	Chapter	Source
troch	run, wheel		G
trop	to turn	11	G
troph	nourish		G
trud~trus	thrust	5	L
tuber	swelling		L
-tude	N		L
tum	swelling		L
-ture~-ure	N	9	L
-ty	N	4, 9	L
-ule (< -*l* diminutive)	little	9	L
ultim	last		L
ultra-	beyond		L
-um~-ium	thing [singular]	9	L
umbr	shade		L
un	one	6	L
und	wave		L
ungu	claw, nail		L
ungu~unc	oil, ointment		L
ur	tail		G
uran~ouran	heavens		G
urb	city		L
-ure~-ture	N		L
urg~erg~org	work	4	G
-us	N, A [masculine singular]	9	L
uter	womb		L
uxor	wife	10	L
vac~van	empty	9	L
vad~vas	go		L
vag	wander		L
vagin	sheath		L
val	strong, useful	10	L
van~vac	empty	9	L
var	change		L
vas	vessel, blood vessel, duct	8	L
vas~vad	go		L
veh~vec	carry		L

Element	Gloss	Chapter	Source
ven	come	2	L
ven	vein	8	L
ventr	belly		L
ver	true	2	L
ver	turn	9	L
verb	word, verb		L
verg (< *ver*)	turn	9	L
verm (< *ver* 'turn')	worm	11	L
vi	path		L
vic~vinc	conquer	4	L
vid~vis	see		L
viginti	twenty	6	L
vin	wine	11	L
vinc~vic	conquer	4	L
vir	man		L
vir	green		L
vis~vid	see		L
vit~viv	live	9	L
vitr	glass		L
viv~vit	live	9	L
voc	call, voice	10	L
vol	will		L
volv	turn		L
vom	regurgitate	3	L
vor	eat	4	L
xanth	yellow		G
xen	foreign	1	G
xer	dry		G
xyl	wood	11	G
-*y*	N	3	G, L
zo	animal	4	G
zyg	yoke		G
zym	ferment		G

Glosses to Elements

Gloss	Element	Chapter	Source
A	-able~-ible~-ble	3, 11	L
A	-al~-ial	9	L
A	-an, -ar, -id, -in, -lent, -ose		L
A	-il	4, 9	L
A	-ous~-os	3	L
A	-tic~-ic		G, L
A, N	-ant, -ary, -ent, -ory, -tive	3	L
abdominal wall	lapar		G
able, powerful	pot~poss	2	L
able to be done, suitable for	-ble		L
abnormal, bad	dys-		G
above, excessive	super-	3	L
above, greater	supra-		L
above, over	hyper-		G
(abstract unit)	-eme	4	G
acceptable	dec	10	L
across, through	trans-~tra-	3, 6	L
act, do	prac	5	G
act, do, drive	ag~ig	5	L
after, behind	post-	3	L
again	palin		G
again, back	re-~red-	3, 4, 6	L
again, up, back	ana-	3	G
against, facing	contra-~counter-	3	L
against, opposite	anti-		G
against, toward	ob-	3	L
age	ev	11	L

Gloss	Element	Chapter	Source
agree, peace	pac		L
air	aer		G
all	omn	2, 6	L
all	pan-~pant-	6	G
all, whole	tot	6	L
almost	pen~paen		L
alone, single	sol		L
among, between	inter-	3	L
angle	gon		G
animal	zo	4	G
ant	formic	11	L
ant	myrmec		G
anus	proct		G
apart	se-~sed-	3, 6	L
apart, reversed	dis-~di-		L
ape	pithec	11	G
appear~show	phan~phen~fan		G
arm	brachi		G
armpit	axill	8	L
around	circum-		L
around, near	peri-	3	G
arouse, move	cit		L
arrange, order	tac	9	G
ashes	cin		L
ask	rog	11	L
augury, god	de~div	4	L
away from, off	apo-	3	G
away from, reverse	de-	3	L
babble, talk	lal		G
back (N)	dors		L
back (N)	terg		L
back, again	re-~red-	3, 4, 6	L
back, reverse	retro-		L
back, up, again	ana-	3	G
backbone, vertebra	spondyl		G
backwards, down	cata-	3	G
bad	dys-		G
bad	mal	11	L
balance, weigh	libr	2	L

Gloss	Element	Chapter	Source
ball	glob~glomer		L
base, bottom	fund		L
battle	mach		G
be	ont		G
be, basic	ent~es~ess		L
beat	batt		L
beautiful	call~cal		G
bee	api	11	L
before	ante-~anti-	3	L
before	pre-	3	L
beget, give birth to	par	2	L
begin	-sc~-esc	6	L
behavior, custom	eth		G
behind, after	post-	3	L
believe	cred	9	L
belly	venter		L
below, after	infra-	3	L
below, under, partial	hypo-	3	G
beside, nearly	para-	3	G
between, among	inter-	3	L
beware	cau~cav		L
beyond	meta-	3	G
beyond	preter-		L
beyond	ultra-		L
billion, giant	giga	6	G
billionth	nano-	6	G
bind tight	sphing~sphinc		G
bird	av	5	L
bird	orn~ornith	11	G
birth	gen~gon	4	G
birth, give birth to	par	2	L
birth, type, origin	gen~gn~na	4	L
black	mel~melan		G
black	nigr		L
blade, layer	lamin		L
blessed	beat		L
blood	hem~haem~em	8	G
blood	sanguin		L
blood vessel	angi		G
blow	fla	6	L

Gloss	Element	Chapter	Source
blue	cyan		G
boat	nau	11	G
boat	nav	11	L
body	som~somat	11	G
body, flesh	corp~corpor	2, 3	L
body tissue	hist	8	G
bone	os~oss	8	L
bone	oste	8	G
book	libr		L
book	bibli		G
both	ambi-		L
both	amphi-		G
bottom, base	fund		L
bottom, low	bas		L
box	caps		L
brain	encephal		G
branch	ram		L
break	frag~frang~fring	4	L
breast	mamm	8	L
breast	mast		G
breathe	spir		L
breathe, lung	pne~pneum	8	G
brief, short	brev		L
brother	adelph		G
brother	fratr	10	L
bud, embryonic	blast		G
build	stru~struc		L
bull	taur		L
burn	ard		L
burn	caus~cauter		G
buttocks	pyg		G
buy, take	em		L
cac	bad	1	G
call, voice	voc	10	L
call out	clam	11	L
cancer	carcin		G
care	cur	6	L
carry	fer	10	L

Gloss	Element	Chapter	Source
carry	pher~phor	10	G
carry	lat	10	L
carry	port		L
carry	veh~vec		L
carry, do	ges~ger		L
cartilage	chondr		G
cat	fel		L
cause, source	eti~aeti		G
cave	spel		G
cell	cyt		G
center	centr		L
change	var		L
change, exchange	mut		L
cheek	bucc		L
chest	pector		L
chest	steth		G
child, teach	ped~paed	10	G
church	eccles		G
circle	orb		L
circle, spin	gyr		G
city	urb		L
city, community	pol	1	G
clap, accept	plaud~plod		L
claw, nail	ungu		L
clean	pur~purg		L
clear, bright	clar		L
clear, white	leuk~leuc		G
climb, steps	scand~scend~scans~scal		L
close (v)	clud~clus	5	L
clot	thromb	8	G
cold, freeze	cry~crym		G
cold, ice	gel~glac		L
color	chrom	1	G
come	ven	2	L
common, public service, gift	mun	11	L
common people	pleb		L
community	pol	1	G
complete, end	tel~tele	11	G
cone	con		G

Gloss	Element	Chapter	Source
conquer	vic~vinc	4	L
contest, struggle	agon		G
convulsion	spas		G
cook	coc		L
copy	mim		G
cornea, hard, horn	kerat		G
correct	orth	10	G
countless, ten thousand	myri	6	G
courage, soul	anim	2	L
cover, roof	steg~teg		G
covering	cortec		L
cow	bov	11	L
cow	bu~bou	11	G
crab, cancer	cancr		L
creep (v), reptile	herp~herpet	11	G
creep (v), snake	serp	11	L
cross, important point	cruc	10	L
crown	coron		L
cry out, call	clam	11	L
custom	eth		G
custom	mor		L
cut	tom~tm	4	G
cut, kill	cid~cis	4	L
cut, split	sec	2	L
cutting out	-ectomy		G
dark, black	mel~melan		G
dawn, early	eo		G
day	hemer		G
death	thanat		G
decay, rot	pu~putr		L
decay, rot	py		G
depth	bath~bathy	9	G
desire	cup		L
devil	diabol (*dia-* + *bol*)		G
diaphragm, mind	phren		G
die	mor		L
dig	foss		L
digest	pept~peps		G
dip, sink	merg~mers		L

Gloss	Element	Chapter	Source
disease	morb		L
dissolve	lu~lv	11	L
divided, split	fid~fiss		L
do, act	prac	4	G
do, act, drive	ag~ig	5	L
do, carry	ges~ger		L
do, make	fac~fec~fic	4	L
dog	can		L
dog	cyn		G
double	dipl	6	G
down, backwards	cata-	3	G
drink	bib		L
drink	po		L
drive	ag~ig	5	L
drop, drip	still		L
dry	ar		L
dry	sicc		L
dry	xer		G
du~bi	two	6	L
dung, feces	copr		G
dung, feces	scat		G
dust	coni		G
dwarf	nan		G
ear	aur	8	L
ear	ot		G
early, dawn	eo		G
earth	chthon		G
earth	ge	10	G
earth	terr	9	L
earth, low	hum		L
eat	ed~es	10	L
eat	phag	11	G
eat	vor	4	L
egg	oo	11	G
egg	ov	11	L
eight	octa	6	G
eight	octo	6	L
eight (each)	octon	6	L
eighth	octav	6	L

Gloss	Element	Chapter	Source
embryonic, bud	blast		G
empty	vac~van	9	L
[empty interfix]	-i-		L
[empty interfix]	-o-		G
end, boundary	fin		L
end, complete	tel~tele	11	G
entreat, pray	prec		L
equal	iso-	3	G
equal	par		L
even, level	equ~iqu	4	L
excessive, above	super-	3	L
exchange	mut		L
eye	ocul	9	L
eye	ophthalm	8	G
eyelash, eyelid	cili		L
eyelid	blephar		G
face of a solid	hedr		G
facing, against	contra-~counter-	3	L
fall	cad~cas~cid	5	L
fall	pto		G
false	pseud	1	G
far	tele	5	G
fast	tach~tachy	9	G
fat	adep~adip		L
fat	steat~stear		G
fat	lip		G
fat, sebum	seb		L
father, country	patr	10	G, L
fault	culp	2	L
fear	phob	8	G
feather	penn~pinn		L
feather, wing	pter	11	G
feces, dung	scat		G
feed	nutri		L
feel	esth~aesth	5	G
feel	sent~sens	5	L
feel, illness	path	1	G
feel, touch	palp		L
ferment, catalyze	zym		G

Gloss	Element	Chapter	Source
fever	febr		L
few	pauc	6	L
few	olig	6	G
field	agr	9	L
fifth	quint	6	L
fight	pug~pung, pugn	9	L
finger	dactyl		G
finger, toe, number	digit		L
fire	ign		L
fire	pyr	1	G
first	prim	6	L
first	prot	6	G
first, govern	arch	5	G
fish	ichthy	11	G
fish	pisc		L
fist, fight	pugn	9	L
fit, capable	apt~ept	4	L
five	penta	6	G
five	quinque	6	L
five (each)	quin	6	L
flat	plac	11	G
flat, broad	plat~platy		G
flax	lin		L
flee	fug	2	L
flesh	carn~car	9	L
flesh	sarc	8	G
flow	rrh~rrhag		G
flow, river	flu~fluc~fluv	9	L
flower	anth		G
flower	flor		L
fluid	liqu		L
fluid, serum	ser		L
fold, times, tangle, entwine	pl~plec~plic	6	L
follow	sequ~secu		L
foot	ped	10	L
foot	pod~pus	10	G
for	pro-	3	L, G
foreign	xen	1	G
fork	furc		L
form, mold	plas		G

Gloss	Element	Chapter	Source
forward, for	pro-	2	L,G
four	quadr	6	L
four	tetra~tessara	6	G
four (each)	quatern	6	L
fourth	quart	6	L
free	liber		L
freeze	cry~crym		G
frog	batrach		G
from, away	ab-~abs-, de-	3	L
front (in front of)	pre-	3	L
fruit, apple	pom	10	L
fruit, produce	fru~frug~fruc		L
full, many	ple	9	L
fungus	myc	10	G
gather, read	leg~lig	5	L
gather, social group	greg	2	L
giant, billion	giga		G
gift, public service	mun	11	L
give	do	9	G
give	do~da~di	9	L
gland	aden	8	G
glass	vitr		L
glue	coll		G
glue	glut		L
go	i		L
go	vad~vas		L
go, let go	ced~cess	5	L
go, step	grad~gred~gress	5	L
go to, seek	pet	2	L
goat	capr		L
god	the	1	G
god, augury	de~div	4	L
gold	chrys		G
good	bon~bene	9	L
good	eu-	3	G
good, test	prob	2	L
goodwill	grat	2	L
govern	crat~crac	6	G
govern, first	arch	5	G

Gloss	Element	Chapter	Source
grain	gran		L
grave, tomb	taph		G
gray (matter of brain/spinal cord)	poli		G
great, large	magn	10	L
great, million	mega~megal	9	G
green	vir		L
greet	salv~salu	10	L
groin	inguin		L
group	-ad		G
grow, inhabit	col~cul	11	L
grow, nurture	al~ol	4	L
grow, produce	cere~cre		L
guard	phylac	8	G
gums	gingiv		L
hair	crin		L
hair	pil		L
hair	trich		G
half	hemi-	6	G
half	semi-	6	L
hand	chir	11	G
hand, handle	man	6	L
hang, weigh, pay, consider	pend~pond	4	L
happy	felic		L
hard	scler	8	G
hard, horn, cornea	kerat		G
hard, lasting	dur		L
harm	nec~noc~nic~nox	4	L
harm, loss	damn~demn	9	L
hate	mis	1	G
head	cap~caput~capit		L
head	cephal	6	G
head	cer~ker~cran		L
heal	iatr	1	G
heap	cumul		L
hear	acou		G
hear	aud	9	L
heart	card	10	G
heart	cord	10	L
heat, temperature	therm		G

Gloss	Element	Chapter	Source
heavens	uran~ouran		G
heavy	bar~bary		G
heavy	grav		L
heel	calc		L
height	hyps		G
height, tip	acr	9	L
hide, secret	cryph~cryp	9	L
high	alt	5	L
hold, maintain	ten~tin	4	L
hollow	cav		L
holy	hagi		G
holy	hier		G
holy	sacr~sanc~secr	4	L
home	ec~oec		L
honey	mel		G
honey	mell		L
horn	corn		L
horn, hard, cornea	kerat		G
horse	equ		L
horse	hipp		G
hostility, soul	anim	2	L
hour	hor	11	G
house	dom		G
house, master	dom		L
human	anthrop	1	G
human	hom	2	L
hundred	cent	6	L
hundred	hecaton	6	G
I	ego		L
ice	gel~glac		L
illness, feel	path	1	G
image	icon		G
in, into	in-	3	L
in, into	en-	3	G
increase	aug		L, G
infected, putrid	sep	8	G
inferior, under	sub-	3, 6, 7	L
inflammation	-itis	8	G
inhabit, grow	col~cul	11	L

Gloss	Element	Chapter	Source
inhabit, home	ec~oec		G
insect	entom		G
inside	endo-	3	G
intense desire	mani		G
intestine	enter		G
into	in-	3	L
into	en-	3	G
inward	eso-		G
inwards	intro-		L
iron	ferr		L
island	insul		L
itch	psor		G
jab	pug		L
join	jug~jung~junc		L
joint	arthr		G
judge	arbitr		L
judge, assess	cens	6	L
judge, law	jus~jur	9	L
juice, sap	succ		L
jump	sal~sil	10	L
key, locked	clav	11	L
kidney	nephr	8	G
kidney	ren		L
kill	cid~cis	4	L
kind, goodwill	grat	2	L
knee	gen		L
knot	nod		L
know	gno	9	G
know	gno~no~gni	9	L
know, discern	sci	2	L
lack, shortage	pen		L
land, state, medical condition	-ia	8	G, L
large	ampl		L
large	macr	1	G
large	magn	10	L
last	ultim		L
lasting	dur		L

Gloss	Element	Chapter	Source
laugh	rid~ris		L
law, deputize	leg	2	L
law, judge	jus	9	L
law, system	nom	1	G
layer, blade	lamin		L
layer, stretch, level	strat	11	L
lead (v)	agog		G
lead (v)	duc	2	L
leaf	phyll	10	G
lean, lie, bed	cli	9	L, G
learn, study	math		G
leave	lic~linqu		L
letter	liter	2	L
level, even	equ~iqu	4	L
lie, lean	cli	9	L, G
lie down, remain	cub~cumb	4	L
life	bi	1	G
life	viv~vit	9	L
life, soul	anim	2	L
light	luc~lumen~lumin	6	L
light	phot~phos	5	G
light, rise	lev		L
liking	phil	1	G
limestone	calc		L
lion	leo~leon		L
lip	lab	8	L
little	-acl~-acul,-cl~-cul, -ell, -icl~-icul, -l, -ule	9	L
little, inferior	min		L
live	viv~vit	9	L
live, inhabit, grow	col~cul	11	L
liver	hepat	8	G
lizard	saur		G
loins, lower back	lumb		L
look, see	spec~spic	4	L
loosen	ly	11	G
loosen	solv~solu		L
loss, harm	damn~demn	9	L
love	am~im	4	L
love, liking	phil	1	G

Gloss	Element	Chapter	Source
love (physical)	ero	5	G
lower back, loins	lumb		L
lung	pulm~pulmon	8	L
lung, breathe	pne~pneum	8	G
lust	lagni		G
mad	fran~fren		L
make	poe~poie		G
make, do	fac~fec~fic	4	L
male	mascul		L
male, man	andr	5	G
man	vir		L
manner, custom	mor		L
many	mult	6	L
many	poly	6	G
many, more	plur	6	L
marrow, spinal cord	myel		G
marry	nub		L
marry, unite	gam	1	G
mass, tumor	onc		G
mature	pub		L
meaning, sign	sem		G
medical condition	-ia	8	G, L
melt, pour, blend	fund~fus	4	L
message	nunci		L
middle	med		L
middle	meso-	3	G
milk	galact	8	G
milk	lact	8	L
mind	psych	1	G
mind, soul	anim	2	L
miracle	thaum~thaumat		G
mix	misc~mix	9	L
mixture	cra		G
moderate, manner	mod		L
mold, form	plas		G
monster	terat		G
moon, madness	lun		L
moon, month	mens		L
mother	matr	10	L

Gloss	Element	Chapter	Source
mother, uterus	metr	10	G
mouse, muscle	mus~mur		L
mouth	os~or	8	L
mouth, opening	stom~stomat	8	G
move	cin~kin		G
move	mov~mo	4	L
move, arouse	cit		L
muscle	mus~mur		L
muscle	my		G
N	-ance, -ence, -ity, -tion	3	L
N	-ia		L, G
N	-ism, -ist		G
N	-ment, -mony	9	L
N	-sis	3	G
N	-tude, -ture~-ure		L
N	-ty	4, 9	L
N	-y	3	G, L
N [gerundive]	-and~-end	9	L
N [plural], things	-a~-ia		L, G
N [singular]	-a		L, G
N [singular]	-os		G
N [singular]	-us	9	L
N [singular], thing	-ma	9	G
N [singular], thing	-on		G
N [singular], thing	-um~-ium	9	L
N, A	-ant, -ary, -ent, -ory	3	L
nail, claw	ungu		L
name	nomen~nomin	10	L
name	onom~onomat~onym	10	G
narrow	sten		G
nation	ethn		G
nature	phys		G
near	proxim		L
near, around	peri-	3	G
nearly, beside	para-	3	G
neck	cervic	8	L
neck	coll		L
nerve	neur		G
net	ret		L

Gloss	Element	Chapter	Source
new	nov	2	L
new	ne	5	G
night	noct	10	L
night	nyct	10	G
nine	ennea	6	G
nine	novem	6	L
nine (each)	noven	6	L
ninth	non	6	L
nose	nas~nar	8	L
nose	rhin	8	G
not	in-	5	L
not, without	a-~an-	3	G
nothing	nihil~nil	9	L
nothing	null	11	L
nourish	troph		G
number	digit		L
nurture, grow	al~ol	4	L
nut	nuc		L
oblique, slanting	plag~plagi		G
off, away from	apo-	3	G
offspring	fil		L
offspring	prol		L
oil	ole		L
oil, ointment	ungu~unc		L
old	pale~palae	10	G
old	presby		G
old person	ger	10	G
old person	sen	11	L
on, over	epi-	3	G
on this side of	cis		L
one	mono	6	G
one	sim		L
one	un	6	L
one and a half	sesqui-	6	L
opinion	doc~dog	5	G
order	mand		L
other	al	10	L
other	all~allel	10	G
other, different	hetero-	3	G

Gloss	Element	Chapter	Source
out	ec-	3	G
out	exo-		G
out	ex-~e-	3, 6, 7	L
outer covering	cortec		L
outside	ecto-	3	G
outside	exter-~extern-		L
outside	extra-	3	L
outside	extro-		L
over, above	hyper-		G
over, above	super-	3	L
over, on	epi-	3	G
owe	deb		L
pain	alg	8	G
pain	odyn		G
painful spasm	angin		L
paint	pig~pic		L
pale	pall		L
parrot	psittac		G
part	mer		G
passage, opening	por		L
path	hod~od		G
path	vi		L
peace, agree	pac		L
pebble, count	calcul		L
penis	phall		G
people	dem	6	G
perceive, feel	esth~aesth	5	G
perceive, taste	sap		L
[perfect participle]	-t	9	L
permit, unrestrained	lic	5	L
personal	idi	1	G
physical love	ero	5	G
pick, read	leg~lig	5	L
pile up	stru~struc		L
pillar, stylus	styl		G
pitch, tension	ton		G
place	-arium	9	L
place	loc	6	L
place	top	1	G

Gloss	Element	Chapter	Source
place, put	pon~pos	9	L
plant	phyt	10	G
play	lud		L
please	plac	11	L
pleased, goodwill	grat	2	L
pleasure	hedon		G
[plural]	-a, -ae, -i	9	L
point, say	dic	9	L
poison	tox		L
poke	pug~pung		L
pouch, purse	burs		L
pour, melt, blend	fund~fus	4	L
power	dyn	11	G
powerful, able	pot	2	L
pray, entreat	prec		L
pray, speak formally	or		L
pregnant	gravid	8	G
preying	pred	10	L
produce	par		L
produce, fruit	fru~frug~fruc		L
produce, grow	cere~cre		L
projéct, threaten	men~min		L
property, wealth	pecu		L
prophesy	mant~manc	11	G
public service, gift	mun	11	L
pull	trac		L
pulse	sphygm		G
punishment	pen~pun	9	L
pupil (of eye)	cor		G
purse	burs		L
push	pell~puls		L
push	osm		G
put, place	pon~pos	9	L
put, place	the	10	G
putrid, infected	sep	8	G
rain	pluvi		L
ray, spoke	radi		L
read, gather	leg~lig	5	L
recent, new	ne	5	G

Gloss	Element	Chapter	Source
red	eryth~erythr		G
red	rub~ruf		L
regurgitate	vom	3	L
remain	man		L
remember	memor		L
remember	mne	4	G
reptile	herp~herpet	11	G
resembling	-oid	3	G
reverse, back	retro-		L
reverse, from	de-	3	L
rib, side	cost		L
ring, circle, spin	gyr		G
ripen, cook	coc		L
rise	or		L
rise, light	lev		L
river	potam		G
rock	petr	1	G
roof, cover	steg~teg		G
root	rhiz	10	G
root, basic	radic		L
rot, decay	pu~putr		L
rot, decay	py		G
rotten	sapr		G
rule, straight	reg~rig	5	L
run	curs~curr	11	L
run, course	drom		G
run, wheel	troch		G
sacred, holy	hagi		G
sacred, holy	hier		G
safe, greet	salv~salu	10	L
salt	hal		G
salt	sal		L
same	homo-	3	G
saw	serr		L
say	dic	9	L
scale	squam		L
scaly	lep~lepr		G
scatter, seed	spor	10	G
sea	mar		L

Gloss	*Element*	*Chapter*	*Source*
sea	thalass		G
seat, face of a solid	hedr		G
second	deuter	6	G
secret, hidden	cryp~cryph	9	G
see	eid~id		G
see	op	8	G
see	vid~vis		L
seed	semen~semin	4	L
seed	sperm		G
seed, scatter	spor	10	G
seek, go to	pet	2	L
seize	rap		L
self	auto~tauto	9	G
self, I	ego		L
send	mitt~miss	3, 4	L
separate (v)	cri~cre~cer	4	L
separate (v), judge	cri	4	G
seven	hepta	6	G
seven	septem	6	L
seven (each)	septen	6	L
seventh	septim	6	L
shade	umbr		L
shadow	sci~ski		G
shake	seism		G
shake	trem		L
shake, strike	cuss		L
shape, form	morph	1	G
share	mer		L
sharp	ac	9	L
sharp	ox~oxy	11	G
sheath	vagin		L
shine, glow	cand		L
short	brach~brachy	9	G
short	brev		L
show, appear	phan~phen~fan		G
shrub	frutic		L
side	later		L
side, rib	cost		L
sign, meaning	sem		G
silent	tac		L

Gloss	Element	Chapter	Source
similar	homeo-		G
sin	pec		L
sing, intone	can~cen		L
single, alone	sol		L
sink, dip	merg~mers		L
sister	soror	10	L
sit	sed~sid~sess		L
six	hexa	6	G
six	sex	6	L
six (apiece)	sen	6	L
sixth	sext	6	L
skin	cut	8	L
skin	dermat~derm	8	G
slanting, oblique	plag~plagi		G
sleep	dorm		L
sleep	narc		G
sleep	somn	2	L
sleep	sop~sopor		L
sleep, trance	hypn		G
small	micr	1	G
smell	od~ol		L
snake	ophi~ophid		G
snake	serp	11	L
social group	greg	2	L
soft, gentle	len		L
solidify, cold, freeze	gel~glac		L
song	od		G
sound	phon	1	G
sound	son	6	L
source, birth, tribe	nat	2	L
source, cause	eti~aeti		G
south	austr		L
speak	leg~lex~log	1	G
speak	loqu~locu	10	L
speak	fa	10	L
speak	pha~phe	10	G
speak, call, voice	voc	10	L
speak, say, point	dic	9	L
speak formally, pray	or		L
speech	phras		G

Gloss	Element	Chapter	Source
speech sound	phon	1	G
spider	arachn	11	G
spin, circle	gyr		G
spinal cord, bone marrow	myel		G
spine, thorn	acanth		G
spine, vertebrae	rach		G
spiral	helic		G
spirit, soul	anim	2	L
spit	pty		G
split	fid~fiss		L
split	schiz~schis		G
split	scind~sciss		L
spoke, ray	radi		L
spot, stain	mac		L
stand, state	sta~ste~sti~st~sist	4	L
stand, state	sta~ste	4	G
star	aster~astr	9	G
star	stell		L
state, condition, stand	sta~ste~sti~st	4	L
state, condition, stand	sta~ste	4	G
state, land, medical condition	-ia	8	G, L
step, go	grad~gred~gress	5	L
steps, climb	scal~scand~scend ~scans		L
stick	gli~gle		G
stick (v), hold back	hes~her	9	L
sticky	muc		L
stomach	gastr	8	G
stone	lapid		L
stone	lith~lit	9	G
straight, correct	orth	10	G
straight, rule	reg~rig	5	L
stretch, level, layer	strat	11	L
stretch, thin	ten~tend~tens	5	L
strike, shake	cuss		L
strike, stroke	pleg~plex		G
strong	robus~robor		L
strong	sthen		G
strong	val	10	L
struggle, contest	agon		G

Gloss	Element	Chapter	Source
study, speak	log	1	G
suffer	dol	9	L
sufficient	sat		L
sun	heli	5	G
sun	sol		L
sweat	sud		L
sweet	dulc		L
sweet	glyc~gluc		G
swelling	tuber		L
swelling	tum		L
swim	nat		L
system, law	nom	1	G
tail	caud~cod	8	L
tail	ur		G
take, buy	em		L
take, contain	cap~cep~cip~cup	4	L
take, seize	prehend~prehens		L
taste	gust		L
taste, perceive	sap		L
teach	doc	5	L
teach, child	ped~paed	10	G
tear /tir/	lacrim~lachrym	8	L
ten	deca	6	G
ten	decem	6	L
ten (each)	den	6	L
ten thousand, countless	myri	6	G
tendency, liking	phil	1	G
tension, pitch	ton		G
tenth	decim	6	L
test, good	prob	2	L
testicle, orchid	orch		G
-th (ordinal number)	-esim	6	L
thankful, goodwill	grat	2	L
thick	pachy		G
thin, stretch	ten~tend~tens	5	L
think, mind	men~mon	4	L
third	terti	6	L
third	trit	6	G
this side of	cis-		L

Gloss	Element	Chapter	Source
thorn, spine	acanth		G
thorough, through	per-	3	L
thousand	chili	6	G
thousand	kilo-	6	G
thousand	mille	6	L
thousandth	milli-	6	L
thread, line	fil		L
threaten, projéct	men~min		L
three	tri	6	G, L
three (each)	tern	6	L
three (parts)	trich	6	G
threshold, border, shore	lim~limen~limin		L
throat	pharyng		G
through	dia-	3	G
through, across	trans-~tra-	3, 6	L
through, thorough	per-	3	L
throw, extend	bol~bl	4	G
throw, lay	jac~jec		L
thrust	trud~trus	5	L
tie	lig	10	L
tie	nect~nex		L
time	chron	1	G
time	tempor	4	L
times, fold, entwine	pl~plec~plic	6	L
tip	apec~apic		L
tip, height	acr	9	L
tissue (body)	hist	8	G
to, toward	ad-	3, 6	L
toe, finger	digit		L
together, with	con-~co-	3	L
together, with	syn-	3, 6	G
tomb, grave	taph		G
tongue	lingu		L
tongue, speech	gloss~glott	9	G
tooth	dent	11	L
tooth	odont	11	G
touch	tag~teg~tig~tang~ting	4	L
toward	ad-	3, 6	L
toward, against	ob-	3	L
tree	arbor		L

Gloss	Element	Chapter	Source
tree	dendr~dry	11	G
tribe, class, race	phyl		G
trillion	tera-		G
true	etym		G
true	ver	2	L
trust	fid		L
tumor, growth	-oma	11	G
tumor, mass	onc		G
turn (v)	trop	11	G
turn (v)	ver	9	L
turn (v)	volv		L
twenty	icosa	6	G
twenty	viginti	6	L
twin	gemin	10	L
twist, drill	torqu~tors		L
two	bi~du	6	L
two	di~dy	6	G
two (each)	bin	6	L
two (parts)	dich	6	G
under, below, partial	hypo-	4	G
under, inferior	sub-	3, 6, 7	L
unite	gam	1	G
universe, adorn, order	cosm	1	G
up, again, back	ana-	3	G
upper jaw	maxill		L
uterus	metr	10	G
v	-ize~-ise	3	G
vein	phleb	8	G
vein	ven	8	L
vertebra	spondyl		G
vessel	angi		G
vessel, blood vessel, duct	vas	8	L
view, see	scop~scep~skep		G
vinegar	acet		L
voice, call	voc	10	L
voice box	laryng	8	G
vomit	eme		G
vulva	episi		G

Gloss	Element	Chapter	Source
walk, go	ambul	5	L
wander	vag		L
wander, do wrong	err		L
war	bell	6	L
warn, beware	cau~cav		L
wash	lav		L
water	aqu		L
water	hydr~hydat	9	G
wave	und		L
wealth	plut		G
wealth, property	pecu		L
weigh, consider	libr	2	L
weigh, hang, consider	pend~pond	4	L
weight	bar~bary		G
well, good	bene~bon	9	L
wheel, run	troch		G
white	alb	9	L
white, clear	leuk~leuc		G
whole	hol		G
whole, all	tot	6	L
wide, broad	lat		L
wife	uxor	10	L
will	vol		L
wind	anem		G
wine	en~oen	11	G
wine	vin	11	L
wing	al	11	L
wing	pter	11	G
wise	soph	11	G
with, together	con-~co-	3	L
with, together	syn-	3, 6	G
within	intra-	3	L
without, not	a-~an-	3	G
woman, female	gyn~gynec	9	G
woman, female	-trix~-ix		L
womb	uter		L
womb, neurotic disorder	hyster	8	G
wood	lign	10	L
wood	xyl	11	G
word	lex	1	G

Gloss	Element	Chapter	Source
word, verb	verb		L
work	erg~urg~org	4	G
work for	serv		L
worm	helminth		G
worm	verm	11	L
worship	latri		G
worthy, fitting	dign		L
write	scrib~script		L
write	graph~gramm	10	G
year	ann~enn	4	L
yellow	xanth		G
yoke	zyg		G
young	juven~jun	10	L

Glossary

ablaut /ˈapˌlaʊt/ An Indo-European morphological pattern whereby roots change their vowel in different contexts (ch. 4, 10). [German *ab* 'away', *laut* 'sound']

ácronym An initialism where the letters are read off as spelling a word, as *scuba*. A **reverse acronym** is one where the form of the acronym is the main justification for the longer phrase, as in the *USA PATRIOT* act (ch. 3). [*acr* 'tip', *onym* 'name']

áctive The active voice indicates that the subject of the active verb (or the noun modified by an active participle) is to be construed as the doer of the action. [*ag* 'act']

adápt When a language adapts a borrowed word or element, it modifies it to conform to sounds and structures of other words and elements already in the language. [*apt* 'fit']

ádjective (A) A word that modifies (i.e., further specifies or labels) a noun. E.g., *Pat is tall; They have an old wooden fence; Jess is wiser than I am.* [*jac~jec* 'throw', 'lay']

ádverb (ADV) A word that either (1) marks the manner or direction in which a verb is performed—e.g., *Sandy slowly walked toward the door; Kim watched silently; The clouds floated away;* or (2) modifies an adjective—e.g., *I became completely frantic; That was rather nice of them;* or (3) comments on an entire sentence, usually from the speaker's perspective—e.g., *Surely Sam won't go; Julie probably went.*

áffix A morphological component that does not contain a root but is only attached to lexical components, which are referred to as the base of the affix. E.g., prefixes and suffixes are affixes. The act of attaching an affix to a word is called **affixátion** (ch. 3). [*fix* 'attach']

áffricate An oral stop produced with a slow release of airflow. Consequently the stop is followed by a fricative at the same place of articulation and with the same voicing as the stop (ch. 5). [*fric* 'rub']

Àfrikáans A language of South Africa closely related to modern Dutch (ch. 2).

airstream The flow of air through the vocal tract that is used in producing speech sounds (ch. 5).

Alfred the Great   King of West Saxons, 871–899 (ch. 2, 8).

állomorph   If two morphs are forms of the same morpheme, we say that those morphs are allomorphs of each other. This variation is known as **állomorphy** (ch. 4). [*all* 'other']

álternate   When different forms with the same function appear in different environments, they alternate with each other and are said to be **altérnatives**. [*al* 'other']

alvéolar   The **alvéoli** are the sockets the teeth are set in. Consonants produced by placing the tongue on or near the gums of the upper front alveolar ridge—the raised area behind the upper front teeth—are called alveolar consonants (ch. 5).

análogy   When a word is formed by correlating form and function with one or more other words, we say that analogy is involved. E.g., *arachnophobia* mimics the structure of previously existing phobia names. [*log* 'speak']

Anatólian   An extinct branch of Indo-European, which contained Hittite (ch. 10).

áncestor   A language X is an ancestor, or parent, of Y if X evolved into Y. E.g., Latin is the ancestor of French. [*ced~cess* 'go']

Angle   A member of the group of West-Germanic speakers who settled north of the Thames in England.

ánglicize   To make a sound or word conform more to English language patterns.

Anglo-Sáxon   A generic name for the West Germanic–speaking tribes that conquered and occupied England in the fifth century.

antícipate   When a sound changes based on the property of a sound that comes after it in a word, the change is **antícipatory**: it anticipates the following sound (ch. 6). [*ante* 'before', *cap~cip* 'take']

ápical   Sounds made with the tip (apex) of the tongue are called apical (ch. 5). [*apec~apic* 'tip']

appróximant   A sonorant consonant produced with a relatively wide opening between the oral articulators (ch. 5). [*proxim* 'near']

archaeólogy   Linguistic **archaeology** is an attempt to infer knowledge about a prehistoric language by studying the vocabulary that is shared among its attested descendant languages (ch. 10). [*arch* 'first', *log* 'study']

artículator   An organ in the vocal tract, such as the tongue or lips, that forms different speech sounds by manipulating the airflow through the vocal tract. An **upper articulator** is a place in the top part of the mouth, including the upper lip, teeth, palate and soft palate; a **lower articulator** is the lower lip or the tongue. **Articulátion** is the production of individual speech sounds. **Manner of articulation** refers to the manner and degree in which the airstream is manipulated when producing a sound. **Place of articulation** refers to the place where the airflow is most characteristically modified when a sound is made (ch. 5). [*art* 'joint']

aspirátion When the glottis is held open when pronouncing a consonant, a puff of air known as aspiration can be heard after the consonant. Such consonants are described as being **áspiràted** (ch. 5). [*spir* 'breathe']

assimilátion If sound X becomes more similar to sound Y, we say that X **assímilates** to Y. If X changes its place of articulation to agree with that of Y, it undergoes **place assimilation**; if it changes its phonation, it is **phonation assimilation**; if it becomes a liquid, it is **liquid assimilation**. If X becomes indistinguishable from Y, the process is a **total assimilation**; otherwise it is **partial assimilation** (ch. 6). [*simil* 'like']

associátion A mental connection made between two or more concepts that seem to be related in some sense, such as by metaphor or metonymy. [*soci* 'companion']

attésted A language is attested if it is presently spoken or if we have found writing in that language. Specific words and word elements are also said to be attested if they have been heard or if they have been found in written texts. [*test* 'witness']

augméntative An augmentative affix has the basic function of making a word that represents something larger than the original word represents. [*aug* 'increase']

back A back vowel is produced when the tongue is drawn back into the mouth (ch. 5).

báck-formation Reversing imputed derivational processes to make a simpler word that did not actually exist previously. E.g., by assuming that *back-formation* had been formed by adding *-ation* to a theoretical ×*back-form*, we can reverse that process to back-form a new word *back-form*.

báckronym A reverse acronym. [blend of *back* and *acronym*]

Báltic The group of Indo-European languages that contains Lithuanian and Latvian (ch. 10).

Balto-Slávic The branch of Indo-European that comprises the Baltic and Slavic languages (ch. 10).

base A lexical component to which affixes are attached. ['bottom']

bilábial A sound produced by bringing the two lips together is called bilabial (ch. 5). [*bi* 'two', *lab* 'lip']

blade The blade of the tongue is its flexible front part.

blend   A new word formed by combining parts of other words; e.g., *motel* from *motor* and *hotel.*

borrow   A language is said to borrow a word or word element when it copies or adapts it from another language. When a language borrows a word, it is under no obligation to pay it back (ch. 2).

bound   A bound morph is one that cannot appear as an independent word (ch. 3).

branch   A set of related languages smaller than a family. English belongs to the Germanic branch of Indo-European (ch. 2).

breathy /ˈbrɛθi/ **voice**   A type of phonation produced when the vocal cords are vibrated even though they are held relatively far apart (ch. 5).

cárdinal numbers   These tell how many of an object you are referring to; e.g., *three.* [*cardin* 'hinge']

case   A grammatical category that marks a noun, pronoun, or adjective as fulfilling a certain type of role in a sentence. E.g., *he* is in the nominative case because it can be used as subject of a verb, *him* is in the accusative case because it can be used as an object of a verb, and *his* is in the genitive because it limits another noun. [*cad~cas* 'fall']

Céltic (traditionally pronounced with initial /s/, now often with /k/)   The branch of Indo-European to which belong Welsh, Irish, Scots Gaelic, and other languages (ch. 2, 10).

céntral   A central vowel is pronounced with the tongue somewhat retracted, but not as far as for a back vowel (ch. 5). [*centr*]

chain shift   A series of sound changes of the form X > Y and Y > Z. The continued existence of Y indicates that the change X > Y couldn't have been completed before the change Y > Z began (ch. 10).

clássical   Classical languages are the language forms used when ancient Latin and Greek literature flourished. The classical Latin period was approximately the three centuries leading to AD 200; classical Greek was the dialect used in Athens from about 500 to 300 BC. Modern loans from Latin and Greek are almost always based on the form the word elements had in the classical period of the respective language.

clip   To clip a word is to shorten it without regard to morph boundaries. E.g., *info* is a clipping of *information* (ch. 3).

closed   A closed syllable is a syllable that ends in a consonant.

cluster   A sequence of two or more consonants.

cógnate Words and word elements are cognate if they descend from the same word in the common ancestor language (ch. 10). [*con-* 'with', *gna* 'birth']

coin To coin a word is to create it.

coloring When consonants affect the quality of vowels, the effect is called **vowel coloring**. **/l/-Coloring** takes place when an /l/ affects the preceding vowel (ch. 6).

common noun A noun that refers to a class of objects and not just to a single individual.

compárative A comparative adjective—also called an adjective in the comparative degree—is one that describe people or things that have more of a certain quality than does another. In English it ends in *-er*, as in *bigger*. [*par* 'equal']

compárative method A technique for discovering what languages are related to each other and what their prehistoric ancestor languages sounded like. The technique relies heavily on the analysis of sound correspondences.

compléx A complex word is a word built from two or more morphs (ch. 3). [*plec* 'tangle']

cómpound A compound word is a complex word formed from two or more stems and therefore containing two or more roots; e.g., *blackbird* or *White House* (ch. 3).

connotátion Secondary associations of a word, including style, mood, and familiarity (ch. 1). [*not* 'mark']

cónsonant A speech sound made with significant narrowing or obstruction in the vocal tract (ch. 5). [*son* 'sound']

constítuent A part of a larger entity. Complex words have two or more morphological constituents (ch. 3). [*sta~sti* 'stand']

convérsion When a word is used as a different part of speech than it originally was used as, the change is known as conversion or zero derivation. E.g., *butter* is basically a noun, but by conversion it is used as a verb in *Don't butter that toast*. [*ver* 'turn']

coronalizátion Moving velar sounds forward in the mouth, especially when conditioned by nearby front vowels. E.g., pronouncing Latin *cent*, which originally had /k/, with initial /s/ instead is a coronalization (ch. 11). [*coron* 'crown']

correspónd When sounds in related languages descend from the same sound in a common ancestor language, they are said to correspond to each other, or to form a **recurrent sound correspóndence**. Documenting recurrent sound correspondences is a scientific way to prove that languages are related and to reconstruct the common ancestor language (ch. 10). [*spond* 'promise']

Cýmric   Another name for Welsh. The name Cymric is closer to the native word *Cymraeg*, and therefore, like it, is now usually pronounced with initial /k/.

degree   In English and many other languages, adjectives and adverbs are inflected when they are used in comparison of degree. E.g., *bigger* is the comparative degree of *big*, and *biggest* is the superlative degree.

deléte   When a rule results in the complete loss of a sound, that sound is said to be deleted, and the phonological process is called **delétion**. In the phrases **vowel deletion**, /s/ **deletion**, and **stop deletion**, the qualifier tells what kind of sound is deleted (ch. 6).

denotátion   The basic meaning of a word (ch. 1). [*not* 'mark']

déntal   A consonant produced with the tongue against the teeth is called dental (ch. 5). [*dent* 'tooth']

deríve   A **derivátional** affix is an affix that turns one lexeme into another; e.g., *un-* or *-less*. A word with a derivational affix is said to be derived from the simpler word. The process of deriving one word from another is called **derivátion** (ch. 3). [*de* 'from', *riv* 'stream']

descénd   Language A has descended from language B if B evolved into A. A is called a descendant of B (ch. 2). [*de-* 'from', *scand~scend* 'climb']

diachrónic   Diachronic linguistics is the study of how language changes. [*dia* 'through', *chron* 'time']

diacrític   Marks added to letters to express nuances of pronunciation. [*cri* 'separate']

díalect   A form of a language associated with a particular geographical region (ch. 8). [*leg* 'speak']

dígraph   Two letters used together to represent one sound. [*di* 'two', *graph* 'write']

dimínutive   Small. A diminutive affix has the basic function of naming something that is smaller than that named by the original word. Often, however, a diminutive form simply expresses affection, familiarity, or some even vaguer notion suggested by smallness. [*min* 'little']

díphthong   (the *ph* is traditionally pronounced /f/, but /p/ is often heard)   When two vowels are pronounced in succession in the same syllable, the result is a diphthong (ch. 5). A **diphthongizátion** is a sound change that turns a simple vowel into a diphthong (ch. 11). [*di* 'two', *phthong* 'sound']

distríbutive numbers   Used in Latin to answer the question "how many each?"; e.g., *terni* 'three each'. [*trib* 'tribe', 'give']

divérge   A language diverges into two or more different languages when changes are localized and do not spread through the entire language community. [*ver~verg* 'turn']

dórsal   Sounds made with the back of the tongue are called dorsal (ch. 5). [*dors* 'back']

double letter   A letter that appears twice in a row in the same word, especially if the sequence represents a single sound, as in *book* and *letter*.

doublet   A pair of words in the same language that differ because of different paths of descent are called doublets. Usually borrowing is involved (ch. 4).

dúal   A grammatical category used in Proto-Indo-European when referring to objects that were two in number (ch. 10). [*du* 'two']

East Germánic   An extinct group of Germanic languages that included Gothic.

élement   A word element is a morphological constituent that is used to build words. A word element may be a single morph or a sequence of morphs.

ellípsis   Omitting one or more words from a longer expression (ch. 7). [*lip* 'leave']

empty   A morph with no discernible meaning or function may be referred to as an empty morph.

ending   An inflectional suffix, such as *-ed* or *-s* in English.

endocéntric   A compound word is endocentric if one of its components names the word's hypernym. E.g., *bookbag* is endocentric because a bookbag is a type of *bag* (ch. 3). [*endo-* 'inside', *centr*]

envíronment   The environment of a sound is the other sounds that may influence its pronunciation. Normally the most salient environment is sounds that occur in fairly close proximity in the same word (ch. 6).

epénthesis   Inserting a sound to a word when it has only a phonetic justification, as the *p* in *redemptive* (ch. 6). [*the* 'put']

etymólogy   The history of a word. Etymologists are linguists who study the histories of individual words. [*etym* 'true', *leg~log* 'speak', 'word']

éuphemism   Referring to a concept by a new or less straightforward term in order to avoid unpleasant connotation (ch. 7). [*eu* 'good', *phe* 'speak']

exocéntric   A compound word is exocentric if none of its components names the word's hypernym. E.g., *killjoy* is exocentric because a killjoy is neither a type of killing nor a type of joy (ch. 3). [*exo-* 'outside', *centr*]

exténsion   An element that is added at the end of a morph. Originally a separate suffix, the element now simply makes a new, **extended**, morph. E.g., *corpor* is an extended allomorph of *corp*. [*ten~tens* 'stretch']

extérnal   When a change occurs in a language due to sociohistorical forces that are not themselves linguistic, such as migration, one speaks of external causes of language change (ch. 8). [*exter* 'outside']

extínct   A language is extinct if it is no longer spoken. [*stingu* 'quench']

fámily   A language together with all the other languages that are related to it constitute a language family. English belongs to the Indo-European family.

Finnish   A national language of Finland. It is not an Indo-European language, but **Finno-Ugric**, related to Hungarian.

folk etymólogy   A morphological reanalysis that leads to a new word. E.g., *pea* by reanalyzing *pease* /piz/ as having a plural ending (ch. 3).

Frank   A member of the tribes that conquered much of what is today France, lending their name and a substantial amount of their West Germanic vocabulary to the Romance language spoken in that region.

free   A free morph is one that can appear as an independent word (ch. 3).

fricative   An obstruent consonant produced by forcing air to pass through the mouth through a narrow opening, creating a rasping sound (ch 5). [*fric* 'rub']

Frísian   A group of West Germanic languages spoken on the coasts of Germany and the Netherlands. These languages are very closely related to English (ch. 2).

front   A front vowel is one made with the body of the tongue not retracted toward the back of the mouth (ch. 5).

gender   An inflectional category used in Latin or Greek to show agreement between adjectives and nouns, among other things. Each noun had one of three genders—masculine, feminine, or neuter—and any adjective that modified that noun would inflect to match that gender.

generalizátion   Using a word to refer to a broader concept that properly includes its former range of usage. Also called *widening* (ch. 7).

genétic   Languages are genetically related to each other if they descend from a common ancestor (ch. 2). [*gen* 'birth']

génitive   A case used especially to show possession; e.g., *his, book's*. [*gen* 'birth']

Gérman This word usually refers to the standard language of Germany, which is a West Germanic language closely related to Yiddish. It may also refer more loosely to related languages, such as Low German.

Germánic The branch of Indo-European to which English belongs. It consists of East, North, and West Germanic languages (ch. 2, 10).

gerúndive A participle in Latin that denotes that something ought to be done; e.g., *agenda* (ch. 9). [*ges~ger* 'do']

glide A sound similar to a vowel, but pronounced very quickly and used in contexts where one would expect a consonant; e.g., /j/, and /w/.

gloss A brief definition of a word. ['tongue']

glóttis The hole in the larynx through which air can pass through, past the vocal cords. Sounds whose primary articulation is at the glottis are called **glóttal** sounds (ch. 5). [*glott* 'tongue']

Gothic An extinct East Germanic language.

grade In Indo-European morphology, the ablaut grade indicates what vowel the element had in Proto-Indo-European: *e*, *o*, or zero (ch. 4). [*grad* 'step']

grammátical fúnction The role a word or phrase plays in the larger clause or sentence; e.g., the subject or direct object of a verb.

Great Vowel Shift A change in the pronunciation of the long vowels of English, which happened in the centuries around 1500. Most long vowels were raised, but the high vowels became diphthongs.

Grimm's law A statement of how obstruent consonants in the Germanic languages correspond to consonants in other Indo-European languages (ch. 10).

head When a word is formed from multiple constituents, the constituent that most strongly determines the property of the word is known as the head. The grammatical head determines how the word can be used in the sentence and what further affixes can be added to the word (ch. 3).

Hellénic The branch of Indo-European that consists of the Greek language (ch. 10).

high A high vowel is produced when the tongue is raised close to the roof of the mouth (ch. 5).

histórical linguístics The branch of linguistics that studies language change.

homeland The homeland of a language family is the region where the common ancestral protolanguage was spoken (ch. 2, 10).

hómograph Two words or elements are homographs if they are spelled the same way. [*homo-* 'same', *graph* 'write']

hómonym Words that are unrelated in origin and meaning but have the same form are called homonyms and are said to be **homónymous** and exhibit **homónymy**; e.g., *ring* 'circular band' and *ring* 'bell sound' (ch. 7). [*homo-* 'same', *onym* 'name']

Hungárian The national language of Hungary. It is not an Indo-European language but Finno-Ugric, related to Finnish.

hýpernym A word that names something more general than the corresponding hyponym. E.g., *bag* is a hypernym of *bookbag* (ch. 3). [*hyper-* 'over', *onym* 'name']

hýponym A word that names something more specific than the corresponding hypernym. E.g., *bookbag* is a hyponym of *bag* (ch. 3). [*hypo-* 'under', *onym* 'name']

illégal A form that would violate the rules of a language's grammar is called illegal. [*in~il* 'not', *leg* 'law']

Índic A group of languages that contains Sanskrit and its many modern descendants such as Hindi, Bengali, and Urdu (ch. 10).

indícative Verbs that express simple statements or questions are generally inflected with what is called indicative mood. E.g., *The children are playing* is in the indicative mood. [*in* 'in', *dic* 'point']

Indo-Európean The language family to which belong English, French, Latin, Greek, and dozens of other languages (ch. 2, 10).

Indo-Iránian A branch of Indo-European, which contains the Indic and Iranian languages (ch. 10).

ínfix An affix that is inserted inside its base. Proto-Indo-European and several of its daughter languages have a nasal infix (ch. 5, 10). [*in* 'in', *fix* 'attach']

infléction A modification of a word to show some grammatical function such as number, degree, tense, person, and case. This modification is often accomplished through **infléctional affixes**, which in English and Latin are almost always suffixes (**inflectional endings**). Words undergoing inflection are said to **infléct** for the grammatical function in question, or to be **inflécted**. [*in* 'in', *flect* 'bend']

inhérit A language inherits a word from an ancestral language the word is passed down from speaker to speaker from that language.

inítialism A word form from the initial letters of a phrase, such as *CIA* from *Central Intelligence Agency* (ch. 3). [*in* 'in', *i* 'go']

innovátion   A linguistic change. [*in* 'in', *nov* 'new']

insért   When a sound is added to a word by a phonological process, it is said to be inserted, and the process is called an **insértion** or epenthesis. In phrases like **Vowel Insertion, /d/ Insertion,** and **/s/ Insertion** the qualifier tells what kind of sound is inserted (ch. 6). [*in* 'in', *ser* 'join']

ínterfix   An affix that is only attached between two other morphological consituents, as the *i* in *pedicure*. [*inter* 'between', *fix* 'attach']

intérnal   When the only explanation for language change is in terms of language structure itself, one speaks of internal causes of change (ch. 8). [*inter* 'inside']

Internátional System of Units (SI)   A modern, internationally standardized form of the metric system.

intránsitive   A verb that does not take a direct object; e.g., *dine*. [*in* 'not', *trans* 'across', *i* 'go']

Iránian   A group of Indo-European languages that contains Farsi and Pashto (ch. 10).

irrégular   A word whose form cannot be predicted from the ordinary rules of the language is said to be irregular. [*in~ir* 'not', *reg* 'rule']

Itálic   The branch of Indo-European to which belong Latin and all the Romance languages (ch. 2, 10).

Jones, Sir William   Person noted for the hypothesis of the Indo-European language family (ch. 10).

Kent   A member of the group of West Germanic speakers who settled in the southeast of England.

kurgán   A grave with a mound. This word is also used to describe the possibly Indo-European culture that used this interment technique approximately 6,000 years ago (ch. 10).

lábial   A speech sound produced at the lips is called labial (ch. 5). [*lab* 'lip']

labiodéntal   A consonant produced by bringing the lower lip to the upper teeth is called labiodental (ch. 5). [*lab* 'lip', *dent* 'tooth']

labiovélar   A sound produced with the back of the tongue raised toward the soft palate and the lips rounded (ch. 5). [*lab* 'lip', *vel* 'veil']

láminal   Sounds made with the blade of the tongue are called laminal (ch. 5). [*lamin* 'blade']

larýngeals   Proto-Indo-European sounds of uncertain phonetic value. Some of them colored adjacent vowels, and all of them lengthened preceding vowels when they were deleted from the end of a syllable (ch. 10). [*laryng* 'larynx']

lárynx   The Adam's apple, or voicebox (ch. 5).

láteral   A sound made in such a way that air flows around the sides of the tongue is called lateral (ch. 5). [*later* 'side']

Látin   The Italic language that originated as the language of Rome and environs, then spread throughout Europe with the Roman Empire. The classical language was the basis for an international (or pan-European) scholarly language that was used up to modern times.

Latin Vowel Weakening   A set of rules that change short vowels in noninitial syllables (ch. 6).

Látinate   A word borrowed from Latin, whether directly or indirectly, is called Latinate (ch. 2).

lax   Vowels produced with slightly less lingual effort than tense vowels are called lax (ch. 5).

learnèd   Words borrowed by scholars are known as learned borrowings. Learned borrowings from Latin and Greek agree closely in spelling to the classical Latin and Greek forms (ch. 11).

léxeme   Words, abstracting away from inflection. E.g., *throw, throws, threw, thrown*, and *throwing* are all considered forms of the same lexeme. [*leg~lex* 'speak', 'word']

léxical   Having to do with individual words. More narrowly, a lexical morphologiocal component is one that provides a meaning. A lexical morph or morpheme is a root. [*leg~lex* 'speak', 'word']

lexicógrapher   A person who writes dictionaries. [*leg~lex* 'speak', 'word', *graph* 'write']

línguist   A scientist who studies language. [*lingu* 'tongue']

líquid   An approximant like /r/ and /l/.

long   A phone whose duration lasts longer than other phones is considered to be long.

low   A low vowel is produced when the tongue, and usually the jaw, are lowered (ch. 5).

Low German   German language varieties spoken in northern Germany.

Lower Sáxony   A state in northwestern Germany. Most of the Germanic settlers of England probably came from in or near this region.

mácron   The diacritic ‾ placed over a vowel to indicate that it is long. [*macr* 'large']

másculine   One of three genders a noun can have in Latin and Greek. The masculine is traditionally considered the default gender, so that adjectives (which inflect to match the gender of the noun they modify) are usually cited in the masculine gender [*mascul* 'male'].

meliorátion   A change in the meaning of a word to have a more positive denotation or connotation (ch. 7). [*melior* 'better']

merger   A morphemic merger occurs when word elements that could formerly be analyzed as a sequence of morphs come to be treated as a single morph. E.g., *anim* was originally a root *an* 'breathe' plus a noun suffix, but the two have merged to form a single morph.

métaphor   Using a word to refer to something that is similar in some way to the thing the word represents previously or more basically; e.g., *horse* for a sawhorse. The **spatial metaphor** uses morphemes that basically represent spatial relations to represent more abstract concepts that are felt to be somehow similar to those spatial relations (ch. 7). [*meta* 'beyond', *pher~phor* 'carry']

metónymy   Using a word to represent something that is associated with the thing more basically named by that word. In current usage the term also includes what has traditionally been called synecdoche. However, metonymy excludes association based on resemblance, which is called metaphor (ch. 7). [*onym* 'name']

mid   A mid vowel is produced when the tongue is neither raised nor lowered from a neutral position (ch. 5).

Middle   When languages have a relatively long literary tradition, that tradition is conventionally divided into three periods, of which the second is labeled *middle*. The Middle English period was 1100–1500; Middle French, 1300–1500.

Módern   When living languages have a relatively long literary tradition, that tradition is conventionally divided into three periods, of which the current is called *modern*. The Modern English and Modern French periods began in 1500.

monolíngual   Something is monolingual if it consists of only one language. [*mon* 'one', *lingu* 'tongue']

morph   The smallest unit of meaning or function in word construction (ch. 3). ['shape']

mórpheme   The set of morphs that have the same meaning or function but some differences in pronunciation depending on the other elements in the word. E.g., the plural morpheme *s* comprises the morphs /s/, /z/, and /əz/ (ch. 4).

morphólogy   The systematic study of word structure. Complex words are built up from two or more morphological components. Morphological analysis, or parsing, seeks to reveal the structure of words in terms of their components. A **morphólogist** is a linguist who studies morphology (ch. 3). [*morph* 'shape', *leg~log* 'speak', 'study']

narrowing   Restricting the meaning of a word to a subset of what it formerly represented. Also called *specialization* (ch. 7).

násal   Sounds made with air passing through the nose are known as nasal sounds (ch. 5). [*nas* 'nose']

násal ínfix   A nasal consonant that is added as an affix inside a root; e.g., *n* in *tangible* (ch. 4, 6, 10).

nátive   Words and elements that are not borrowed from another language are called native. [*gen~na* 'birth']

neólogism   A newly created word. [*ne* 'new', *log* 'speak']

nóminative   The case used to mark nouns, pronouns, and adjectives when they are used as subjects of verbs, or cited by themselves out of context. E.g., *he* in English. [*nomen~nomin* 'name']

Nórman   Normans were French-speaking descendants of Vikings who lived in Normandy. Their successful invasion of England in 1066 is called the Norman Conquest.

Norse   The ancestor of the North Germanic languages. Viking Norse is the stage spoken by the Vikings who settled in the English Danelaw; Old Norse is the later literary language.

North Germánic   A branch of Germanic that includes Norse, Icelandic, Norwegian, Swedish, and Danish.

noun (N)   A word that labels an actual or abstract thing that may act as subject or object of a verb. E.g., *That **dog** is barking again; Only **Leigh's pride** was injured; **Running** is supposed to be good **exercise**.*

number   A grammatical category classifying how many objects are comprised by a noun. In English and many other languages nouns inflect depending on whether they refer to one item (singular number) or more than one (plural number).

óbstruent A consonant whose production entails substantial obstruction of airflow: an oral stop, affricate, or fricative (ch. 5). [*ob* 'against', *stru* 'pile up']

Old When languages have a relatively long literary tradition, that tradition is conventionally divided into three periods, of which the first is labeled *old*. The Old English period was 700–1100; Old French, 1000–1300; Old Norse, 1100–1350. Many people also lump in earlier, minimally attested forms of the language under the same label.

onomatopóeia The word-formation process whereby a word is intended to mimic some natural sound; e.g., *creak*. [*onom~onomat* 'name', *poei* 'make']

óral Sounds are those produced with the nasal cavity sealed off by the velum, so that the air stream passes entirely through the mouth (ch. 5). [*os~or* 'mouth']

órdinal numbers These identify which position a referent holds in a series; e.g., *third*. [*ordin* 'order']

orthógraphy The standard, conventional spelling. [*orth* 'straight', 'correct', *graph* 'write']

pálate The hard palate is the bony part of the roof of your mouth. The soft palate, or velum, is the soft part behind it. When people use the unqualified word palate, or the adjective **pálatal**, the hard palate is meant (ch. 5). **Pàlatalizátion** refers to many different sound changes that bring the tongue closer to the hard palate or beyond; see also *coronalization* (ch. 11).

párent Language X is a parent, or ancestor, of Y if X evolved into Y. E.g., Latin is the parent of French (ch. 2). [*par* 'give birth to']

parse When you parse a word, you analyze it in terms of its component morphemes. E.g., *blackbirds* can be parsed into *blackbird* plus *s*, and *blackbird* itself parses into *black* plus *bird*.

párticiple A verb that is used as an adjective to modify a noun. E.g., *fall* is used as in **present participle** form in *Watch out for falling rocks*. In Latin loanwords participles not infrequently can also be nouns. **Present participles** tend to have active meaning, and **perfect participles** have passive meaning or describe a state (ch. 9). [*part, cap~cip* 'take']

pássive The passive voice indicates that the subject of the passive verb (or the noun modified by a passive participle) is to be construed as the object upon which the action is done. E.g., *The piñata was struck by the children*. [*pat, pass* 'suffer']

pejorátion A shift in the meaning of a word to have a more negative denotation or connotation (ch. 7). [*pejor* 'worse']

person A grammatical category referring to whether the speaker is referring to self (first person), the addressee (second person), or something or someone else (third person).

In English and several other languages, the verb may change its inflection depending on which person the subject of the verb has.

phonátion   The type of vibration made by the vocal cords when a sound is produced (ch. 5). [*phon* 'sound']

phonétics   The sounds of language, or their systematic study (ch. 5). [*phon* 'sound']

phonólogy   The way sounds function in language, or the systematic study of the functioning of sounds. [*phon* 'sound', *log* 'study']

plúral   A value of the grammatical category of number, used when referring to more than one object; e.g., *books* is the plural of *book*. [*plur* 'many']

pólysemy   A word or morpheme that has multiple meanings is called **polysémous** and is said to exhibit polysemy (ch. 7). [*poly* 'many', *sem* 'meaning']

pópular   Words that are inherited from the ancestor language in the normal way, without interference from scholars who want to maintain or restore classical spelling and pronunciation, are referred to as popular vocabulary. Popular Romance words are often very much different from the classical Latin form; e.g., popular French *chef* as opposed to classical *capit-* 'head'. A somewhat different use of the word *popular* is to refer to a variety of language that is highly colloquial and not strongly influenced by high literary style; e.g., **popular Latin** (ch. 11).

postalvéolar   Sounds produced by raising the blade of the tongue to an intermediate position between the alveolar ridge and the palate are called postalveolar (ch. 5). [*post-* 'after', *alveol*]

préfix   An affix that is attached before its base. [*pre-* 'before', *fix* 'attach']

Prehistóric English   English in its formative period before the development of substantial writing, ca. 400–700.

preposítion (PREP)   A word that marks a spatial relationship, usually with regard to something labeled by a noun. E.g., *The key is on the table; She stood in the box; It came to a conclusion.* [*pre-* 'before', *pos* 'place']

prescríptive   A prescriptive approach to language tells people how they ought to speak, rather than describing how they do speak (ch. 8). [*pre-* 'before', *scrib~scrip* 'write']

prívative   A privative affix negates the meaning of the base to which it is attached. [*priv* 'alone']

próper noun   A noun that is used to refer to a particular individual. In English proper nouns are capitalized. E.g., *Jim* and *Nevada* are proper nouns. [*propri* 'one's own']

Proto-*X*   The reconstructed language that is the ancestor of all languages of family or branch *X*. E.g., Proto-Germanic is the ancestor of all Germanic languages, and

Proto-Indo-European (PIE) is the ancestor of all the Indo-European languages (ch. 2). [*prot* 'first']

reanálysis   Giving a historically incorrect analysis to a linguistic construction, such as taking *uproar* to be a compound of *up* plus *roar* 'make a loud noise' (ch. 3). [*re-* 'again', *ana* 'thoroughly', *ly* 'loosen']

reconstrúct   When you reconstruct a protolanguage, you infer what it sounded like based on evidence from attested languages that descended from it (ch. 2, 10). [*re-* 'back', *stru* 'pile up']

recúrsion   When a rule can take its own output as input, the rule is called recursive, and the process is described as recursion. E.g., a prefix can attach to a base, forming a base to which a prefix can be added: *post-post-modern* (ch. 3). [*re-* 'again', *curs* 'run']

régular   A form is regular if it can be predicted by the rules of the language. [*reg* 'rule']

reláted   Languages are related to each other if they diverged from the same ancestral language (ch. 2). [*lat* 'carry']

repair   If certain linguistic rules or historical circumstances would produce a word that violates other rules of the language, the word may be changed to conform to those other rules. Such a change is called a repair (ch. 4).

rhótacism   The change of /s/ to /r/ (ch. 6). [*rho*, the name of the Greek letter for the sound /r/]

Romance   Languages that descended from Latin are called Romance languages. They include Italian, French, Spanish, Portuguese, and Romanian, among other languages.

rómanize   When a language that is normally written in a different script, such as Greek, is written in Latin letters, it is said to be romanized.

root   A lexical morph or morpheme (ch. 3).

round   When we say that a speech sound is round, or rounded, we mean that the lips are at least partially rounded, or pursed. **Rounding** is the state of being rounded (ch. 5).

runes   A variant of the Latin alphabet formerly used for carving inscriptions in Germanic languages.

Sánskrit   An ancient Indo-European language that served as the classical language of India and the ecclesiastical language of Hinduism (ch. 10).

Sáxon   A member of the Germanic-speaking peoples who settled in England south of the Thames.

schwa /ʃwa/   A mid central vowel, /ə/ (ch. 5). [Hebrew]

scientífic notation   A method of representing numbers as a number from 0 to 10 multiplied by a power of ten expressed as an exponent; e.g., 35,000,000 is 3.5×10^7. [*sci* 'know', *not* 'mark']

semántics   Meaning, or the systematic study of how language expresses meaning. **Semantic change** is change in the meaning of a word. [*sem* 'meaning']

short   A speech sound that is not held for the same length of time as a long sound. **Consonant Shortening** is a rule that makes long consonants short (ch. 6).

sílent *e*   An *e* found at the end of many English words. It rarely corresponds to an *e* in the classical languages but is introduced in English to indicate how other letters in the word are to be pronounced.

símplex   A simplex word or morphological component has no internal structure but consists of only one morpheme. [*sim* 'one', *plec* 'fold']

simplificátion   A reduction in complexity. **Cluster Simplification** reduces the number of consonants in a cluster (ch. 6).

síngular   A value of the grammatical category of number, used when referring to a single object. [*sim* 'one']

Slávic   A group of Indo-European languages that contains Russian, Polish, Serbian, and several other languages (ch. 10).

sociolinguístics   The study of social factors in language variation and change. [*soci* 'companion', *lingu* 'tongue']

sónorant   A sound that permits relatively unobstructed flow of air through the vocal tract (ch. 5). [*son* 'sound']

sound sýmbolism   The unusual situation in which a sound bears some natural connection to the object it names; e.g., *teeny* (ch. 3). [*syn-~sym-* 'with', *bol* 'throw']

specializátion   Using a word to represent only a subset of what it formerly applied to. Also called *narrowing* (ch. 7). [*spec* 'look']

split   A morph split occurs when a single morph turns into two or more different morphs over time, which usually end up functioning as allomorphs of the same morpheme (ch. 4).

standard   A set of linguistic norms accepted by a social group (ch. 8).

stem   A lexical base to which an inflectional affix may be attached. E.g., *book-* and *booklet-* are both stems to which the inflectional affix *-s* may be attached (ch. 3).

stop A sound whose production entails the a complete stopping of the airflow through the mouth. If the airflow is blocked entirely, an **oral stop** is produced; if air escapes through the nose, a **nasal stop** is produced (ch. 5).

strong In Germanic languages, a strong verb is one that forms its past tense and past participle by changing the vowel rather than by adding a suffix; e.g., *sing, sang, sung.*

súbject The part of the sentence that typically names the doer of the action. In English, it almost always precedes the main verb, with which it agrees in number: *He plays music; They play music.* [*jac~jec* 'throw', 'place']

súffix An affix that is attached after its base. E.g., the derivational affix *-less* and the ending *-ing* are affixes. The act of attaching a suffix is called **suffixátion**. [*sub* 'under', *fix* 'attach']

súperfix A morph that operates not by adding more sounds to a word but by changing some more abstract property like stress. E.g., the difference between the noun *cóntract* and the verb *contráct* can be attributed to a superfix (ch. 3). [*super-* 'above', *fix* 'attach']

supérlative The superlative degree of an adjective or adverb is used to indicate the highest degree of the quality named by the modifier; e.g., *biggest* is the superlative of *big.* [*super-* 'above', *lat* 'carry']

supplétion The use of different roots in different inflected forms of the same lexeme. E.g., the comparative of *good* is **supplétive** because it is made by adding *-er* to the unrelated root *bett.* [*ple* 'full']

syllábic consonants Consonants that can be used as the core of a syllable, in place of a vowel (ch. 10).

sýnonym. Words are synonyms of each other if they have nearly the same meaning. [*syn-* 'with', *onym* 'name']

tense (1) An inflectional category of verbs that indicates the relative time an event took place, such as the present or the past. (2) A vowel produced with slightly more lingual effort than another is called a tense vowel; that phonetic property is called **tenseness** (ch. 5).

Tochárian An extinct Indo-European language of Western China that constitutes its own branch of that language family (ch. 10).

Tower of Babel (traditionally /ˈbebļ/, now often /ˈbæbļ/) A narrative in the Hebrew Bible (Genesis 11:4–9) that states that people attempted to build a tower to reach heaven. In punishment, God changed the language of each of its builders so that they could no longer understand each other.

tránsitive A verb that takes a direct object; e.g., *I broke the vase.* [*trans* 'across', *i* 'go']

umlaut /ˈumˌlaʊt / A phonological rule that makes back vowels like /u/ be pronounced further front in the mouth, like /i/. Historically, this was caused by a front vowel or glide later in the word. [German *um* 'around', *laut* 'sound']

unattésted If a word or element is unattested, we know of no written document containing the word. [*test* 'witness']

ungrammátical A word or phrase is ungrammatical if people would not say such a thing in ordinary speech. E.g., ×*killedjoy* would be an ungrammatical type of compound word. [*graph~gramm* 'write']

úvula The part of the soft palate that dangles at the back of your mouth. Sounds made there are called **úvular** (ch 5). [*uv* 'grape']

váriant One of multiple linguistic elements that can have the same meaning or function.

vélar Sounds made at the soft palate, or **velum**, are called velar (ch. 5). [*vel* 'veil']

verb (v) A word that details activity, process or state of being or becoming in a construction with a subject or object noun. E.g., *Tony **slapped** the wall; Jan **wears** running shoes every day; On Monday I **learned** how sick she **was**.*

Viking Norse The North Germanic language spoken by the Vikings who conquered and settled in the east of England. In Scandinavia, Viking Norse developed into literary Old Norse and further into Icelandic, Norwegian, Swedish, and Danish (ch. 2).

vócal cords (or vocal folds) Membranes that are capable of closing the glottis. They can also vibrate many times a second, creating the characteristic buzzing known as voice (ch. 5). [*voc* 'voice']

vócal tract The part of the mouth and nasal cavities above the larynx that is used to produce different speech sounds (ch. 5). [*trah~trac* 'pull']

voice A type of phonation in which the vocal folds are held close together and vibrate rapidly, producing a buzzing sound (ch. 5).

vowel A sound made with air passing through a relatively unobstructed mouth (ch. 5).

vúlgar Vulgar Latin is another word for popular Latin. Vulgar Latin was spoken at the same time as classical Latin, but it had many differences in pronunciation, grammar, and vocabulary (ch. 11). [*vulg* 'common folk']

weaken Latin Vowel Weakening is a sound change whereby vowels become higher, and therefore less sonorous, in less prominent positions in the word (ch. 6).

West Germánic   A branch of Germanic that includes English, Dutch, Frisian, German, and Yiddish (ch. 2).

widening   Using a word to refer to a broader concept that properly includes its former ranger of usage. Also called *generalization* (ch. 7).

word   A morphological construct that can be moved about relatively freely and independently within a sentence. The word *word* sometimes is used to refer to lexemes (q.v.) and sometimes to **word forms**. When we speak of word forms we take account of inflections; thus *throw* and *thrown* are considered two separate word forms (ch. 3).

Yíddish   A West Germanic language spoken originally by Jews in Central Europe. It is closely related to German.

zero   When no audible or visible element appears where one is logically expected by analogy with other forms, one may speak of a zero element. E.g., one may speak of forming the plural of *sheep* by adding a zero plural ending, or of converting the noun *butter* to a verb by zero derivation. Often represented by the symbol ∅.

Further Reading and Research Tools

Sources of Information on Complex Morphology and Vocabulary

The word elements assigned in each chapter may be supplemented by others found in appendix 1. The following elaborated dictionaries of morphemes may also be useful for reference to morphemes not found in the glossary.

Borror, Donald J. *Dictionary of Word Roots and Combining Forms, Compiled from the Greek, Latin and Other Languages, with Special Reference to Biological and Scientific Terms.* Palo Alto, Calif.: Mayfield Publishing Co., 1960.

Hogben, Lancelot. *The Vocabulary of Science.* New York: Stein and Day, 1969.

Smith, Robert W. L. *Dictionary of English Word-Roots: English–Roots and Roots–English, with Examples and Exercises.* Totowa, N.J.: Littlefield, Adams, 1966.

Other works on specific categories of English word elements include the following:

Prefixes and Other Word-Initial Elements of English. Detroit, Mich.: Gale Research, 1984.

Suffixes and Other Word-Final Elements of English. Detroit, Mich.: Gale Research, 1982.

Urdang, Laurence, ed. *-Ologies and -Isms.* 3rd ed. Detroit, Mich: Gale Research, 1986.

Lists of English words from Latin, Greek, and other sources can be found in the following works:

Mawson, C. O. Sylvester. 3rd ed., rev. and ed. by Eugene Ehrlich. *The Harper Dictionary of Foreign Terms.* New York: Harper & Row, 1987.

Urdang, Laurence, and Frank R. Abate, eds. *Dictionary of Borrowed Words.* New York: Wynwood Press, 1991.

In addition to the books listed, there exist numerous useful specialized dictionaries, glossaries, and encyclopedias that treat vocabulary and serve as guides to the nomenclature and terminology of specific fields.

Etymological Dictionaries

The most comprehensive of all historical treatments of English is the renowned *Oxford English Dictionary* (OED). Now in its second edition and available online and on CD-ROM, it is without doubt the single most valuable source available on English etymology. The printed version of the dictionary exists in both its original twenty-volume format and a photographically reduced one-volume edition (sold with a good magnifying glass!). The printed books have been supplemented by three additional volumes of material incorporated in the electronic sources. Other recommended etymological dictionaries include the following:

> *The American Heritage Dictionary of the English Language.* 4th ed. 2000. Boston: Houghton Mifflin. This is a regular desktop dictionary that is especially strong on Indo-European etymology. It is also available on CD-ROM and online at http://bartleby.com/.
>
> Onions, C. T., ed. *The Oxford Dictionary of English Etymology.* Oxford, Eng.: Clarendon Press, 1966. This dictionary contains abridged material from the first edition of the OED.
>
> Partridge, Eric. *Origins: A Short Etymological Dictionary of Modern English.* 4th ed. New York: Macmillan, 1966.

Sources on Relevant Areas of Linguistics

The student may want to refer to the following introductory works for additional information and reading in the various subdisciplines of linguistics discussed in this book.

General Linguistics

> Burling, Robbins. *Patterns of Language: Structure, Variation, Change.* San Diego: Academic Press, 1992.
>
> Clark, Virginia P., Paul A. Eschholz, and Alfred E. Rosa, eds. *Language: Introductory Readings.* 5th ed. New York: St. Martin's Press, 1994.
>
> Crystal, David. *The Cambridge Encyclopedia of Language.* 2nd ed. Cambridge, Eng.: Cambridge University Press, 1997.

Finegan, Edward. *Language: Its Structure and Use.* 4th ed. Boston, Mass.: Heinle
    & Heinle, 2003.
Fromkin, Victoria, Robert Rodman, and Nina Hyams. *An Introduction to Lan-*
    guage. 8th ed. Boston, Mass.: Thomson, 2007.

History of English

Algeo, John, and Thomas Pyles. *The Origins and Development of the English*
    Language. 5th ed. Boston, Mass.: Thomas/Wadsworth, 2005. (There is also a
    companion workbook for this volume.)
Baugh, Albert C., and Thomas Cable. *A History of the English Language.* 5th ed.
    Upper Saddle River, N.J.: Prentice Hall, 2002. (There is also a companion
    workbook by Thomas Cable.)
Claiborne, Robert. *Our Marvelous Native Tongue.* New York: Times Books, 1983.
Millward, C. M. *A Biography of the English Language.* 2nd ed. Fort Worth, Tex.:
    Harcourt Brace, 1996. (There is also a companion workbook for this volume.)

Phonetics

Ladefoged, Peter. *A Course in Phonetics.* 5th ed. Boston, Mass.: Thomson/Wads-
    worth, 2006. (Includes a CD-ROM.)

Usage and Rhetoric

Bolinger, Dwight L. *Language, the Loaded Weapon: The Use and Abuse of Lan-*
    guage Today. London: Longman, 1980.
Eschholz, Paul A. and Alfred E. Rosa. *Language Awareness.* 9th ed. New York:
    St. Martin's Press, 2004.
Quinn, Jim. *American Tongue and Cheek.* Middlesex, Eng.: Penguin Books, 1980.

Sociolinguistics and Dialectology

Cassidy, Frederick J., ed. *The Dictionary of American Regional English.* Cam-
    bridge, Mass.: Belknap Press of Harvard University Press, 1985–.
Trudgill, Peter. *Sociolinguistics: An Introduction to Language and Society.* 4th ed.
    London: Penguin.
Wardhaugh, Ronald. *An Introduction to Sociolinguistics.* 4th ed. Oxford, Eng.:
    Blackwell, 2001.
Wolfram, Walt. *Dialects and American English.* Englewood Cliffs, N.J.: Prentice-
    Hall, 1991.

Language and Culture

Bonvillain, Nancy. *Language, Culture, and Communication: The Meaning of Messages.* 4th ed. Englewood Cliffs, N.J.: Prentice-Hall, 2002.

Language Change, Historical Linguistics, and Language Classification

Aitchison, Jean. *Language Change: Progress or Decay?* 3rd ed. Cambridge, Eng.: Cambridge University Press, 2000.

Baldi, Philip. *An Introduction to the Indo-European Languages.* Carbondale, Ill.: Southern Illinois University Press, 1983.

Buck, Carl D. *A Dictionary of Selected Synonyms in the Principal Indo-European Languages: A Contribution to the History of Ideas.* Chicago: The University of Chicago Press, 1949, reprinted 1988.

Ruhlen, Merritt. *A Guide to the World's Languages.* Stanford, Calif.: Stanford University Press, 1987, reprinted 1991.

Sihler, Andrew L. *New Comparative Grammar of Greek and Latin.* New York: Oxford University Press, 1995.

Latin and Greek Grammar and Vocabulary

Crane, Gregory, ed. *Perseus Digital Library.* http://www.perseus.tufts.edu/ cache/perscoll_Greco-Roman.html/. Online collection of classic reference sources for Greek and Latin, including searchable dictionaries and grammars.

Ehrlich, Eugene. *Amo, Amas, Amat, and More: How to Use Latin to Your Own Advantage and to the Astonishment of Others.* New York: Harper & Row, 1985.

Gildersleeve, B. L., and Gonzalez Lodge. *Latin Grammar.* 3rd ed. New York: Macmillan, 1895; reprinted Wauconda, Ill.: Bolchazy-Carducci, 1997.

Glare, P. G. W., ed. *Oxford Latin Dictionary.* Oxford, Eng.: Oxford University Press, 1982.

Liddell, Henry G., and Robert Scott. *A Greek–English Lexicon.* 9th ed., with rev. supplement. Oxford, Eng.: Oxford University Press, 1996.

Smyth, Herbert W. *Greek Grammar, rev. by Gordon M. Messing.* Cambridge, Mass.: Harvard University Press, 1956.

Woodhouse, S. C. *English–Greek Dictionary: A Vocabulary of the Attic Language.* London: Routledge, 1910, reprinted 1979.

Changes from Latin to French to English

Pope, M. K. *From Latin to Modern French.* Rev. ed. Manchester, Eng.: Manchester University Press, 1961.

Spelling

Cummings, D. W. *American English Spelling.* Baltimore: Johns Hopkins University Press, 1988.

Index